THE SOCIAL CONTRACT REVISITED

*A Conference Sponsored by
the Changing Domestic Priorities Project
of The Urban Institute*

THE SOCIAL CONTRACT REVISITED

Aims and Outcomes
of President Reagan's Social Welfare Policy

Edited by D. Lee Bawden

The Changing Domestic Priorities Series
John L. Palmer and Isabel V. Sawhill, Editors

 THE URBAN INSTITUTE PRESS · WASHINGTON, D.C.

Distributed by arrangement with
UPA, Inc.
4720 Boston Way
Lanham, MD 20706

9 8 7 6 5 4 3 2

Copyright © 1984
THE URBAN INSTITUTE
2100 M Street, N.W.
Washington, D.C. 20037

Library of Congress Cataloging in Publication Data
Main entry under title:

The Social contract revisited.

    (The Changing domestic priorities series)
    Includes bibliographical references.
    1. Public welfare—United States—Addresses, essays,
lectures. 2. United States—Social policy—Addresses, essays,
lectures. 1. Bawden, D. Lee. II. Series.
HV95.S59   1984   361.6'0973   84–7209
ISBN 0–87766–335–1 (pbk.)
ISBN 0–87766–362–9 (cloth)

Printed in the United States of America

THE URBAN INSTITUTE is a nonprofit policy research and educational organization established in Washington, D.C. in 1968. Its staff investigates the social and economic problems confronting the nation and government policies and programs designed to alleviate such problems. The Institute disseminates significant findings of its research through the publications program of its Press. The Institute has two goals for work in each of its research areas: to help shape thinking about societal problems and efforts to solve them, and to improve government decisions and performance by providing better information and analytic tools.

Through work that ranges from broad conceptual studies to administrative and technical assistance, Institute researchers contribute to the stock of knowledge available to public officials and to private individuals and groups concerned with formulating and implementing more efficient and effective government policy.

Conclusions or opinions expressed in Institute publications are those of the authors and do not necessarily reflect the views of other staff members, officers or trustees of the Institute, advisory groups, or any organizations which provide financial support to the Institute.

THE CHANGING DOMESTIC PRIORITIES SERIES

Listed below are the titles available, or soon to be available, in the Changing Domestic Priorities Series

Books

THE REAGAN EXPERIMENT
An Examination of Economic and Social Policies under the Reagan Administration (1982), John L. Palmer and Isabel V. Sawhill, editors

HOUSING ASSISTANCE FOR OLDER AMERICANS
The Reagan Prescription (1982), James P. Zais, Raymond J. Struyk, and Thomas Thibodeau

MEDICAID IN THE REAGAN ERA
Federal Policy and State Choices (1982), Randall R. Bovbjerg and John Holahan

WAGE INFLATION
Prospects for Deceleration (1983), Wayne Vroman

OLDER AMERICANS IN THE REAGAN ERA
Impacts of Federal Policy Changes (1983), James R. Storey

FEDERAL HOUSING POLICY AT PRESIDENT REAGAN'S MIDTERM
(1983), Raymond J. Struyk, Neil Mayer, and John A. Tuccillo

STATE AND LOCAL FISCAL RELATIONS IN THE EARLY 1980s
(1983), Steven D. Gold

THE DEFICIT DILEMMA
Budget Policy in the Reagan Era (1983), Gregory B. Mills and John L. Palmer

HOUSING FINANCE
A Changing System in the Reagan Era (1983), John A. Tuccillo with John L. Goodman, Jr.

PUBLIC OPINION DURING THE REAGAN ADMINISTRATION
National Issues, Private Concerns (1983), John L. Goodman, Jr.

RELIEF OR REFORM?
Reagan's Regulatory Dilemma (1984), George C. Eads and Michael Fix

THE REAGAN RECORD
An Assessment of America's Changing Domestic Priorities (1984), John L. Palmer and Isabel V. Sawhill, editors (Ballinger Publishing Co.)

Conference Volumes

THE SOCIAL CONTRACT REVISITED
Aims and Outcomes of President Reagan's Social Welfare Policy (1984), edited by D. Lee Bawden

NATURAL RESOURCES AND THE ENVIRONMENT
The Reagan Approach (1984), edited by Paul R. Portney

FEDERAL BUDGET POLICY IN THE 1980s (1984), edited by Gregory B. Mills and John L. Palmer

THE REAGAN REGULATORY STRATEGY
An Assessment (1984), edited by George C. Eads and Michael Fix

THE LEGACY OF REAGANOMICS
Prospects for Long-term Growth (1984), edited by Charles R. Hulten and Isabel V. Sawhill

THE REAGAN PRESIDENCY AND THE GOVERNING OF AMERICA
(1984), edited by Lester M. Salamon and Michael S. Lund

Advisory Board of the
Changing Domestic Priorities Project

CONTENTS

FOREWORD

In late 1981 The Urban Institute initiated a three-year project—Changing Domestic Priorities—to examine the shifts in domestic policy occurring under the Reagan administration and the consequences of those shifts. This volume, a product of the Changing Domestic Priorities project, is one of six collections of analyses by leading scholars on subjects of considerable national interest in the 1980s. The other five volumes are focused upon budget policy, economic growth, governance, natural resources and the environment, and regulatory policy.

Broadly speaking, the social contract defines the rights of citizens and their responsibility to government, and the government's duty and responsibility to its citizens. In a narrower sense the term has come to stand for the social welfare policy of a government—the set of low-income assistance and social insurance programs that aid citizens in time of need. So defined, the social contract in the United States, as in most developed nations, has greatly expanded over time; programs have proliferated and social welfare expenditures have grown relative to the economy.

When President Reagan came to office he wanted to "curb the growth" of this social welfare spending and generally reduce the role of the federal government in favor of much greater state and local government and private sector involvement in meeting social welfare needs. At the same time, he promised the preservation of a reliable safety net of social programs and a healthy economy that would provide jobs and better wages for many who had become wholly or partially dependent on such programs. Both the president's policies and the premises upon which they are based have proven controversial.

The papers in this volume were first presented at an Urban Institute conference held in July 1983 to address the aims and outcomes of the Reagan
administration's social welfare policy.

The first essay, by William Gorham, provides an overview of both the
conference papers and discussion. This is followed by a statement of the
philosophy and objectives of President Reagan's social welfare policies by
Martin Anderson, his first chief domestic policy advisor. Subsequent papers
by Blanche Bernstein, Jack A. Meyer, and Timothy M. Smeeding consider
the merits of the administration's policies, both proposed and enacted, and
their implications for future spending growth, welfare dependency, and the
social safety net; while those by Sheldon Danziger, Peter Gottschalk, Edward
M. Gramlich, and Deborah S. Laren focus on the distribution of unemployment among income classes and the extent to which the poor benefit from
public transfer programs and economic growth. In the final paper Nathan
Glazer addresses the significance of President Reagan's social welfare policies
from an historical perspective.

We believe this volume will be of considerable interest both to those
involved in the continuing redefinition of the social contract in this country
and to those who wish to understand it.

John L. Palmer
Isabel V. Sawhill
Editors
Changing Domestic Priorities Series

ACKNOWLEDGMENTS

I have many people to thank for the quality of this volume. The authors were diligent and fair minded, and they revised their papers after the conference in light of the discussion by participants. The commentators took their charge seriously. Their efforts are not fully reflected in the comments contained in this volume because some of their remarks, rendered irrelevant by postconference revisions of the papers, were deleted. Other conference participants made many useful comments and contributed importantly to the overview paper. Mildred Woodhouse did a superb job of organizing the conference, recording the discussions, and providing typewritten transcripts for authors' use. Theresa Walker efficiently managed the editing and publication process, and Martha Thomson improved the papers by her skillful editing.

Finally, the support of the Ford Foundation and the John D. and Catherine T. MacArthur Foundation is gratefully acknowledged.

D. Lee Bawden
Editor

OVERVIEW

William Gorham

The United States had no federal social welfare policy in 1930—no Social Security, no unemployment insurance, no welfare benefits. And the only federal grant-in-aid to states was for education.[1] Responsibility for taking care of the aged, the sick, and the unemployed fell upon state and local governments, concerned citizens, and primarily on the families of the needy.

The federal government assumed part of this responsibility with passage of the Social Security Act of 1935, which remains the cornerstone of federal social welfare policy to this day. Nevertheless, as the United States entered World World II, federal social welfare expenditures (including grants-in-aid to states) comprised only 2.3 percent of the gross national product (GNP).[2] Social welfare policy evolved slowly until the mid-1960s, when the Johnson administration declared the War on Poverty. From 1965 to 1975 federal social welfare expenditures as a proportion of GNP more than doubled, from 5.1 to 10.6 percent. While this growth slowed markedly in the latter half of the 1970s, by 1980 the federal government spent 11.6 percent of GNP for social welfare purposes—nearly $1,500 for each man, woman, and child.

Besides diverting private funds to public social purposes, the government extended its regulation and control over heretofore private domains during the 1960s and early 1970s. The Civil Rights Act of 1964, the National

---

1. The first federal grants-in-aid to states, other than for education, were for child and maternal health in 1921, but these grants were terminated in 1929. For a history of social welfare policy in the United States, see Walter I. Trattner, *From Poor Law to Welfare State*, 2d ed. (New York: The Free Press, 1979).

2. These and the numbers that follow refer to "payments to individuals" as reported by the Office of Management and Budget, Fiscal Analysis Branch, *Federal Government Finances*, March 1981.

Environmental Policy Act of 1969, the Occupational Safety and Health Act of 1970, and dozens of other laws and regulations increasingly constrained the behavior of individuals and firms in order to protect the rights and interests of other individuals and groups.

Ronald Reagan entered the presidency as an antagonist of federal social welfare spending and social regulation and as a critic of federal government performance. Candidate Reagan promised to examine, reshape, and generally leash "runaway" social welfare spending and intrusions into private and corporate life. He spoke of enhanced personal responsibility, family responsibility, community responsibility, and private-sector responsibility as the primary line of defense against the vicissitudes of life. He did not repudiate the goals of the majority of social programs enacted since the mid-1930s, but aimed to reduce their size (or at least their rate of growth) and to improve their administration. At the same time, he lauded the traditional virtues and proclaimed economic growth to be the ultimate source of economic well-being.

Although Reagan's campaign rhetoric sounded revolutionary, or counterrevolutionary, his specific goals, as they emerged, were not radically different from those of his predecessor, Jimmy Carter, who also came into office as a strong critic of the federal government (although Carter did not advocate curtailing social welfare spending or regulation). However, the magnitude of Reagan's proposed tax cut and his first proposals to trim social welfare spending growth were unprecedented. Reagan's first budget, converting his campaign rhetoric into action, was impressive, tangible evidence that social welfare interests were near the top of his agenda. The conference that this book records is a review of President Reagan's social welfare goals and his success in implementing them to date.

Because less than three years have elapsed since Reagan took office and less than two years since his first budget took effect, the conference papers are unavoidably light on direct measurement of the impacts of his policies on neighborhoods and on the lives of families and individuals. Policy changes must be transmitted through successive layers of government and other institutions having various capacities to delay or attenuate the federal changes before their full impact can be felt and therefore judged. Still, it is not too early to record the Reagan administration's goals (and changes in them), to detail its specific proposals to implement those goals, to record their disposition by the Congress, and to use reliable models to predict the ultimate impacts of Reagan's policies in certain arenas.

This early assessment provides limited though timely information to those currently involved in further legislative and administrative actions—either to extend or to reverse Reagan administration initiatives.

Conclusions of this Conference

This conference addressed several objectives of social welfare policy, some of which have been embraced by the Reagan administration, the extent to which these objectives have been met, and their long-run consequences. The conclusions reached by the authors of the papers in this volume are as follows:

- The budget reductions for social welfare were not equally distributed across programs: the deepest cuts were made in means-tested programs targeted on the nonaged poor, while the social insurance programs— Social Security, Medicare, and veterans' benefits—were affected much less; *within* programs, benefits were reduced most for the less needy.

- The safety net, defined by the administration to exclude assistance to the working poor, is still largely intact in terms of coverage and benefit levels for the poorest single-parent and aged families. Part of the credit must go to Congress, however, for it rebuffed several administration proposals that would have lowered the safety net. Because the budget cuts in social programs were aimed primarily at the less needy, single mothers working at low wages and their children bore the brunt of the reduction in social welfare expenditures.

- The Reagan administration's program will have little impact on long-term welfare dependency because it has done little to redress the root causes of long-term poverty, such as out-of-wedlock births among teenagers, the dissolution of families, and inadequate job skills of welfare mothers.

- The sharp rise in unemployment due to the recession has been the major source of economic hardship. Low-income family heads have the highest rate of unemployment. Overall transfer income makes up less than half of the lost wages.

- The incidence of poverty in 1982 was the highest in over a decade. The projected rate of economic growth through the 1980s will not be able to reduce the incidence of poverty to its 1979 level. Compared with earlier times, the ability of economic growth to reduce poverty is more limited because the poor increasingly are children and single mothers, many of whom have few job skills.

- The success of the Reagan administration's social welfare program will be judged on the fairness of the sacrifices required to simultaneously promote economic growth and build a stronger military and— as the president would wish—on the success of his overall economic policy. On the first score, the conference consensus was that the budget cuts and unemployment due to the recession fell more heavily on low-income families than on those in the middle- and high-income brackets. There are signs, however, that the administration is attempting to spread the budget cuts more widely by reining in expenditures on social insurance and other programs benefiting the middle class. On the second criterion, the current high unemployment manifests a failure of the president's economic policy, at least in the short run. Future prospects for full employment with low inflation and good growth are clouded by huge projected deficits. There seems to be no solution to the deficit problem except substantial tax increases, a slower military buildup, and further cuts in social welfare expenditures.

The Social Welfare Objectives of the Reagan Administration

The Reagan administration has not explicitly stated its social welfare objectives. Like most administrations, its objectives must be surmised from official pronouncements such as State of the Union messages, annual budget messages to the Congress, other speeches by the president and his social welfare policy advisors, and the arguments accompanying proposed substantive legislation.

The following excerpts are from President Reagan's State of the Union and budget messages:

Our goal was and remains economic recovery—the return of non-inflationary and sustained prosperity. We seek a larger economic pie to provide all Americans more jobs, more after-tax income, and a better life. (FY 1983 budget message)

Where Government had passively tolerated the swift, continuous growth of automatic entitlements, . . . a long-overdue reordering of priorities has begun, entitlement growth is being checked. . . . (FY 1983 budget message)

We will continue to direct our resources to our two highest budget priorities: a strong national defense . . . and a reliable safety net of social programs for those who have contributed and those who are in need. (State of the Union message, 1982)

(Our proposals) include new steps to tighten eligibility, reduce errors and abuse and curtail unwarranted benefits in the welfare, medical, and nutrition programs. (FY 1983 budget message)

Martin Anderson, formerly President Reagan's principal domestic policy advisor, says in his conference paper that the administration's basic domestic objective has been to reform social welfare programs so that they would more effectively achieve their original goals. Specifically he lists the following objectives:

1. Reduce poverty and ensure the opportunity for prosperity for every-one by promoting growth;

2. Introduce reasonable limits as to who qualifies for aid;

3. Reduce fraud, waste, and extravagance;

4. Improve certain program operations by returning them to the states and localities together with the tax resources necessary to fund them; and

5. Do not provide a guaranteed income.

Official documents and Anderson's list of social welfare objectives of the Reagan administration are in essential agreement. Other conferees saw the administration goals as follows:

1. The government should have a markedly reduced social role;

2. The private market should be more heavily relied upon to meet social welfare needs;

3. National priorities should shift from domestic to defense programs; and

4. Responsibility for social welfare should shift from federal to state and local governments (not unlike Anderson's fourth objective, but broader in scope).

The differences between the goals as implied in official documents, as stated by Anderson, and as stated by the other conferees are modest. The areas of disagreement revolve around the definition of what are ends and what are means. For example, Anderson views devolution of program responsibility to the states and localities as a means of improving programs, not as an end in itself. (If devolution to state and local governments is seen as a goal, it would be promoted whether or not it improved program effectiveness.) How-ever, the administration evidently believes that devolution is correct policy and not simply a way to improve program administration.

On a related issue, some conferees state that the Reagan administration is aiming to reduce the social role of all government. (This objective can be deduced from other objectives—for example, lowering program eligibility standards and providing assistance only to the truly needy.) Much of the rhetoric of the Reagan administration supports this view, although official documents do not identify this as a goal. Nor does Anderson. However, reducing the social role of the *federal* government does seem to be an objective of the Reagan administration.

Some conferees cite reduction of welfare dependency as a social policy goal of the administration, although official documents do not include this as a goal, nor does Anderson. It must be seen as a corollary to "providing benefits only to the truly needy," which in Reagan's view, excludes those who are able to work. The Reagan administration has attempted to wean these individuals from public benefits by imposing stiffer work requirements for the receipt of unemployment benefits, and by promoting "workfare"—requiring welfare recipients to work for their benefits. Requiring stepparents to assume economic responsibility for their stepchildren and increasing pressure on absent fathers to make child support payments are two administration initiatives that also can be interpreted as attempts to reduce welfare dependency.

Despite much public debate over the administration's general social welfare policy goals, the only discernible shift in social welfare proposals by the administration during its first two and a half years in office has been to give more attention to controlling social insurance expenditures, especially Social Security, civil service retirement, and Medicare. This constitutes more a change in emphasis than a change in policy objectives.

The Reagan administration's goals seem generally compatible with one another, although the extreme pursuit of any one could substantially undermine the others. For example, to virtually eliminate welfare fraud and abuse would probably require a level of policing that would cost far more than would be saved in welfare expenditures. Likewise, shifting certain social welfare programs to the states may be inconsistent with other objectives, such as confining spending to the truly needy, improving the efficiency of programs, and curtailing fraud and abuse. In general, however, the social welfare policies implemented by the Reagan administration appear to be fairly consistent.

Consequences of the Reagan Administration's
Social Welfare Policies

The conference papers assess the degree to which the Reagan administration has succeeded in achieving selected policy objectives and analyze the impacts of these policies. The papers do not address welfare program devolution to the states (which largely has not occurred) nor administration initiatives to reduce fraud and abuse and to increase program effectiveness (evidence on the outcomes of which is scanty to date).

The major issues addressed in the papers and the authors' conclusions are briefly summarized below.

Fairness of the Administration's Actions

Any administration expects its programs and actions to be subject to a "fairness" test. Legitimacy in a democracy, perhaps in any nontotalitarian form of government, in large measure is rooted in the perception that its behavior meets its public's sense of evenhandedness and justice. Jack Meyer, whose paper addresses the fairness question, uses two income criteria to assess fairness: vertical proportionality and horizontal equity. The former standard measures the proportion of benefits or costs borne by individuals in various income categories; the latter measures the equality of treatment among individuals or groups in the same circumstances. Meyer confines his analysis to the distribution of budget cuts across and within social programs; he does not address the effects of the tax cut and unemployment caused by the recession.

Meyer finds that during its first two years the legislative proposals of the Reagan administration, when viewed *across* programs, were generally unfair by both criteria. The budgetary and program actions were more costly to those at the low end of the income distribution than those at the high end, and programs for the low-income elderly and veterans were largely unaffected while those for the nonelderly poor, particularly female-headed families, were cut substantially.

He reaches this conclusion by classifying social programs into two categories: (1) means-tested programs aimed at assisting low-income individuals and families and (2) programs that direct benefits to individuals or families with little or no regard for income. Based on legislation enacted to date and on administration proposals in the FY 1984 budget, he shows expenditures for means-tested programs declining from 13 percent of total federal expenditures in FY 1981 to a projected 9 percent in FY 1988. Meanwhile, he sees expenditures for the various social insurance programs that benefit all income groups declining only slightly, from 42 percent in FY 1981 to 40.5 percent in FY 1988. The low-income programs accounted for 25 percent of federal social welfare expenditures in 1980, but would decrease to less than 20 percent in 1988. Expenditures for the social insurance programs, which comprised three-fourths of the social welfare budget in 1980, are projected to grow to 82 percent of that budget by 1988.

Thus, he concludes that like people in similar economic circumstances were not affected equally and that, viewed across programs, individuals and families with low incomes were more adversely affected than those with higher incomes.

Meyer gives the Reagan administration higher marks for its proposals and administrative actions that affect the allocation of resources within programs. These changes have moved resources toward the most needy and away from those higher in the income distribution. While the overall benefits are less, a higher proportion of them go to those most in need.

Apart from an abortive Social Security proposal in the spring of 1982, the Reagan administration initially made few proposals to reduce spending in the two biggest social programs—Social Security retirement and Medicare. More recently, however, the administration embraced the Social Security Commission's recommendation for scaling back benefits and increasing taxes, and supported a congressional initiative to change the way hospitals are reimbursed under Medicare.

Is the Safety Net Intact?

Timothy Smeeding's paper addresses changes in the safety net, but he defines it differently, more substantively, than has the administration. The administration has defined the safety net in terms of *programs*; Smeeding defines it as the amount of assistance available to those with no other income.

Martin Anderson argues that the term "safety net" was used by the Reagan administration to "describe a set of social welfare programs that would not be closely examined on the first round of budget changes because of the fierce political pressures (to changing them)," and that the idea of a safety net "was political shorthand that only made sense for a limited period of time." More to the point of Smeeding's definition of the safety net, Anderson says that "providing a safety net for those who cannot or are not expected to work was not really a social policy objective (of the Reagan administration)." Yet there remains much discussion of the safety net and the degree to which it has remained intact. Whatever it is called, how benefits have changed under the Reagan administration for the poorest of the poor is an important question to address in assessing the consequences of the administration's social welfare policy.

Smeeding finds that the social safety net has been pretty much unchanged by the Reagan administration for female-headed families and the aged with no other incomes. The level of their combined program benefits, adjusted for inflation, has continued its slow decline of the late 1970s, mostly due to state rather than federal actions. The same cannot be said for nonaged two-parent families experiencing unemployment. Their principal safety net is unemployment insurance, where extended benefits have been curtailed and a less generous Federal Supplemental Benefit program has been provided than in recent, milder recessions. The sagging safety net for nonaged two-parent families is manifested in recent large increases in their rate of poverty.

Congress must receive much of the credit for keeping the level of the safety net intact for single-parent families and the aged, according to Smeeding. The administration proposed several reductions in basic benefit levels that were rejected by Congress. He states that, "Had the administration's proposals been adopted wholesale (by Congress), even the truly needy would have suffered substantial income losses. Altogether the real combined AFDC, Food Stamp, and LIEA (Low-Income Energy Assistance) benefit guarantees would have dropped from 1981 to 1983 by 4.0 percent per year, almost three times the actual annual (rate of decline). If the Reagan administration proposals had been adopted, combined OASI (Social Security), Food Stamp, and LIEA benefit levels (for the elderly) would have declined by an average of 1.7 percent per year from 1981 to 1983, in contrast to the nominal 0.2 percent average gain actually observed over this period."

The administration's proposals support Martin Anderson's assertion that maintaining the safety net has not been one of Reagan's social policy objectives. Nevertheless, the built-in checks and balances between the executive and legislative branches resulted in the level of the safety net staying about the same in real terms from 1981 to 1983 for single-parent families and the aged with no other incomes.

Welfare Dependency

Blanche Bernstein's paper addresses the issue of whether welfare dependency will be reduced by the policy and programmatic changes of the Reagan administration. Two measures taken by the administration to reduce welfare dependency—tougher enforcement of child support payments by absent fathers and the requirement that stepparents support their stepchildren—are judged by Bernstein to be sensible and effective actions. She also supports the administration's efforts to impose "workfare" on welfare recipients, but believes that the program will be ineffective because of a flawed design (no provision of funds to cover administrative and capital costs incurred by agencies in creating workfare jobs) and resistance by the social welfare community. She believes that elimination of the "$30-and-a-third" rule after four months in AFDC will lead to less welfare dependency and that some of the other program changes were long overdue.

Citing evidence that a major portion of welfare dollars goes to long-term welfare recipients, Bernstein faults the administration for not addressing—and not initiating proposals to alleviate—the causes of long-term poverty. The administration has given weak support, at best, to family planning counseling and the teaching of sex education in the schools, programs addressed to the two largest causes of long-term welfare dependency—teenage child-bearing and the breakup of intact families. Also, the administration has done little new to train and otherwise help welfare mothers to obtain jobs.

The Economy

The linchpin of the Reagan administration's social welfare policy is its economic policies. Robust economic growth was to be the tide that lifted all boats. It was intended to reduce poverty and insure "the opportunity for prosperity for everyone," according to Martin Anderson. Thus the impact of the economy on the economic well-being of the population is of considerable significance in assessing the performance of the Reagan administration's social policies. The first order of economic business when the administration came to office was to reduce the rate of inflation, the second was to promote economic growth. The inflation target was attacked largely through a contin-uation of the tight monetary policy begun in 1979 by the Federal Reserve Board. The success of this effort is manifest in a reduction in the rise of the Consumer Price Index (CPI) from over 12 percent in 1980 to under 4 percent in 1983.

The benefits of declining inflation are widely shared. The conference did not address the distribution of those benefits. However, the price of reduced inflation has been depressed total output and total earned income. Isabel Sawhill, in her comments on the Gramlich and Laren paper, states that "the (estimated) losses in real GNP from the first quarter of 1981 through the fourth quarter of 1982 (using reasonable assumptions of potential CPI growth and full employment) were $412 billion. . . ."

The Impact of Rising Unemployment. The economic burden of the recession was the major short-term social welfare outcome of the first half of the Reagan administration. Overall, it dwarfed the impact of federal cuts in social welfare programs. The distribution of this burden is the subject of the conference paper by Ned Gramlich and Deborah Laren. Using the Panel Study of Income Dynamics, they estimated the incidence of family unem-ployment and income losses over business cycles from 1967 to 1980. They estimated four main types of relationships: the incidence of direct unemployment, the amount of time spent unemployed for those who were employed, the nature of intrafamily cushioning of income losses, and the extent to which the tax-transfer system cushioned income losses. They made separate calculations for white male, nonwhite male, and female heads of households and their families, subdividing each of these categories in turn based on eight income classes.

Their main conclusion is that economic downturns hit low-income families harder than high-income families, generating percentage losses in income from three to five times as great. The disparities would be even worse but for a substantial amount of cushioning accomplished by the tax-transfer system. They found almost no cushioning resulting from adjustment of labor income within the family. Across groups, families of nonwhite males generally experienced more unemployment than families of white males in any income class, and families of females had less unemployment than the families of males—white or nonwhite.

When these results are extended to a comparison of horizontal incidence, to see how many families in a given income class actually experience large losses, Gramlich and Laren find that as long as cycles do not become too severe, a fairly small segment of the population suffers significant losses, most of whom are typically at the low end of the income distribution. When the cycles are large, as in the recent recession, the share of people experiencing significant employment and income losses rises sharply.

"The main macroeconomic policy lesson from all this appears to be that moderate doses of anti-inflationary medicine, in the form of moderate cycles, do appear to be digestible, as they do not make very many people significantly worse off; while serious cycles are much less digestible." The principal message relevant to policymakers is that, while recessions affect all income groups, they have their greatest impact on poor people, who experience the largest income losses.

Economic Growth and Poverty. A fundamental premise of the Reagan administration's program is that robust economic growth is good for all. Its social welfare policy presumes a sound economy in which the benefits of growth extend down the income distribution to lift individuals and families above minimal economic conditions by providing work opportunities. How well does this premise agree with reality? To what extent does a rising tide lift all boats?

Peter Gottschalk and Sheldon Danziger address this question in their conference paper. They conclude that economic growth does have a significant effect on the rate of poverty, but that its effect is limited—a rising tide does not lift *all* boats. The poor aged and, to a lesser extent, female-headed families are not helped much by economic growth, whereas nonaged, two-parent poor families are helped. Based on an analysis of the *Current Population Survey* data from 1967 to 1982, the authors find that growth in both market incomes and income transfers are important to reducing poverty and that "the relative importance of these efforts differs widely by demographic group."

Because of the demographic makeup of the poverty population, Gottschalk and Danziger are not sanguine that rising real incomes in the next few years will reduce poverty much below the level in the late 1970s. "Much of the decline in poverty since the mid-1960s resulted from increased transfers to the elderly, a pattern that has come to an end. Sustained growth in market incomes would further reduce the poverty levels of persons living in households headed by nonaged males. However, this would have limited impact on poverty, since this group represents only about 45 percent of all poor persons and already has relatively low rates of poverty."

The implications of these findings are that reductions in social welfare benefits will be only partially offset by the fruits of economic growth, and that both a vigorous economy and substantial welfare expenditures—at least equal to those in the past (in real terms)—will be necessary to significantly reduce the incidence of poverty over the next decade.

The Long-Run View

The paper by Nathan Glazer looks at the philosophy behind the Reagan administration's social welfare policy and assesses the effects on future welfare policy in this country. He argues that this administration has rejected the "social engineering" approach to social policy—that welfare programs could be fine tuned to both accurately meet the needs of the low-income population and to provide the "correct" economic incentives to the dependent population to become more self-supporting—an approach that dominated welfare reform thinking in the late 1960s and most of the 1970s. Instead, the administration has emphasized the work ethic and personal and family responsibility. As Glazer states, "The traditional incentives, to work and support one's family, were now assumed rather than paid for." The (liberal) incentives-based approach to human behavior was to be replaced by higher moral standards and a strengthening of traditional beliefs in the values of family and work.

The main legislative impact of the Reagan administration on social welfare to date was contained in the Omnibus Budget Reconciliation Act of 1981. While many programs were affected and some were severely cut back, Glazer concludes that the overall scale of change "is not very large." He notes that many of the proposed changes "were fully developed prior to the Reagan administration and had considerable bipartisan support."

The devolution of many programs to states (via block grants) and the proposed return to the states of many other programs reflect a belief by this administration that the federal government does not necessarily know what is best. The rationale for a strong federal role has declined, Glazer argues, as regions have come closer together in economic strength, as minority political power has increased, and as several past federal interventions have been seen as failures. While not explicitly stated, he implies that shifting decision making and responsibility for social welfare programs to lower levels of government is desirable and will not soon be reversed.

Glazer faults the administration, not for its ideology, but for its lack of "political courage" in implementing it. Large tax cuts and a huge increase in defense expenditures require massive cuts in domestic programs; yet, the administration has mainly cut programs for the poor, leaving the much larger—and more politically sensitive—social insurance programs relatively unchanged. The consequence is a huge budget deficit, which remains to be dealt with by the administration.

Glazer concludes that the change in social welfare policy under the Reagan administration has not been large. But the belief that the poor should be more responsible for their own welfare, that the best way for the government to assist the poor is by providing jobs via a strong economy, and that the federal government is limited in its ability to intervene through a plethora of special programs—all represent a shift in social welfare thinking that "was due" and that will remain for several years.

Concluding Comments

The Reagan administration's most important social welfare goal is to maximize the role of the private economy in meeting the economic needs of individuals and families. Campaign rhetoric centered on taking the government off people's backs, and a number of measures proposed and enacted sought to give life to that objective. Equally clearly, the Reagan administration wished to get some people off the backs of the government (the taxpayers). Both sets of actions were thought to be consistent with the aforementioned overriding goal.

The big guns in the fight to restore growth—and, with it, greater prosperity for all—have been (1) tax cuts and (2) initial support for the tight monetary policy of the Federal Reserve Board to meet the concerns of inflation. So far, however, the Reagan administration has not fulfilled its goal of enlarging the role of the private economy in meeting the economic needs of people.

The nation has suffered the harshest recession since the Great Depression. Inflation rates are down, but unemployment remains high and the poverty rate is the highest in a decade. More, not fewer, individuals and families are receiving support from the government, despite more stringent eligibility standards for welfare. Sustained, long-run economic growth may reverse this, but the promised benefits from economic growth have not yet been realized.

The future is also clouded. The projected structural budget deficit (at full employment) is estimated at over $200 billion, which most authorities believe threatens to reduce the rate of long-term growth. Shrinking the deficit will require increased taxes, lower defense expenditures, and a further scaling back of social programs.

The Reagan administration, with the substantial impetus of Congress, has kept the safety net pretty much intact. Benefits for the working poor and near poor have been cut, and some ineffective programs have been eliminated. States and localities now have more say in how to spend federal social welfare dollars than before.

Social welfare programs in general and social insurance programs in particular will come under tremendous pressure in the next few years because of the budget deficit; cuts will be less motivated by ideology than by the need to reduce federal expenditures. The economy and actions to reduce the deficit will be the dominant forces influencing the well-being of low-income individuals and families over the next few years—and will have far greater impact than the changes in social welfare policy inspired to date by the Reagan administration.

THE OBJECTIVES OF THE REAGAN ADMINISTRATION'S SOCIAL WELFARE POLICY

Martin Anderson

Today there is a fairly widely held perception that the Reagan administration does not care much for the poor, has pursued programs that are unfair to the poor, and has succeeded in hurting them. The basic reason for this public perception, which is perhaps even more widely held among professors and reporters, is that so many who have chosen to write or talk about this issue are either cheerfully ignorant of Reagan's social welfare philosophy or, worse, are quite aware of its main parameters and have chosen to deliberately ignore or misrepresent it.

The Urban Institute is making an important contribution to advancing the level of scholarship in this area by holding this conference on the topic: "An Assessment of Reagan's Social Welfare Policy." As far as I know it is the only attempt being made to objectively and comprehensively assess these policies.

Misconceptions about the Objectives of the Reagan Administration

Unfortunately there is a long way to go. For example, even in the prospectus of this conference, the statement of what the conference is about is incomplete and, in some places, in error about the objectives of the social welfare policy of the Reagan administration. The first sentence of the conference prospectus states: "The Reagan administration came to office with a clear mandate to reduce government spending on social welfare programs." That is wrong. During the campaign Reagan pledged to limit and control the *growth* of spending on social welfare programs and to reduce fraud, waste, and any extravagant use of the taxpayers' money. The only two issues for which he had anything resembling a clear mandate were (1) increasing our national defense capability and (2) restoring the economic health of the country.

During the last three years I have spent a lot of time talking to pollsters and reading national polls and have never gotten the slightest hint that the voters of America gave Reagan a mandate to cut spending on social welfare programs from the 1980 level. Moreover, Reagan never believed he had a mandate to reduce that spending, and he was right.

The second and third sentences of the prospectus are a little longer. They say "The administration's plan was not to cut programs across the board, however, but to reduce spending in ways to accomplish certain objectives:

(1) reduce welfare dependency,

(2) provide a safety net for those who cannot or are not expected to work,

(3) eliminate ineffective programs, and

(4) shift a large share of the control and fiscal responsibility to the states.

"At the same time the administration took actions to increase the rate of long-term economic growth, arguing that the 'trickle down' effects of this growth would substantially reduce poverty—and attendant social welfare expenditures—in the long run."

Those two sentences, as an example of the current state of the art in understanding the objectives of Reagan's social welfare policy, are very good. But one must feel somewhat chagrined and embarrassed that these are statements of fact contained in the prospectus of a conference held by one of the best research institutions in the country. They are incomplete, wrong in certain aspects, and misrepresentative in others. Let us see why.

Point one. In listing the major objectives of the Reagan administration's social welfare policy, reducing *welfare dependency* comes first. This is somewhat misleading.

On the one hand, there is a question as to what *reducing welfare dependency* means. In the context of the administration's social welfare policy it represents certain reforms of our welfare programs to remove some incentives that were encouraging people to remain on welfare rather than going to work. These reforms were apparently successful. A recent evaluation of the 1981 amendments to the Aid to Families with Dependent Children (AFDC) program concluded that removal of some of the disincentives resulted in a substantially higher percentage of welfare recipients going off the AFDC rolls.[1]

On the other hand, the term *welfare dependency* can have a much broader and more literal meaning. When used in this other way, it is the top social welfare policy objective of many professionals in the field. As Senator Moynihan put it in opening his well-known book on the politics of a guaranteed income, "The issue of welfare is the issue of dependence."[2] He then went on to describe how poverty, in his view, is quite different from dependency. "This is not to say that dependent people are not brave, resourceful, admirable, but simply that their situation is never enviable, and rarely admired. It is an incomplete state in life; normal in the child, abnormal in the adult."[3]

President Reagan obviously does not feel that dependency is something good in and of itself. Like millions of other Americans, he feels that to be independent is better than to be dependent. However, that does not mean that the very fact of being dependent, especially when that state occurs through no fault of one's own, is something to be ashamed of. The Reagan administration has always been concerned about the more literal form of welfare dependency, but is far, far more concerned about ensuring that people who cannot help themselves receive help, than it is about resolving the unsolvable dilemma that the very fact of receiving help, by definition, makes the person dependent.

Point two. Providing a safety net for those who cannot or are not expected to work was not really a social policy objective. The term *safety net* was used in the 1980 Republican Platform and then adopted by the Office of Management and Budget to describe a set of social welfare programs that would not be closely examined on the first round of budget changes because of the fierce political pressures that made it impossible to even discuss these programs without invoking a torrent of passionate, often irrational, criticism. If a social welfare program was not part of what was euphemistically called the safety net, it did not mean that the administration did not support the kind of assistance that program was providing. And if a program was labeled as part of the safety net, it did not mean that all was well with that program.

The term safety net was political shorthand that only made sense for a limited period of time. Its use was unfortunate because it gave the impression

---

1. Research Triangle Institute, *Final Report: Evaluation of the 1981 AFDC Amendments* (submitted to Office of Family Assistance, Social Security Administration, Department of Health and Human Services), April 15, 1983, p. 5.

2. Moynihan, Daniel P., *The Politics of a Guaranteed Income: The Nixon Administration and the Family Assistance Plan* (Random House, New York, 1973), p. 17.

3. Ibid.

that only those programs in the safety net were valid programs in providing help to low-income people, and that those programs were somehow to be immune from criticism or close budget scrutiny.

Point three. Asserting that a major social policy objective was to "eliminate ineffective programs" misrepresents the case. When we call a program ineffective, we usually mean that the program does not work very well in achieving what we believe are essentially legitimate goals. Reagan's basic objective was to reform existing social welfare programs so that they could more effectively achieve their original goals.

The few programs the administration sought to eliminate generally had some question about the legitimacy of their goals, as well as the effectiveness of their operation. It is misleading to state that elimination of ineffective programs is a major objective when, in fact, the major objective was to reform and improve ineffective programs, while reserving the elimination option for those few programs that had demonstrated clearly that they were either inappropriate or redundant.

Point four. As far as it goes, the statement that Reagan wanted to "shift a large share of the control and fiscal responsibility to the states" is true. Unfortunately it only states *half* the case, and the statement, thus crippled, makes it appear that Reagan wants to dump certain social welfare programs on the states and localities and let them figure out how to pay for their operation. The half of the case that is left out, and that is as vital to the argument for the *New Federalism* as vermouth is to a good martini, is the transfer of the federal tax resources necessary to pay for the continuation of the programs.

Point five. It is stated that the administration has argued "that the 'trickle down' effects of this economic growth would substantially reduce poverty—and attendant social welfare expenditures—in the long run." Where and when has the administration ever argued this? Except for a single mention in the early morning musings of David Stockman to a *Washington Post* editor, I am unaware of the concept ever being discussed, let alone advocated by any member of the administration, and certainly never by President Reagan.

It is true that many people believe that Reagan endorses the so-called trickle down theory. But beliefs do not make things true. Perhaps a small reward should be offered to any scholar who can provide us with an accurate reference in regard to precisely who in the administration has seriously advocated such a theory.

President Reagan and, as far as I know, all the senior policy people in his administration believe very strongly in the efficacy of the power of economic growth for all people, including the poor. But they have never expressed belief or even interest in the discredited economic straw man of trickle down—

that if you help the rich, after a time some economic prosperity will trickle down to the poor.

The list of the social welfare policy objectives of the Reagan administration in the conference prospectus is most deficient not in what it lists, but in what it does not list. No mention is made of the objectives of reducing fraud, waste, and extravagance, of cutting back on inappropriate eligibility levels, and of an implacable opposition to a guaranteed income. All of these have been key elements in Reagan's philosophical approach to welfare for many years, and they still are.

I apologize for having dwelled so long on the content of our conference prospectus, but I believe it exemplifies the conventional wisdom about the social welfare philosophy attributed to the Reagan administration. Seeing and hearing statements like this about the social welfare philosophy of the Reagan administration is somewhat like looking at a reflection in a badly cracked mirror. Now I would like to attempt to explain what that philosophy looks like in an unbroken mirror.

The Reagan Administration's Social Welfare Philosophy

Five important elements of the Reagan administration's social welfare philosophy seem to me to define and explain its basic thrust:

1. A sound and growing economy is vital to reducing poverty and ensuring the opportunity for prosperity for everyone.

2. Eligibility standards for social welfare programs should be fair, setting reasonable limits as to who qualifies for aid.

3. Fraud, waste, and extravagance in social welfare programs should be substantially reduced.

4. In order to improve effectiveness and to lower costs, the responsibility for certain social welfare programs, together with the tax resources necessary to fund them, should be returned to the states and localities (the New Federalism).

5. A guaranteed income is unconscionable and impractical. To the extent that people are able to take care of themselves, they should do so.

A Sound and Growing Economy

The general level of economic prosperity largely determines the personal prosperity of those in the society who are relatively poor.

First, the level of government support and the extent of that support is largely determined by the size of government tax revenues and that, in turn, is largely determined by the size and health of the economy. There is no way that a country like India, with its weak and relatively stagnant economy, could provide—even if it wished to do so—anywhere near the extent of social welfare benefits that exist in the United States.

Second, how well the economy is functioning can have a powerful effect on low-income people. How much money they have is important, but what they can buy with the money is equally important. The devastating effect of inflation on poor people is often overlooked. One would expect that low-income people would be less able to adapt quickly to a rapidly escalating cost of living than their more financially agile brothers and sisters with higher incomes. The differences in well-being that result from not being able to adjust one's income to inflation can be very large.

For example, if sound economic policies kept the rate of inflation at zero instead of, say, 10 percent, it would mean that after just two years someone with a low, fixed income would have real purchasing power that would be roughly one fifth higher than it would have been under the higher rate of inflation. There are few social welfare programs that could expect to enjoy growth of this magnitude.

High interest rates are another manifestation of high inflation. The higher cost of borrowing money can be especially painful to those without substantial liquid assets who must borrow if they want to use and enjoy something while they pay for it, rather than wait until they have saved enough to buy it outright.

High tax rates, especially high marginal tax rates, can have a severely inhibiting effect on people's work effort. And they can be particularly discouraging to someone who is considering entering the work force at low- to moderate-income levels. Our tax system, if we look just at federal taxes, or state taxes, or Social Security taxes, is fairly reasonable. But if we look at it from the perspective of a low- or moderate-income taxpayer who must pay all these taxes simultaneously, it becomes quite irrational. The effect of federal, state, and Social Security taxes acting together often produces effective marginal tax rates of almost 30 percent for incomes only slightly above the poverty level.

A high unemployment rate, especially if it is sustained and unemployment benefits run out, can make a lot of people poor very quickly.

In sum, all the characteristics of a poorly functioning economy—high inflation and high interest rates, rising unemployment, and high marginal tax rates—produce a powerful economic effect that constitutes a double whammy on the poor. It hurts them directly by reducing the purchasing power of their money, throwing them out of work, and eroding their incentives to work if they can find work. At the same time, a poorly functioning economy reduces the tax revenues that must pay for the social welfare programs that provide aid to them.

For anyone concerned about the long-term well-being of the poor in the United States, the achievement and maintenance of a healthy, growing economy should be of paramount importance.

Eligibility Standards

Another important aspect of the Reagan administration's social welfare philosophy is the determination of who should receive social welfare benefits. Over the years, as the size and scope of our social welfare programs have grown, there has been a gradual increase in income eligibility levels.

The purpose of welfare, as understood by most Americans, is to provide help and support to poor people, to those who cannot care for themselves. One of the primary reasons we developed poverty statistics was to determine what kinds and what degree of help should be provided by government social welfare programs. Unfortunately, two developments in recent years have combined to blur our understanding of poverty in the United States and to compromise the validity of those programs in the eyes of the public.

The official poverty statistics published each year by the Bureau of the Census consistently and deliberately overstate the incidence of poverty in the United States. Many years ago, when this series was first put together, it was decided to focus on cash income only, disregarding the value of in-kind services received by the poor, such as medical care or housing assistance. At the time, this was a reasonable decision because in-kind benefits were then only a small fraction of total welfare benefits received, and the loss of completeness in the statistics was more than made up by the savings in the effort of compiling those statistics.

But as the years rolled by, the value of in-kind benefits grew and grew and grew. As the relative amount of in-kind benefits increased, the validity of the poverty statistics decreased. This problem is further compounded by the consistent underreporting of income to the Bureau of the Census. The extent of this underreporting is known, but the poverty series is not adjusted to take it into account.

The benign neglect of in-kind benefits and the disregarding of underreporting of income have gradually eroded the validity of the official poverty statistics to the point where they are not only unreliable but are very misleading. The census statistics, according to estimates by the Congressional Budget Office and independent scholars, indicate that poverty is at least twice as great as it really is.

The truly regrettable part of this whole affair is that social welfare experts who have been aware of the problem for many years continue to use discredited data while efforts to correct the data proceed with "all deliberate speed." The Bureau of the Census now has a significant effort underway to correct these statistics, but for at least five or more years the numbers have been badly misleading to those who are unfamiliar with their deficiencies.

An interesting question arises as to why otherwise reputable scholars would continue to use the discredited official poverty numbers. It may be that they do not know any better or that it is too much trouble to change. But these are unlikely explanations.

As time goes on one has to give more and more credence to the suspicion that the discredited numbers continue to be used because of, not in spite of, the fact that they grossly overstate the incidence of poverty and thus buttress the ideological view shared by most scholars in the field. To the extent that this is perceived to be true, it causes injury to the professional reputation of the entire field. The time appears long overdue for a little intellectual self-policing.

As we have gradually lost track of the true nature and extent of poverty in the United States, we have also begun to slide away from a clear idea of who should be eligible for social welfare benefits. Most Americans probably share the rather uncomplicated view that by and large only poor people should be eligible for benefits. One problem with this view is that as soon as you draw a clear line between the *poor* and *nonpoor* you create an insoluble problem, namely that those a few dollars over the line are very, very close in the nature of their financial circumstances to those just below the line. Yet those above the line are not eligible, while their neighbors just below the line are eligible for many social welfare benefits.

Partly in response to this, the eligibility levels of many programs have been increased far above the poverty level, so that many individuals and families who are not classified as officially poor receive social welfare benefits. For example, a family is eligible for Food Stamps if its income is less than 130 percent of the povery level, and for child health care if family income is less than 185 percent of the poverty level. To qualify for certain rent subsidies, income must be less than 50 percent of the area median income (it used to be 80 percent but was recently changed). Families asking for student financial aid at one time had no income restrictions at all, and the spectacle of wealthy students investing their subsidized loans in the financial markets finally resulted in a rather generous ceiling of $30,000 being placed on "countable" family income.

These and other expansions of eligibility standards have greatly blurred our common understanding of who is poor and who should be eligible to receive government aid. As the eligibility levels are raised, the number of people at the margin who qualify for social welfare programs increases rapidly and this, in turn, sharply boosts the cost of these programs. At the same time, the public sees more and more people receiving aid whose justification for receiving that aid becomes increasingly questionable as the income eligibility levels rise.

There is no easy way to draw the line on eligibility. What the Reagan administration has done as one of the main thrusts of its social welfare policy has been to restore more of a sense of balance and fairness in federal programs designed to aid the poor. In proposing slower rates of spending growth— and, in some cases, reductions—for certain social welfare programs, the guiding principle has been that the adjustments be made primarily at the expense of those people at the upper end of the eligibility scale. To use one of the most glaring examples, it was felt to be somewhat unseemly for people with six-figure incomes to be bellying up to the federal bar for their share of the guaranteed student loan money for their precocious offspring, especially when many low- and moderate-income taxpayers were paying the bill.

A major objective of the Reagan administration's social welfare policy is to restore fairer standards of eligibility so that the available resources can be focused on those least able to take care of themselves.

The extent to which this has been achieved is still unclear, but there are some signs it is working. Last year *New York Times* reporters interviewed state welfare officials in all fifty states in an effort to ascertain the consequences of the Reagan administration's adjustments to the social welfare budget. They were expecting reports of "protests, demonstrations, and lobbying campaigns in behalf of the poor."[4] What they found was silence—no protests, no demonstrations, and no lobbying campaigns. And the major reason for this may be found in the explanation given by John T. Dempsey, director of the Michigan Department of Social Services, who was reported to have "said that he thought Mr. Reagan had cut benefits in a way that minimized the effect on the poorest people, by reducing welfare benefits for

---

4. Pear, Robert, *New York Times*, February 10, 1982, p. A-1.

those who could work or who had income exceeding 150 percent of the subsistence income level set by each state."[5]

Fraud, Waste, and Extravagance

While past studies by the General Accounting Office, the Department of Health and Human Services, and various state governments have shown massive amounts of fraud and mismanagement in social welfare programs, there has been very little rigorous analysis by social welfare scholars of the extent and causes of this phenomenon. But this has done little to deter the problem from continuing in the real world.

One of the major objectives of the social welfare policy of the Reagan administration is to reduce and some day eliminate the massive fraud and abuse that characterizes so many of those programs. There are two basic reasons for doing so. The obvious one is to save a considerable amount of money, money that could be given to those who qualify and money that would not have to be spent at all. Another reason is to remove the stigma that attaches to all people receiving social welfare benefits, because those who are cheating and getting away with it have convinced the vast majority of the American public that fraud is widespread in social welfare programs. Not knowing which recipients are fraudulent, the public tends to be suspicious of them all. If there is anything that infuriates the American taxpayer it is the idea that someone is getting his tax money who should not be.

The New Federalism

The question of the proper division of responsibility for government social welfare programs between the federal government and the states and localities is one that has been with us for a long time. What has been called the *New Federalism* of the Reagan administration is, for the most part, an old federalism concept that has been discussed for decades. Over thirty years ago President Eisenhower established the Commission on Intergovernmental Relations. The commission, which included such distinguished Americans as Marion B. Folsom, Oveta Culp Hobby, Clark Kerr, Wayne Morse, and Hubert Humphrey, deliberated for two years and delivered a far-reaching report that concluded that we should:

1. Leave to private initiative all the functions that citizens can perform privately.

---

5. Ibid., p. A-26.

2. Use the level of government closest to the community for all public functions it can handle.

3. Utilize cooperative intergovernmental arrangements where appropriate to attain economical performance and popular approval.

4. Reserve National action for residual participation where State and local governments are not fully adequate, and for the continuing responsibilities that only the National Government can undertake.

A major objective of the Reagan administration is to systematically transfer authority and responsibility for some social welfare programs to the states and localities along with the tax resources necessary to finance them. This is the thrust of the New Federalism.

The objective is not to eliminate the programs.

The objective is not to dump the programs on the states and localities, forcing them to raise taxes to whatever extent they can in order to continue programs.

The objective is to improve the operation of those social welfare programs, and to reduce their costs, by returning responsibility and resources to a level of government that is more appropriate for these programs. There is a good deal of sympathy for the view that Dan Lufkin expressed after serving for two years as Connecticut's first commissioner of environmental protection: "The more the administration of policies and programs is brought down to the state and local level, the better the people will be able to judge who is fair, who is honest, who is creative, and who is productive and efficient."[6]

Opposition to a Guaranteed Income

Sometimes what is not said or done is just as important as what is said and what is done. Before President Reagan took office there had been a string of administration efforts—both Republican and Democratic—to radically change the existing welfare system and to establish guaranteed income for all Americans. President Nixon proposed the Family Assistance Plan. President Ford explored the Income Supplementation Plan. And President Carter tried the Program for Better Jobs and Income.

All these programs were spawned by a small, largely liberal, intellectual elite, some of whom were well aware that what they were trying to foist on an unsuspecting public was a guaranteed income. Unfortunately for the pro-

---

6. Dan W. Lufkin, *Many Sovereign States: A Case for Strengthening State Government—An Insider's Account* (New York: David McKay, 1975), p. 194.

grams, the public, which has a keen abhorrence of any guaranteed income scheme, sensed the true nature of these programs and our elected representatives thoroughly drubbed those proposals when they reached the Congress.

One of the more important social policy objectives of the Reagan administration is to *not* propose any disguised guaranteed income programs. This deliberate neglect of one of the hallowed canons of social welfare policy in this country for the last twenty years or so is, and I believe will continue to be, a major social policy objective of the Reagan administration.

Conclusion

The concern of the Reagan administration for the poor is as deep and compassionate as that of any previous administration, perhaps not in the volume of cant, but certainly in terms of developing an integrated, comprehensive program aimed at achieving a substantial and lasting reduction of poverty in the United States.

The broad objectives of this social welfare philosophy complement and reinforce one another, and they all work to the advantage of those who are poor or cannot care for themselves.

The major objectives are as follows:

1. The achievement of economic growth and the kind of a healthy economy that provides direct, immediate benefits to the poor

2. The restoration of fair, sensible eligibility levels in all federal social welfare programs

3. The reduction of fraud, waste, and extravagance in social welfare programs

4. The improvement of the operation of certain social welfare programs by returning authority and responsibility for them to the states and localities, *along with the tax resources necessary to pay for them*

5. The avoidance of any attempts to establish a guaranteed income.

These are the broad social welfare policy objectives that Reagan spoke of during the presidential campaign of 1980 and acted upon in the early years of his administration.

The specific agenda and statements of others in the administration may not always follow these broad strategies with full faithfulness, and sometimes may even contradict them. To the extent the strategies were followed, they may not have been executed with the greatest deftness, and to the degree that they were, they may not have achieved all that was intended.

But the driving thrust of Reagan's social welfare policy remains—to follow social policies that will work well, not just sound good, policies that are not only fair and just to the poor, but to the rest of us as well.

COMMENTS

Stuart E. Eizenstat

I have great respect for Martin Anderson as a scholar and serious student of public policy, although we come from different ends of the political spectrum. However, I could not disagree more with the basic message in his paper—nor with the absence of supporting evidence for that message—namely, that the president's program is good for the poor, and that scholars, the press, and the public simply misunderstand the administration's motives. It seems odd that an administration which prides itself on its ability to communicate should have so utterly failed in this area.

Before I state my views on the objectives of the Reagan administration regarding social welfare policy, I will first note some disagreements I have with portions of Anderson's paper.

First, Anderson propounds the theory that President Reagan did not believe he had a mandate to cut spending, but only to reduce the rate of growth of spending on social welfare programs. This is nowhere sustained by data in the paper, nor can it be. In program after program, real reductions have been the order of the day, particularly in discretionary social programs upon which many low-income citizens are dependent.

Second, Anderson gives a new twist to the once-sacred safety net programs, which the president assured Congress and the country were immune from budget reductions. He says that they were simply not "closely examined on the first round of budget change," because of political pressures which were "often irrational." He goes further to add that the whole safety net concept was political shorthand that only made sense for a limited period of time, and that the safety net should not be immune to close budget scrutiny, a euphemism for more cuts. If this were true, it would seem that the whole safety net concept was cynically used to convince Congress to support budget cuts at the beginning, something I hope—and believe—was not the case.

Third, Anderson argues that the states would not be unfairly burdened by the New Federalism, since new tax resources would be transferred to the states for the continuation of these programs. Yet most of the programs have been transferred at 75 percent of their prior levels and, after 1988, states will be expected to raise the revenues to pay for the continuation of the transferred programs.

Fourth, Anderson asserts that the president's economic policy is unfairly characterized as a trickle-down policy, despite that description by his own budget director. Yet a disproportionate percentage of the tax cut goes to the wealthy under the theory that this will ultimately help the rest of the nation.

Fifth, Anderson argues against high marginal tax rates, saying that they inhibit work effort. Yet the administration's welfare reform proposals instituted a dollar-for-dollar reduction in welfare benefits for earnings, which experts feel will cause a tremendous work disincentive, particularly for the near poor.

Sixth, Anderson argues, as he has for years, that the poverty figures overstate the extent of actual poverty by not counting in-kind benefits to the poor, like Food Stamps, subsidized housing, and Medicaid. Yet these are the very programs receiving budget cuts. If they are keeping people from poverty and should be counted to determine poverty levels, then what is the justification for cutting them, bringing families below the poverty line in many instances?

Last, Anderson tries to discredit past Republican and Democratic efforts in welfare reform, from Nixon and Ford to Carter, by calling them guaranteed income devices. I can say authoritatively that the Carter program was nothing of the sort, having a heavy work requirement and a job component.

Now I will briefly describe what I believe constitutes the Reagan social welfare program. First, the administration, more fundamentally than any of its predecessors, believes that the government should have a markedly reduced social role. David Stockman's contention that the people are not "entitled" to any services from the federal government provides the philosophical underpinning of this policy. FY 1983 domestic spending was reduced by $43 billion below that needed to maintain programs at their current levels. By FY 1986 the president's budget would reduce outlays for these domestic programs from 65 percent of the total budget to about 55 percent. The FY 1984 budget proposes reducing grants to states and localities by $5 billion below the amount necessary to provide the same services as offered in FY 1983. Income security programs such as AFDC, Medicaid, Food Stamps, Low Income Energy Assistance, and child nutrition programs will be cut to $2.3 billion below their projected maintenance costs. The president has called for a FY 1984 budget freeze for all areas except defense and interest payments, which in real terms would mean a 5 percent reduction in all other spending. Sixty percent of the proposed budget reductions affect programs for low-income people. One study indicated that two-thirds of the federal savings from budget cuts devolves upon those making $20,000 or less, compared to 10 percent upon those with incomes over $40,000.[1]

This first element of the Reagan program is a celebration of the private marketplace over government. While cutting funds for public education, Reagan favors tuition tax credits to provide parents with incentives to send their children to private schools. While sharply reducing public enforcement of environmental programs, Reagan gives private companies more latitude in complying with environmental requirements. He has systematically cut or eliminated federally supported alternate energy and conservation programs, while opening public lands for private development. He has eliminated public service jobs and public subsidies for legal services, training of physicians, and health maintenance organizations.

A second element of the Reagan agenda is a major shift in national priorities from domestic to defense programs. In 1981 the president proposed an increase of 9 percent in real terms for defense, or $1.6 trillion over five years. Defense spending would rise from 5.6 percent of the Gross National Product (GNP) to 7 percent. Defense outlays would rise from 24 percent of the budget to 36 percent in five years, while at the same time large real declines are proposed for discretionary nondefense programs. Grants to state and local governments and other federal operations would experience real declines of 30 to 50 percent over prior levels. From 1981 to 1986 all areas not dominated by entitlement programs—including education, social services, employment and training, and transportation—will be reduced from 16 to 63 percent, depending on the program.

A third element of the Reagan program is a massive shift in responsibilities from the national government to state and local governments. This would be accomplished under the president's New Federalism in two ways. First, President Reagan proposed a swap of major programs. The federal government would assume Medicaid costs in exchange for states taking over Food Stamps and AFDC; in addition, the federal government would turn some forty other programs over to the states at lower rates of spending. Second, President Reagan proposed that seventy-seven specific federal programs be abolished and consolidated into nine block grants. In 1980 federal funding constituted about 25 percent of state and local expenditures. The administration's goal is to reduce this to the 4 to 5 percent level by 1991, as low a share of state and local budgets as existed in 1933.

Lastly, the administration has sharply departed from Keynesian economics. Reagan's tax cuts were not only mammoth, but heavily weighted to benefit

---

1. Congressional Budget Office, *Major Legislative Changes in Human Resources Programs Since January 1981*, table 11 (August 1983), p. 76.

the wealthy. In 1983, persons earning less than $10,000 will pay $120 less than last year in taxes, while those making over $80,000 will pay on the average $15,000 less.[2] By 1985 the tax reduction as a percentage of income will be 2.3 percent for those earning less than $10,000, 5.0 percent for those earning from $20,000 to $40,000, and 8.5 percent for those earning $80,000 or more.[3] As a percentage of income, those in the highest bracket have a tax cut five times as large as those in the lowest bracket.[4] The combined impact of the budget cuts and tax cuts represents a significant shift of resources from public to private ends, from lower- to upper-income taxpayers, from poorer states and regions (e.g., the East and South) to richer states and regions (e.g., the West and Southwest). Households earning less than $10,000 will suffer an annual net loss from budget and tax cuts of $240, while those making $80,000 or over will have a net benefit of more than $15,000.[5] In other words, the Reagan program offers no significant benefits for those making less than $15,000, modest benefits for those in the middle class, and substantial gains for higher-income families.

In addition to benefiting the rich, the tax cuts play another critical function in the Reagan revolution—namely, to deprive the federal government of money that might otherwise go toward new social programs. These tax cuts are seen not only as an economic necessity to stimulate growth, but as an ideological imperative as well. Federal tax receipts as a percentage of GNP will decline in only four years (1981–1985) from 21 to 18.5 percent, resulting in a growth in the federal deficit from 2 to 6.5 percent of GNP. President Reagan intends to use these deficits to push Congress to cut still more in social spending.

Franklin Delano Roosevelt's revolution long outlived him. It institutionalized a relationship between the American people and the federal government which persists to this day; it created a set of responsibilities for the federal government in areas of economic management, social services, and income support. It has been a durable foundation, the policy of Republican and Democratic administrations alike. In contrast to the legacy of FDR, President Reagan—if he is reelected in 1984—will outlive his own revolution. This is not to denigrate Reagan's accomplishments. He has caused the rethinking of basic assumptions and changed the entire framework of the social welfare debate. But his revolution has been essentially a counterrevolution,

2. Congressional Budget Office. *Effects of Tax and Benefit Reductions Enacted in 1981 for Households in Different Income Categories*, table 3 (February 1982), p. 8.
3. Ibid., p. 9.
4. Ibid.
5. Ibid., p. 26.

one which has run its course. It constitutes a significant midcourse correction, but not a basic underlying change. His social and economic programs have been unable to accomplish all that they promised but, more fundamentally, their impact will be shortlived because of their fundamental dissidence from mainstream Democratic and Republican thought.

Government has certain unavoidable roles in a complex modern industrial democracy. Americans have come to expect a certain level of service. Tax cuts cannot be used to explain away massive deficits. There are limits to prudent defense spending. The goals of reduced taxes, greater defense spending, and a balanced budget were inconsistent. The 1983 agreement by Republicans in the Senate and Democrats in the House on a budget which fundamentally departs from the Reagan administration program demonstrates that the public will not tolerate any further reorientation of public resources.

BUDGET CUTS IN THE REAGAN ADMINISTRATION: A QUESTION OF FAIRNESS

Jack A. Meyer

Introduction

This paper attempts to ascertain whether the budget cuts in social programs under the Reagan administration have been sensible and fair. It does not directly address the appropriateness of the overall magnitude of the cuts, relative to some prior trend or baseline projection. Rather, it analyzes whether cuts were equitable, given the overall expenditure reductions.

Clearly, the issue of the right mix of cuts is subjective. I propose to offer some basic criteria for judging the appropriateness of changed trends in federal outlays, and let the reader judge whether the criteria posed here are the pertinent ones. The principal criterion is one of fairness.

President Reagan's call for some austerity in federal social spending arose from a desire (and supposed political mandate) to give greater emphasis to other objectives such as national security and to halt the gradually rising federal tax burden. Some argue that the squeeze on nondefense spending resulted from a miscalculation of the economic stimulus arising from tax cuts, which led the Reagan administration to underestimate the size of the ensuing deficits. Indeed, I believe that the tax cuts enacted in 1981 were too large in view of the administration's ambitious defense spending plans, since the combination led to an unfortunate choice between severe cuts in social programs or deficits claiming so much of available savings as to dampen private investment and retard productivity growth.

The author would like to thank Joel Menges for valuable research assistance in the preparation of this article.

The priorities of the Reagan administration, for the purpose of this paper, are taken as given. However, this policy mix itself has important implications in determining the resultant fairness. In this sense, I am analyzing a kind of "derivative" fairness issue. An overall report card on this issue would evaluate the distribution of tax cuts and the fairness of policies leading to substantially lower inflation in light of the attendant costs (in the short run, at least) of substantially higher unemployment.

In addition to the basic criterion of fairness—a relatively greater share of the burden of belt-tightening on those who can best afford to make the sacrifice—I propose a second criterion: to what extent were savings generated simply by cuts in benefits within existing programs as opposed to savings generated through basic redesign or restructuring of programs?

This paper analyzes these issues involving the degree of fairness and structural or design changes in federal budget policy through three basic concepts. First, the fairness of cuts *across* programs will be assessed by comparing cuts in means-tested programs to cuts in other social programs. Second, the fairness of cuts *within* programs will be addressed by examining whether restrictions in eligibility and benefits in particular programs affected mainly the less needy recipients. Third, the *type* of cuts will be considered, with a distinction drawn between cuts yielding one-time savings (followed by a resumption of prior spending growth paths) and those achieving a lower growth path over the long run.

An Overview

Federal spending for social programs grew sharply during the 1960s and 1970s. About $314 billion was spent by the federal government for social programs in 1980, more than ten times as much as the $24 billion spent in 1960. In real terms the 1980 figure was about 4.6 times as large as the 1960 figure. Federal outlays for social programs nearly doubled as a proportion of all federal outlays over these two decades, rising from 28.5 percent in 1960 to 54.1 percent in 1980 (see table 1).

The sharp increase in the share of outlays for social programs was financed in three ways. First, as table 1 shows, the increased social spending was offset by a decline in the share of national defense spending, which accounted for 48.6 percent of all federal spending in 1960, but only 21.4 percent, or less than half as large a share, in 1980. Second, this major shift in the composition of the federal budget was accompanied by an increase in the size of the government, with a corresponding increase in the tax burden.

TABLE 1

FEDERAL SPENDING FOR SOCIAL PROGRAMS AND DEFENSE

Fiscal Year	Real Spending on Social Programs (in Billions of 1980 Dollars)	Percentage of Total Federal Spending	
		Social Programs	Defense
1960	67.6	28.5	48.6
1965	93.5	30.2	38.9
1970	158.3	38.0	38.5
1975	264.1	52.9	24.3
1980	313.8	54.1	21.4

SOURCE: Calculated from data compiled by the Office of Management and Budget, *Payments to Individuals*, Washington, D.C.

Federal taxes as a percent of GNP rose from 18.8 percent in 1960 to 21.5 percent in 1980. Third, despite this increase in taxes, revenues fell short of taxes in almost every year during this period. Thus, the three sources of growth in spending for social programs were real defense cuts, tax increases, and budget deficits. These factors, taken together, enabled social programs to rise from 8 percent of GNP in 1960 to 19 percent in 1980.[1]

Most of the shift in budget allocations between social programs and national defense spending had occurred by 1976. While overall government spending continued to grow sharply in the Carter years, the relative shares of defense and social spending remained relatively stable during the late 1970s. Indeed, as table 2 shows, the bulk of the buildup in the share of the budget going to social programs over the past two decades occurred during the Nixon administration. The share of social spending rose from 32.7 percent in 1968 to 50.1 percent in 1974.

In order to examine the fairness of the cuts in federal social programs, one must categorize the various social programs and ascertain differences in spending trends between these categories.

To this end, I grouped those programs targeted primarily to low-income groups (hereafter called "L" programs) and those social programs available to all economic groups (hereafter called "A" programs). "L" programs targeted primarily to lower economic groups (means-tested programs) include Medicaid; housing assistance; food and nutrition assistance; public assistance; elementary, secondary, and vocational education; job training; employment;

1. Rudolph G. Penner, "The Future Growth of Government Budgets," in William Fellner, ed., *Contemporary Economic Problems* (Washington, D.C.: American Enterprise Institute), p. 107.

TABLE 2

SPENDING FOR SOCIAL PROGRAMS AS A PERCENTAGE OF TOTAL FEDERAL SPENDING

Fiscal Year	Social Programs
1963	29.5
1964	29.0
1965	30.2
1966	31.3
1967	32.4
1968	32.7
1969	35.4
1970	38.0
1971	43.5
1972	46.2
1973	48.3
1974	50.1
1975	52.9
1976	55.3
1977	55.0
1978	53.7
1979	54.2
1980	54.1

Total Percentage Increase

1963–1980:	24.6
1963–1968:	3.2
1968–1974:	17.4
1974–1980:	4.0

SOURCE: Calculated from data compiled by the Office of Management and Budget, *Payments to Individuals*.

and social services. "A" programs that are accessible to all economic groups include Social Security and railroad retirement; federal employee and military retirement; unemployment compensation; medical care, except Medicaid; assistance to students, including the GI Bill; higher-education and research and education aids; and other payments to individuals.

Each of these broad groupings contains a small amount of funding that could fall into the other category. Some of the "A" programs have a poverty-reducing effect, and although they are not means-tested, they may redistribute income equitably. Nonetheless, the means-tested "L" programs provide benefits to a lower-income population than the programs available to all, even if the "A" programs go to households with average incomes below the mean for all U.S. households.

Table 3 illustrates the relatively small share of federal outlays for social programs targeted to low-income persons. About 10 percent of federal dollars are spent on means-tested programs compared to about 40 percent of federal dollars that are spent on social programs available to all income groups. The share allocated to the "L" programs roughly doubled between 1965 and 1975 (5.9 percent to 12.6 percent) and then leveled off for the next six years.

The "Reagan I" Period: 1981–1983

During the first two years of the Reagan administration, only a slight reversal in the trends noted in the previous section is apparent. As shown in table 4, defense spending began to edge up between 1980 and 1983. This increase, along with higher outlays for interest, was not "financed" by any significant decline in social spending, but by sharply rising federal deficits. As tax revenues began to melt away, overall outlays grew, albeit at a somewhat diminished pace.

The recession prevented federal spending for social programs from falling further during this period by causing increased outlays under such programs as unemployment insurance and Food Stamps. The recession was accom-

TABLE 3

COST OF SOCIAL PROGRAMS AS A PERCENTAGE OF TOTAL EXPENDITURES

Fiscal Year	"A" Programs[a]	"L" Programs[b]
1965	24.3	5.9
1970	29.2	8.8
1975	40.3	12.6
1980	40.8	13.3
1981	42.0	13.0
1982	42.3	11.3
1983*	42.9	11.1
1984*	41.9	10.3
1985*	41.1	9.9
1986*	40.7	9.5
1987*	40.3	9.2
1988*	40.5	9.0

SOURCE: Calculated from data compiled by the Office of Management and Budget, *Payments to Individuals*.
*Figures for 1983–1988 are based on OMB projections made in the first quarter of 1983.
a.   "A" programs are social programs available to all income groups.
b.   "L" programs are social programs available only to low-income persons.

TABLE 4

PERCENTAGE DISTRIBUTION OF FEDERAL OUTLAYS

Fiscal Year	Social Programs	Defense	Interest	General Purpose and Other	Federal Deficit (in Billions of Dollars)
1980	54.1	21.4	9.1	15.4	$ 59.6
1981	55.0	22.2	10.5	12.3	57.9
1982	53.5	23.7	11.6	11.2	110.6
1983[a]	54.0	24.7	11.0	10.3	207.7

SOURCE: Calculated from data compiled by the Office of Management and Budget, *Payment to Individuals;* and *Budget of the United States Government, Fiscal Year 1984* (Washington, D.C.: GPO, 1983).
   a. Estimated figures.

panied by a significant deceleration in inflation, however, which slowed the growth of indexed benefit programs and reduced the outlay growth needed to avoid real cuts in discretionary outlays.[2]

The beginning of the defense buildup in the early 1980s was also accommodated by a sharp drop in the share of spending attributable to general-purpose government programs. These programs, including general revenue sharing, agricultural programs, transportation, and law enforcement assistance, claimed 15–17 percent of all outlays in the 1970s. In 1982 this figure had fallen to 11.2 percent and is estimated at 10.3 percent for 1983, a share of total government spending that is about 50 percent below the 1980 level.

The steadiness of overall spending for social programs masks a new trend that is uncovered by examining the "L" and "A" programs separately. From a peak of 13.3 percent of all federal spending in 1980, the "L" programs fell to an estimated 11.1 percent in 1983. This decline of about 17 percent in the share of "L" programs occurred over a period (1980–1983) in which the share of the "A" programs actually *rose slightly*, from 40.8 percent to 42.9 percent (see table 3). Indeed, while "L" programs accounted for one of four federal dollars going to social programs in 1980 (24.6 percent), this figure had fallen to one in five (20.5 percent) by 1983 (see table 5).

Meanwhile, federal revenues foregone as a result of tax exemptions, deductions, and exclusions grew steadily during the 1960s and 1970s, and did not change much during the early 1980s. The benefits of these tax provisions flow mainly to middle- and upper-income households. For example, excluding employer contributions to health-benefit programs from workers'

2. Congressional Budget Office, "Major Legislative Changes in Human Resource Programs Since January 1981" (Staff Memorandum, August 1983), p. 6.

TABLE 5

DISTRIBUTION OF EXPENDITURES FOR FEDERAL SOCIAL PROGRAMS

Fiscal Year	"A" Programs[a] as Percentage of Total	"L" Programs[b] as Percentage of Total
1965	80.4	19.6
1970	76.8	23.2
1975	76.2	23.8
1980	75.4	24.6
1981	76.3	23.7
1982	79.0	21.0
1983	79.5	20.5
1984	80.4	19.6
1985	80.6	19.4
1986	81.1	18.9
1987	81.5	18.5
1988	81.8	18.2

SOURCE: Calculated from data compiled by the Office of Management and Budget, *Payments to Individuals*.
   a.   "A" programs are social programs available to all income groups.
   b.   "L" programs are social programs available only to low-income persons.

taxable income saved taxpayers an estimated $31 billion in 1983.[3] A large share of that amount flows to households with incomes over $30,000. Thus, middle-income and upper-income households were shielded from Reagan's fiscal austerity in two ways—the cuts in non-means-tested ("A") programs were minimal and their tax advantages were left intact.

In my view the first two years of the Reagan administration can be distinguished from the second two years (as they are shaping up so far) insofar as the administration and the Congress now seem more willing to make a significant dent in the growth of income security programs paying benefits to all economic groups. In the first two budget cycles (FY 1982 and FY 1983), the administration proposed only minor cuts in this major category of federal outlays, while working for substantial cuts in means-tested programs. In fact, in some means-tested programs, the administration sought considerably larger cuts than Congress enacted. For example, in the Aid to Families with Dependent Children (AFDC) program the Reagan proposals for fiscal years 1982 through 1984 would have cut outlays by $5.2 billion, while

---

   3. Gail R. Wilensky and Amy K. Taylor, "The Effect of Tax Policies on Expenditures for Private Health Insurance," in Jack A. Meyer, ed., *Market Reforms in Health Care* (Washington, D.C.: American Enterprise Institute, 1983), p. 175.

Congress enacted reductions totaling $4.1 billion. The cumulative difference over the three-year period between Reagan's proposals for AFDC and congressional action was $1.1 billion, or about 15 percent of total outlays projected by the administration for the AFDC program in FY 1984.[4]

In the Food Stamp program, the cuts proposed by the administration in its FY 1982 budget (a 14.6 percent reduction from current policy over the FY 1982–FY 1985 period) were slightly exceeded by congressional action (a 16.0 percent reduction). By contrast, further cuts proposed by Reagan in 1983 (18.2 percent from current policy through 1985) were sharply trimmed by Congress to a 4.9 percent reduction, and another administration effort in the FY 1984 budget to cut 9.5 percent was dropped entirely by Congress.[5]

In the low-income energy assistance program, the administration's proposed cuts over this same three-year period exceeded the cuts enacted by Congress by $1.3 billion, a figure equal to the estimated spending under the program in FY 1984.[6]

Thus, in 1981 and 1982 the Reagan administration proposed significant reductions in social programs targeted to low-income households. Congress trimmed back these proposed reductions, but the net result was still a substantial slowdown in outlay growth that reduced real benefit levels or restricted eligibility under these programs. By contrast, the administration did not propose many cuts in the non-means-tested programs, and when it did, Congress balked. For example, Congress resoundingly rejected the administration's proposal in the spring of 1981 to significantly reduce benefits for Social Security, an "A" program. The administration seemed to retreat on this issue for the next year and a half. Indeed, the 1981–1982 period reflected a politically passive stance toward the elderly. In the first two years, which I call the "Reagan I" period, programs affecting the elderly were hardly touched. The elderly accounted for an estimated 26 percent of federal outlays in FY 1981, compared to 27 percent in the budget enacted for FY 1983.[7]

4. These figures were obtained from unpublished Urban Institute data tabulated by James R. Storey.

5. G. William Hoagland, "The Reagan Domestic Food Assistance Policies: Proposals, Accomplishments, and Issues," paper presented to the American Enterprise Institute conference on "The 'Safety Net' After Three Years: Income Maintenance and Redistribution Programs in the Reagan Administration," Washington, D.C., December 6, 1983.

6. These figures were obtained from unpublished Urban Institute data tabulated by James R. Storey.

7. James R. Storey, *Older Americans in the Reagan Era* (Washington, D.C.: The Urban Institute Press, 1983), pp. 3–4.

An Assessment of the "Reagan I" Period

In its first two years, the administration mistakenly relied on two forces to reconcile its tax cuts with its ambitious defense spending plans. First, it vastly overestimated the impact of tax cuts on the pace of economic activity. Second, the administration was overly optimistic about the extent to which spending cuts for low-income programs, administrative decentralization, and improved program management could bridge the growing gap between outlays and revenues.

Its considerable faith in tax incentives and management reforms may have caused the administration to underestimate the need for long-term changes in non-means-tested entitlement programs. Alternatively, the administration may have purposefully planned to take one step at a time, relying on the pressure of looming deficits to sustain the momentum of budget cutting.

Whether driven by excessive faith in tax cuts and improved management or a kind of Proposition 13 strategy designed to cut spending by shrinking revenues, the Reagan administration did not set out to control the spending growth of social programs providing benefits to all economic groups (the "A" programs). The administration's Social Security proposal hastily assembled in 1981 would have cut benefits significantly, but Congress reacted negatively to this sudden policy shift. At the outset, the administration had no game plan for Medicare and was not prepared to initiate long-term reforms in Civil Service pay and benefits or veterans' programs. Cuts proposed by the administration in these programs were minuscule in comparison with the magnitude of the funding problems.

This lack of a strategy for the non-means-tested entitlement programs stands in sharp contrast to other facets of President Reagan's fiscal policy. The administration came to office with a clear program for action in the areas of tax policy and national defense. It also had a strategy for expenditure control in means-tested entitlement programs and developed a cost-control policy for discretionary or general-purpose government programs. In the case of low-income programs, the administration planned to avoid the trade-off between work incentives, benefit levels, and break-even or eligibility levels by categorizing the welfare population into working and dependent segments. Public assistance benefits would be more tightly targeted to nonworking low-income households, with able-bodied heads of household required to participate in *workfare* programs. Many discretionary programs were earmarked for new block grants, with either reduced funding or flat spending (implying cuts in real outlays).

Thus, the philosophical underpinnings of the administration—involving increased reliance on private-sector helping networks, decentralization, and workfare—did not have a counterpart with respect to middle-class entitlement programs. As a result, a substantial share of the budget cuts involved low-income programs, discretionary programs, and general-purpose programs. With only limited possibility for cuts in such programs, the combination of large tax cuts and a sharp buildup in spending for national defense would inevitably yield huge federal deficits. Cuts in programs such as AFDC and Food Stamps were offset, if not exceeded, by annual cost-of-living increases under such programs as Social Security. Thus, the growth in overall federal spending for social programs declined only slightly.

To conclude, the budget cuts made through FY 1983 were unfairly distributed. Large percentage cuts were made in programs targeted to low-income groups while other entitlement programs and tax benefits flowing to all economic groups were hardly touched.

The "Reagan II" Period: 1983–1984

Federal spending projections incorporated in President Reagan's proposed FY 1984 budget reveal that the Reagan administration has more sweeping plans than simply a capping of the Great Society agenda. According to these estimates, as shown in table 6, the share of social spending will continue to edge downward, falling from 54 percent in 1983 to 49.5 percent in 1988 (its lowest level since 1973).

TABLE 6

PERCENTAGE DISTRIBUTION OF FEDERAL OUTLAYS

Fiscal Year	Social Programs	National Defense	Net Interest	General Purpose and Other
1980	54.1	21.4	9.1	15.4
1981	55.0	22.2	10.5	12.3
1982	53.5	23.7	11.6	11.2
1983*	54.0	24.7	11.0	10.3
1984*	52.2	26.8	12.2	8.8
1985*	50.9	29.0	12.4	7.6
1986*	50.2	30.5	12.4	6.9
1987*	49.4	31.0	12.2	7.3
1988*	49.5	31.8	11.8	6.8

SOURCE: Calculated from data compiled by the Office of Management and Budget, *Payments to Individuals.*
*Estimated figures.

By contrast, the share of defense spending is projected to be almost 50 percent greater in 1988 than in 1980 (31.8 percent of the federal budget versus 21.4 percent). (Recall, however, that national defense outlays had been as high as 48.6 percent of the federal budget in 1960.) The share of interest payments is projected to remain roughly level, while general-purpose spending will fall significantly from 10.3 percent in 1983 to an estimated 6.8 percent in 1988. These general-purpose programs were 22-23 percent of total federal outlays in the mid-1960s.

The projections presented here are based on administration forecasts prepared by the Office of Management and Budget. As a result, they are based on policy goals that may or may not be realized. The general trends noted here, however, are unlikely to be significantly affected by the success of these policy objectives, largely reflecting the future implications of action already taken by the government.

The figures presented here suggest that a snapshot of the present situation may provide a misleading picture of the impact of altered budget policies. The developments over the past three years must be analyzed both against the backdrop of prior trends and as a prelude to future trends that are partially determined by budget decisions that have already been made. For example, an analysis of spending trends over the 1981–1983 period compared to the final budget proposed by President Carter might lead one to conclude that very little change is taking place. But when earlier trends and future projections are taken into account, the picture looks quite different. From this longer view, the early 1980s appear to be the gateway to a significantly different set of budgetary priorities, with a sharp buildup in defense, a gradual tapering off of entitlement programs (disproportionately affecting low-income households), and a continued decline in general-purpose government functions.

Projections through 1988 show a widening gap between "L" and "A" programs. The disparity between these two groups of programs can be illustrated by comparing retirement and disability programs with other income security programs (see table 7). Except for Supplemental Security Income (SSI), the former programs provide benefits to all income groups, while the latter programs provide mostly means-tested benefits. (Unemployment insurance is partially means-tested insofar as benefits are taxed above certain threshold levels.) Table 7 shows projected percentage changes in outlays relative to baseline forecasts as a result of legislative actions since 1981, for fiscal years 1982–1985.

The retirement and disability program cuts range from 1 to 3 percent, except for SSI, where legislative changes increased outlays somewhat. By contrast, the income security programs that comprise the core of the social safety net face cuts ranging from 4 to 28 percent except for WIC (a nutrition

TABLE 7

PROJECTED OUTLAYS RELATIVE TO BASELINE FORECASTS

Retirement and Disability Programs	Percentage Changes	Other Income Security Programs	Percentage Changes
Social Security	− 3.3	Unemployment Insurance	− 6.9
Railroad Retirement	− 2.2	Aid to Families with	
Civil Service Retirement	− 2.8	Dependent Children	− 12.7
Veterans' Compensation	− 0.8	Food Stamps	− 12.6
Veterans' Pensions	− 1.7	Child Nutrition	− 27.7
Supplemental Security		Women, Infants, and	
Income	4.5	Children (WIC)	4.4
		Housing Assistance	− 4.4
		Low Income Energy	
		Assistance	− 8.3

SOURCE: Congressional Budget Office, "Major Legislative Changes in Human Resource Programs Since January 1981," Washington, D.C., 1983, pp. 24, 34.

NOTE: CBO uses a 1981 baseline, revised to reflect February 1983 economic assumptions, as the basis for computing the percentage changes for fiscal years 1982–1985 resulting from legislative actions since 1981.

program for pregnant women, infants, and children) which will receive higher funding. Particularly telling here is a comparison between AFDC and Food Stamps, on the one hand, where cuts over the 1982–1985 period are about 12.5 percent, and Social Security and Civil Service Retirement, on the other hand, where cuts are only 3.3 and 2.8 percent, respectively.

The percentage reductions in health care spending are somewhat larger than for the retirement and disability programs, but less than for most of the other income security programs. The percentage changes in outlays over the 1982–1985 period as a result of legislative changes since 1981 under Medicare and Medicaid are 5.0 percent and 4.5 percent, respectively (see table 8).

Mid-Course Corrections

While budget cuts in the early 1980s were clearly greater for means-tested programs than for other entitlement programs, the Congress and the administration began making mid-course corrections in the winter of 1982–1983. These changes ushered in the "Reagan II" era of 1983–1984. The Social Security compromise that emerged during this period has broad, long-term significance. It reflects not only the precarious position of the Old Age and Survivors Insurance (OASI) program, but the growing realization that the upward-spiraling budget deficit could not possibly be contained without

TABLE 8

PROJECTED OUTLAYS IN MEDICARE AND MEDICAID
RELATIVE TO BASELINE FORECASTS

	Percentage Change				
Program	1982	1983	1984	1985	Total 1982–1985
Medicare	−1.1	−4.8	−5.9	−6.9	−5.0
Medicaid	−4.7	−5.0	−5.9	−2.8	−4.5

SOURCE: Congressional Budget Office, "Major Legislative Changes in Human Resource Programs Since January 1981," Washington, D.C., August 1983, p. 47.

NOTE: CBO uses a 1981 baseline, revised to reflect February 1983 economic assumptions, as the basis for computing percentage changes resulting from legislative actions since 1981.

changing the giant income security programs offering benefits to all income groups.

Social Security. As noted earlier, during the administration's first two years, benefits for the elderly were hardly touched. The Social Security compromise, however, reflected a growing understanding among the electorate (and perhaps among many elderly people themselves) that a balance must be created between the nonworking elderly and taxpayers who are working and contributing to income security programs, as well as a balance between beneficiaries of programs for the elderly and other groups receiving federal assistance.

A significant portion of the short-term deficit in the OASI fund was averted by accelerating scheduled increases in payroll taxes. But, longer-term changes, such as taxing Social Security benefits (even at the margin, initially) and raising the retirement age in the early part of the next century are benefit alterations that, however small they seem, would have been politically unthinkable a few years ago. In late 1982, Congress began to come to grips with two important problems in federal social programs. First, when huge programs paying out over $200 billion in benefits are only cut by a billion dollars or so, while relatively small programs such as AFDC (paying out about $7–8 billion) are cut by the same dollar amount, before too long the latter will disappear. While the public undoubtedly supports some trimming and cleanup of the "L" programs, it generally does not support sacrificing them entirely in order that elderly groups, veterans, and civil servants should remain unaffected by the austerity program. Second, the failure to address the Social Security funding crisis for another year would threaten the continuation of Social Security checks. These two realizations lead to a tilt in budget

policy toward a relatively greater share of the burden of fiscal tightness for
the nonpoor elderly.

Medicare and Medicaid.   The change in budget policy between the
first two years and second two years of the Reagan administration can also
be seen in the gradual tightening of the Medicare program, combined with a
gradual easing of the cuts in the Medicaid program. The Omnibus Reconciliation Act (OBRA) of 1981 made few changes in Medicare, but cut about
$0.5 billion from Medicaid in FY 1982, or about 2.7 percent of federal outlays
for this program.[8] The corresponding percentage cut for Medicare was 1.2
percent. The cumulative effect of these Medicaid cuts through FY 1984 has
been estimated at $2.0 billion. Moreover, the administration's proposed bud-
get for FY 1983 called for percentage cuts in the Medicaid program that were
twice as great as for Medicare (10 percent versus 5 percent, respectively).[9]

The *cumulative* 1982–1985 percentage outlay reductions for Medicare
and Medicaid presented in the previous section were roughly equal—5.0
percent and 4.5 percent, respectively. But these totals hide a turnaround in
the middle of this administration in the mid-course correction. From a 1982
comparison of a 4.7 percent reduction from baseline projections for Medicaid
and a 1.1 percent reduction for Medicare, the relationship began to reverse,
as table 8 illustrates.

Tightening of Medicare spending began with the health care provisions
of the Tax Equity and Fiscal Responsibility Act of 1982 (TEFRA). This
legislation included a formula limiting increases in Medicare reimbursement
of hospitals, along with a ceiling on reimbursement for physicians under
Medicare. The TEFRA legislation demolished the myth that Medicare was
untouchable.

Proposals developed for Medicare in the early months of 1983 further
tightened the grip on this program. With little debate, Congress in March
1983 attached to the Social Security amendments a new plan for reimbursement of hospitals by Medicare. Under this plan, the government would pay
hospitals a fixed amount for each of 467 diagnostically related groups. Basically, the government is developing a fixed price that it will pay for each
type of illness, with some adjustment for regional differences in labor costs,
the complication of the cases, and so on.

This *prospective* payment system is viewed as a first line of defense
against the imminent crisis in Medicare financing. A Congressional Budget

---

8. Judith Feder, John Holohan, Randall R. Bovbjerg, and Jack Hadley, "Health," in John
L. Palmer and Isabel V. Sawhill, eds., *The Reagan Experiment* (Washington, D.C.: The Urban
Institute Press, 1982), p. 279.

9. Ibid., p. 281.

Office study predicts a $300 *billion* deficit in the hospital insurance trust fund by 1994.[10] However, even if the new payment plan works as designed, it can make only a small dent in the impending deficits. It would be premature to conclude that the long-term growth path of spending under Medicare has been reversed or even contained by the program changes enacted to date.

The magnitude of the funding crisis is reflected in the projection that to maintain the current Medicare benefit structure for another two decades would require an increase in the Medicare portion of payroll taxes from the current level of 2.6 percent (1.3 percent each for employers and employees) to a range of 7 to 11 percent.[11] Under current law, the Medicare portion of the payroll tax is scheduled to rise from 2.6 percent to 2.9 percent in 1986, and to remain at that level indefinitely.

Further changes in the Medicare reimbursement system are desirable to achieve greater fairness and efficiency in the program, and these changes will be outlined below. But some clear choices must be made. The Medicare Board of Trustees' 1983 report explains that to avoid depletion of the health insurance funds would require that either outlays will have to be reduced by 30 percent or income increased by 43 percent.[12]

Civil Service Retirement. The steady progression in budgetary restrictions under Medicare from 1981 to 1983 was paralleled in the Civil Service Retirement budget. The FY 1983 budget served as a kind of bridge between a largely business-as-usual approach the prior year and a significantly tougher set of proposals in the administration's FY 1984 budget.

In the FY 1983 budget the administration proposed that cost-of-living adjustments (COLA) in civilian and military employee retirement benefits be limited to the lesser of the increase in the Consumer Price Index or the annual "comparability" pay increase. This proposal, which could save an estimated $2 billion per year when fully implemented, was designed to limit the incentive to retire early and ride an annuity up a steeper slope than could be achieved through regular pay increases. Congress did not enact the administration's proposal, but the 1982 budget act stipulated that retirees under age 62 could receive less than the full cost-of-living adjustment. The COLA for early retirees would equal half the full adjustment if COLAs do not exceed a target amount—set at 6.6 percent for 1983; only if inflation exceeds the expectations

---

10. Congressional Budget Office, "Prospects for Medicare's Hospital Insurance Trust Fund" (February 1983), p. 3.
11. Mickey D. Levy, "Reforming Income Security and Health Care for the Elderly: The Need to Match Benefit Adequacy and Program Affordability" (Paper prepared for the American Enterprise Institute, Public Policy Week, December 6, 1982), p. 6.
12. Health Care Finance Administration, *Summary of the 1983 Annual Reports of the Medicare Board of Trustees* (June 1983), p. 13.

built into the targets would their COLA be increased. Under this formula, younger retirees would receive a COLA a few percentage points less than older retirees.

As in the case of Medicare, the administration's FY 1984 proposals for civil service retirement are much tougher than earlier proposals or changes enacted by Congress in the 1981–1982 period. Indeed, a striking similarity is apparent in the budget cycles for Social Security, Medicare, and civil service retirement, three of the major non-means-tested programs. This pattern is characterized by a business-as-usual approach in the first year (FY 1982), some cleanup and trimming in the second year (FY 1983), and a far tougher set of proposals for FY 1984 that finally begin to come to terms with the forces driving nondefense spending upward.

In the FY 1984 budget, the administration proposed to freeze the COLA for federal retirees in 1984. The administration also proposed to make permanent the current limitation on full COLAs for nondisability retirees under age sixty-two by allowing one-half of the full COLA increase after 1985. This limitation had been scheduled to expire at the end of FY 1985. In addition, the administration asked Congress to phase in over ten years a plan that would eventually provide only one-half of full annuities to federal workers retiring at 55 years of age. It also proposed to increase the amount withheld from government employees' salaries for pensions from 7 percent, where it has stood since 1969, to 9 percent in 1984 and 11 percent in 1985. Moreover, the government's contribution to the retirement system would be reduced. The total contribution, which is well over 30 percent of payroll, would be brought down to 22 percent of payroll by lowering the earnings replacement rate. Thus, the administration is proposing both a substantial shrinking of the total contribution and an increase in the employees' share in order to bring the civil service retirement system more closely into line with private sector practices.

Unemployment Insurance.   Another example of administration interest in scaling back the growth in benefits under non-means-tested programs is its handling of unemployment insurance benefits. The Omnibus Budget Reconciliation Act of 1981 (OBRA) made it more difficult for a state to qualify for extended unemployment insurance benefits. A state's unemployment rate must now be 5 percent (up from 4 percent) to trigger the extended benefit program (which provides unemployment compensation for 39 weeks, rather than the usual 26 weeks). OBRA also prohibited states from including those who are receiving the extended benefits in the calculation of their Insured Unemployment Rate, the rate used to determine each state's eligibility for extended benefits.

Unemployment benefits were previously subject to federal taxation for married couples with incomes exceeding $25,000 and for individuals with incomes over $20,000; in 1982 Congress lowered those limits to $15,000 and $12,000 respectively. The administration has also expressed interest in taxing all unemployment benefits. This idea, however, was floated at the trough of the recession (late 1982 and early 1983), and was withdrawn when it elicited an angry political reaction.

In this sense, congressional action in 1982 to tighten the caps on the amount of income (in nominal terms) that escapes taxation for a class of non-means-tested beneficiaries—the unemployed—was a precursor of the 1983 congressional action that subjected Social Security benefits to taxation for recipients with total income, including benefits, of $32,000 per year for married couples and $25,000 for individuals. Less than one of ten Social Security recipients will be initially affected by this ceiling on the tax-exempt status of benefits. However, if Congress allows these nominal caps to erode through time with inflation (as it has done so far in the unemployment insurance program), the "bite" of the ceilings will gradually increase.

An Assessment of the "Reagan II" Period

In summary, the Reagan administration began with a budget plan that virtually exempted the large non-means-tested social programs from the movement to decelerate the growth in federal spending. This strategy was doomed to fail, particularly in the face of a corresponding set of tax cuts intended to return the federal tax burden in a few years' time to a range of 18–19 percent of GNP (where it had stood in the late 1970s).[13] This paper contends that cuts of whatever size in the means-tested programs could not begin to reconcile the twin objectives of the Reagan administration in the areas of federal income taxes and national security, and that initial attempts in this direction were quite unfair to low-income households.

This paper further argues that the government's fiscal policy has been shifting over the past year toward a more balanced approach to the slowdown in the growth of federal spending. In part, this reflects congressional balking at the priorities established by the administration in 1981–1982. But it also reflects some change in those priorities within the administration, as manifested in the administration's FY 1984 budget. I do not suggest that priorities have been reversed, but I do believe that they have been altered significantly. Moreover, while the end of 1982 appears to me to be a watershed period in

---

13. Federal tax receipts averaged 19.3 percent of GNP over the 1976–1980 period. See Palmer and Sawhill, *The Reagan Experiment,* Appendix table A-3, p. 487.

federal budget policy and a noticeable period of transition in Reagan administration budget policy, the transition was a gradual evolution. In some areas of social policy, the FY 1983 budget was a kind of bridge between the previous budget, in which non-means-tested entitlement programs were hardly touched, and the subsequent budget which incorporated some major reform proposal for these programs.

Finally, I conclude that the Reagan administration is only *beginning* to fashion a policy of fair fiscal control. The Social Security amendments averted deficits in the OASI trust fund that could have massively increased the overall federal deficit, and changes in Medicare may postpone the exhaustion of the HI trust fund for a short period.[14] But significant changes in Medicare and civil service pay have yet to gain the political consensus that brought about the Social Security compromise. Tax subsidies have not been altered noticeably; and projected national defense outlays for the remainder of the decade have been only slightly altered, so far, by the Congress.

Thus, the American public still faces some difficult decisions and further sacrifices if the nation is to avoid continuously burgeoning deficits. The huge deficits claim a substantial share of the pool of private savings, reducing private investment, which in turn hampers productivity growth and long-term improvements in the nation's standard of living.

Targeting within Programs

The foregoing sections have illustrated how federal programs available to all economic groups were cut proportionately less than means-tested programs. In this section I will examine attempts to target benefits within programs and assess such attempts against two criteria—the impact on work incentives, and fairness.

The administration deserves higher marks for fairness in its targeting within programs than on the fairness of cuts across social programs. Generally speaking, cuts were made within programs from the top down, with the relatively better-off beneficiaries either losing eligibility or receiving reduced benefits. In other words, assuming that cuts of a given magnitude were to be made in a given program, the Reagan cuts were for the most part vertically equitable.

---

14. An estimated 50–60 percent of the funding arising from the Social Security reforms involved general revenue financing. Thus, the 1983 Social Security amendments reduced the anticipated deficit increase, but only by about half.

Several examples can be cited where benefits flowing mainly to middle-income households were trimmed while low-income households were shielded from cuts in the same program.

Education, Disability, and Unemployment Benefits

In education the administration has taken steps to limit benefits under the Guaranteed Student Loan program (GSL) to families with some degree of financial need. In 1981 a ceiling of $30,000 in "countable" income (net of allowable deductions) was placed on the eligibility for student loans at below-market interest rates without analysis of need.

In its FY 1984 budget the administration renewed its FY 1983 request for two further changes in the student loan program. It proposed that *all* loan applications be subject to a need analysis, not just those of families with income above $30,000. Graduate and professional students would continue to be eligible for regular GSLs, but would pay a 10 percent loan origination fee (up from 5 percent).[15]

The administration has also tightened up the management and oversight of the student loan program in an effort to reduce defaults, improve collection efforts, and ensure that the loans are used for educational purposes.

Another administration proposal is designed to encourage student self-help efforts and to change the regulations under which a student can assemble loans from as many as six federal programs on top of other sources of aid without contributing anything himself.[16] The administration plans to submit legislation requiring every student receiving a federal grant to contribute something to the cost of higher education.

In keeping with this theme, the college work-study program would be increased by more than 50 percent, while the Pell grant program—a means-tested program assisting students in low-income households—would be converted to a grant program supplementing students' self-help efforts. The grant program would be funded at about the same level as the current Pell program. Additional student loan programs, such as supplemental educational opportunity grants and state student incentive grants, would be terminated in 1984.

These changes seem to meet the fairness criterion discussed here, provided that any program conversion of the Pell grants does not impose unreasonable contribution requirements on students with limited financial means. The changes largely attempt to target assistance on those who cannot obtain

---

15. Office of Management and Budget, *Budget of the United States Government, FY 1984* (Washington, D.C.: GPO, 1983), pp. 5–91.

16. Ibid., pp. 5–90.

higher education through their own sources, while removing incentives for well-heeled individuals and families to use the loan programs unnecessarily, as well as to improve loan payments through tighter management. Allowing below-market interest loans to families with incomes of $100,000, as occurred prior to 1981, seems unconscionable. Cost-sharing by students seems reasonable, as long as this does not precipitate a gradual and total withdrawal of all federal aid to low-income students. And certainly any policy that reduces the default rate on student loans is laudable.

In the areas of elementary, secondary, and vocational education, Reagan's principal policy change was the enactment in 1981 of the Education Consolidation and Improvement Act which combined about thirty small grant programs into one state and local block grant.

Changes in federal child nutrition programs are probably more controversial, but they also were comprised of such elements as targeting assistance on needy youth in the school lunch program and reducing duplication in subsidies.

In other programs, such as Black Lung, Disability Insurance (DI), and Federal Employees Compensation (a disability program for federal employees), the Reagan administration has attempted to tighten up the review of initial claims and continued eligibility. Following a congressional mandate to review the status of DI recipients, as well as a statutory criterion for ongoing eligibility that stresses the capacity for working at any job in any area of the country, the administration dropped some beneficiaries who could not meet this standard. Supporters of the policy contend that the administration was simply complying with a congressional mandate to limit eligibility to those whose disability prevented them from working. Critics contend that the administration dropped large numbers of beneficiaries who remain incapacitated.

Skilled workers in manufacturing industries faced a strong work disincentive in the late 1970s due to the cumulative structure of unemployment compensation, Trade Adjustment Assistance (TAA), and private supplemental unemployment benefits. While taxing unemployment benefits had been initiated by the Carter administration, President Reagan proposed changes (adopted by the Congress in 1981) to further reduce the work disincentive arising when some workers actually received more after-tax income when they were laid off than when they were working. Tightened eligibility standards for TAA, along with the administration's plan to start TAA benefits only after unemployment insurance benefits were exhausted, helped return this program to the original intent of Congress—providing temporary aid and relocation assistance for workers in dying industries. In this case, the changes initiated by the administration reduced program overlap, and were both equitable and efficient.

Welfare Benefits

An assessment of changes in public assistance programs is more diffi-cult.[17] Here the administration's move toward one goal—vertical equity—seems to take it further away from the other goal—encouraging work effort. Savings were achieved in welfare programs not so much through reducing program overlap as by dividing those eligible for benefits under a given program (such as AFDC) into two groups based upon their dependency status. Specifically, the administration attempted to target benefits to the dependent poor, while making those who could work ineligible for benefits or forcing them to work in order to retain benefits.

A generation ago, earned income reduced the benefits of welfare recip-ients dollar for dollar. In effect, the "tax rate" on earned income was 100 percent. In the late 1960s, Congress passed the "$30-plus-a-third" rule, which exempted a portion of earned income from reducing welfare benefits. This lowered the effective tax rate to about two-thirds for recipients of Aid to Families with Dependent Children. In addition, AFDC beneficiaries were allowed to deduct a certain amount of work expenses from earned income. This deduction further lowered the effective tax rate on earnings.

In the ensuing fifteen years, the relatively small incentive to work pro-vided by the "$30-plus-a-third" rule has apparently failed to produce sig-nificant results, since roughly the same proportion of welfare mothers have earnings now as when the change was initiated. Other factors, of course, have changed, including the broadening of benefits under overlapping programs such as Food Stamps, as well as sluggish economic conditions over much of the past decade. Thus, the constancy of the percentage of AFDC recipients who are working does not necessarily mean that the work incentive provided by Congress in 1967 had no positive effect. It may have helped to prevent a drop in the proportion of welfare recipients who work.[18]

Nonetheless, there is little evidence of any strong positive effect on labor supply resulting from a lowering of the effective tax rate to AFDC mothers. In fact, there is evidence that such a lower tax rate, by raising the "break-even" level of income where households no longer qualify for welfare ben-efits, leads to a decline in the labor supply of newly qualified families with

---

17. This section draws upon the author's prior work in this area. See, for example, Jack A. Meyer's testimony in the U.S. Congress, Senate, Committee on the Budget, "Controllability of Entitlements," Hearings. 95th Congress, 2d Sess., March 1982.

18. For analysis of experimental studies, see Robert A. Moffitt, "The Effect of a Negative Income Tax on Work Effort: A Summary of the Experimental Results," in Paul M. Somers, ed., *Welfare Reform in America: Perspectives and Prospects* (Boston: Kluwer-Nijhoff Publishing, 1982).

somewhat higher incomes. This negative labor supply effect has been shown to accompany and largely offset the positive effect on the labor supply of poor women.[19]

However, research suggests that significantly increased work incentives would provide some positive stimulus to the work effort of AFDC beneficiaries although it may provide no net increase (and possibly a slight decline) in total labor supply as a result of offsetting effects.[20] In my view, this possible offset effect does not mean we should discard the incentives approach. The increased stimulus to work among welfare recipients could possibly break the cycle of dependency plaguing the welfare class. Even if the disincentives to work are not penny-wise and pound-foolish, they are dispiriting to beneficiaries whose sense of self-worth and usefulness might be enhanced by participation in the work force. Moreover, basic fairness dictates that people should have higher incomes when they work than when they do not.

Citing the lack of evidence that it reduces the welfare rolls significantly, critics of the incentives approach advocated "workfare"—the notion that welfare recipients be compelled to work as a condition of receiving benefits. As earnings increased, benefits would be reduced correspondingly. A third alternative—cutting benefit levels to induce work effort—is not popularly advocated, despite evidence suggesting that this strategy might be effective. Despite erosion of AFDC benefits in real terms, Food Stamps and other programs providing assistance for fuel, medical bills, and rent have kept overall benefits as high as or higher than potential earnings for many low-income individuals.

This situation may change if spending cuts in public assistance programs become more severe. But, at present, the government has chosen neither to lower effective tax rates (because of its short-term budget effects and partial dependency status for many lower-middle-class families) nor to pare potential total benefits for those unable to work (a harsh and politically unpopular move). Instead, the administration and the Congress have maintained both high benefits levels relative to earnings and effective tax rates on earnings

---

19. See, for example, Frank Levy, "The Labor Supply of Female Household Heads, or AFDC Work Incentives Don't Work Too Well," *Journal of Human Resources,* vol. 14, no. 1 (Winter 1979), pp. 76–97.

20. See, for example, Irwin Garfinkel and Larry Orr, "Welfare Policy and Employment Rate of AFDC Mothers," *National Tax Journal,* vol. 24, no. 2 (June 1974), pp. 275–84; Robert Williams, "Public Assistance and Work Effort," Princeton, NJ: Princeton University, Industrial Relations Section, 1974; and Daniel H. Saks, "Public Assistance for Mothers in an Urban Labor Market," Princeton, NJ: Princeton University, Industrial Relations Section, 1975. For a thorough review of the literature on this subject, see Sheldon Danziger, Robert Haveman, and Robert Plotnick, "How Income Transfer Programs Affect Work, Savings, and the Income Distribution," *Journal of Economic Literature,* vol. XIX (September 1981), pp. 975–1028.

higher than the rates paid by those in the highest tax brackets. Shunning the incentives approach, they have grasped instead at a *regulatory* solution to the problem—state workfare programs. In my view, this strategy will fail to crack the cycle of welfare dependency.

Congress effectively repealed the $30-plus-a-third incentive in 1981. At the urging of the administration, Congress placed a time limit on the work incentive bonus and a dollar limit on the work expense deduction. The $30-plus-a-third rule may now be applied to only the first four months of employment. After four months, every penny of net earnings is subtracted from welfare benefits. The work-expense deduction was limited to $160 per month per child for day-care expenses and $75 per month for other work-related expenses.

Congress also tightened eligibility standards, denying AFDC assistance (and often Medicaid benefits) to many working poor families. And it authorized states to institute workfare programs requiring welfare recipients to take jobs.

A similar trend is evident in the Food Stamp program, where the earnings disregard was lowered from 20 percent to 18 percent in 1981 and would have been eliminated entirely in 1983 under President Reagan's proposed budget. Congress balked at this recommendation and did not further reduce this disregard.

The Reagan administration's alternative to lower effective tax rates on earnings is to require AFDC applicants to seek work; able-bodied recipients who cannot find work would be required to participate in a Community Work Experience Program. States would be allowed to develop job programs reflecting both their own needs and the needs of program participants.

Despite its good intentions, workfare may not achieve its objectives.[21] Workfare programs and other work tests in social programs (programs like the Work Incentive program (WIN), unemployment insurance, etc.) have had limited accomplishments. Of course, some workfare programs have succeeded in reducing welfare outlays. But, in my view, workfare conflicts with the administration's prudent preference for incentives approaches to social policy over rigid regulatory schemes.

The changes in AFDC adopted by Congress seem unfair to the working poor and only worsen the adverse work incentives facing our lowest-income households. These changes target benefits to the *dependent* poor, while those

---

21. See, for example, Leonard Hausman et al., *An Evaluation of the Massachusetts Work Experience Program*, Brandeis University, October 1980. The authors concluded that "neither of the two treatments tried in the Massachusetts Work Experience Program lead to a reduction in welfare payments among the men in the experimental groups," p. 153.

who have the ability to work (and are therefore deemed *independent*) get no help, even if their means are about the same. Low-income households have been somewhat arbitrarily divided into two discrete categories—working and nonworking—with a callous approach to the former and a "business as usual" approach to the latter.

The administration contends that it would be a waste of money to give "permanent" help to working, low-income households. Yet, the wide array of special tax breaks and other subsidies flowing permanently to middle- and upper-income households remains unchecked. This unique treatment of the working poor is a major source of unfairness in administration policy.

Public assistance recipients are not the only federal beneficiaries to face stiff work disincentives. In several other program areas, the Reagan administration has worked—often successfully—to reduce adverse work incentives. The heavy penalty on earnings above $6,600 per year for Social Security recipients discourages work among the elderly who can and wish to work. The Reagan administration's 1981 Social Security reform plan would have phased out this earnings ceiling, but Congress defeated the entire reform plan. The 1983 Social Security amendments, however, did lower the benefit withholding rate under the retirement earnings test from one-half to one-third, beginning in 1990.

Summary and Conclusions

In summary, the fairness of the Reagan administration's fiscal policies depends on the perspective from which they are viewed. A rather narrow, program-by-program assessment shows that programs were generally cut "from the top down," a basically fair approach. In means-tested programs, the near-poor were more likely than the poor to have benefits reduced; likewise in programs previously available to all economic groups—such as student loans, Trade Adjustment Assistance, or school lunch programs—the relatively more prosperous program participants generally lost benefits.

One exception to this overall assessment is the unfair treatment of the working poor. The Reagan administration heightened the horizontal inequity among people of equal means by treating the working poor less generously than the nonworking poor. The Reagan administration did not, of course, invent this unfair treatment of the working poor. Categorical eligibility restrictions have screened two-parent poor families out of social programs for many years. But the tighter eligibility restrictions proposed by the administration and adopted by the Congress heightened the long-standing inequity.

From a broader perspective, looking across the budget, this administration's social welfare policies seem blatantly unfair. In the 1981–1982 period, it made virtually no cuts in the huge non-means-tested programs—Social Security, Medicare, and civil service retirement—with a combined price tag of over $250 billion in FY 1984. The budget cuts disproportionately affected the nation's poorest households. Exceptions, such as in the area of education, are quite small compared to programs such as Social Security. Nevertheless, in the past year a noticeable change has occurred as to what programs are considered fair prey for budget cuts. Congress has enacted a top-down approach in Social Security (e.g., taxing benefits for households with incomes above a given threshold), and a gradual tightening of the Medicare program, and the administration has offered some tough proposals for pension changes for federal civilian white-collar workers. At the same time, there are signs of an easing of further cuts in programs geared to low-income households.

Basic Design Changes in Social Programs

Thus far, this paper has focused primarily on the targeting of benefits under federal social programs and the impact of program changes on work incentives. This section addresses the issue of the extent to which the Reagan administration has redesigned federal social programs in ways that promise to improve outcomes or reduce program costs. To what extent were outlay reductions achieved simply by restricting eligibility or delaying benefit payments, as opposed to a wholesale restructuring of programs? To some extent, this will determine how lasting an impact the budget cuts will have.

I conclude that, in most cases, the Reagan administration reduced federal outlays without fundamentally changing programs or influencing the long-term growth of outlays. I will cite some notable exceptions to this generalization and briefly highlight some program areas where the Reagan administration has embarked on a major change of course. Moreover, the previous distinction made between the first two years and the second two years of the Reagan administration is relevant not only to an analysis of the *distribution* of the spending cuts, but also in considering the *nature* of the program design changes. In 1983 the administration appeared more willing to redesign programs while de-emphasizing management reform and program decentralization.

Generally speaking, the Reagan administration has made three types of changes in federal social programs. First, it has made basic design changes in some programs (changes that are likely to control the growth of spending in the long run). Recent changes in unemployment insurance, housing policy, and employment and training programs fall into this group, as do changes in

Guaranteed Student Loans, school lunches, AFDC, and Food Stamps. Second, it made "one-time" budget reductions in some of the discretionary programs, including many of the block grants to states and localities, without changing eligibility levels or the basic intent and design of the programs. Third, neither major design changes nor major budget cuts were made in some programs, at least in the first two years of this administration. I will cite three examples of programs in this last category—Medicare, Medicaid, and civil service pay—noting some important initial steps or proposals toward reform that have emerged in recent months.

Medicare

The cost of Medicare and Medicaid has been doubling every four to five years, and amounted to about $70 billion in FY 1983. Including the federal tax subsidy arising from the exclusion from workers' income of employer contributions to health insurance, the federal government's share of health care surpasses $100 billion a year.

Medicare and Medicaid have both inefficient and inequitable features. In Medicare, for example, hospital costs are shared at the "back end," when people have incurred huge medical bills, but much less so for routine services at the "front end." Moreover, federal medical aid to the poor is inequitable, systematically excluding millions of people on the basis of family status. Open-ended tax subsidies encourage first-dollar insurance coverage for a wide variety of health services, which in turn has led to increased demand for services. The government has stacked the deck against innovative health care delivery systems that promise to compete with the dominant delivery system, and has entangled the health care system in a labyrinth of largely ineffective regulations.

Reliance on rigid regulatory controls has failed to arrest the sharp growth in health care costs. Furthermore, exclusive or even primary reliance on prospective payment (the plan now envisioned for Medicare) could not contain significantly the cost of Medicare. In my view, the complex, yet incomplete, system of prospective payment may be as well-intentioned but ineffective as certificates of need, professional standards review organizations, and rate-setting have proved—unless it is coupled with cost-sharing, vouchers, and tax reform. The administration and Congress should give more attention to these reforms and place on the back burner the array of complicated formulas and target rates for allowable increases specified under the Tax Equity and Fiscal Responsibility Act of 1982 (TEFRA).

In its FY 1984 budget, the Reagan administration endorsed several of these more promising proposals, including a tax subsidy ceiling, Medicare benefit redesign, and a voucher system for Medicare. The administration deserves credit for proposing these politically unpopular steps that finally address the cause of the nation's health care financing problems instead of the symptoms.

My concern is that the Reagan administration and Congress will remain the prisoners of past policies, becoming ensnared in the implementation of the TEFRA legislation and the prospective payment plan embodied in the 1983 Social Security legislation. Both of these laws suggest that Congress has not yet confronted the real problems with our health care finance system. The fundamental features of the finance system that have driven up the costs of health care are (1) open-ended federal tax subsidies for the purchase of increasingly comprehensive insurance, which inflates the demand for health-care services, (2) a lack of choice in the purchase of health insurance for employees and government beneficiaries, and (3) government regulation it-self, which tends to maintain the status quo protecting those who provide too much health care too expensively, while impeding innovative efforts to lower costs.

Both prospective reimbursement and the new health maintenance organization (HMO) reimbursement policy need to be broadened and converted into a voucher system for Medicare. With this approach, Medicare would give beneficiaries a voucher for the purchase of any qualified health plan in their area. If the premium of the selected plan was lower than the voucher amount, Medicare would reimburse the beneficiary for the difference in cash; those choosing plans with premiums higher than the voucher would pay the extra amount themselves. The value of the voucher could vary according to such factors as age, sex, and local medical costs. A voucher system for public programs and a ceiling on the tax subsidy would foster both greater equity and greater choice of health plans. Even so, much greater contributing by those recipients who are able to pay, and tax increases would be necessary to make Medicare financially viable.

Medicaid

The administration has not yet addressed the basic design problem in the Medicaid program. The program still follows an inefficient cost-based reimbursement system and provides much assistance to some poor people and none to others in equally adverse financial straits.

Recent signs of some meaningful program reforms, however, have been fostered by federal legislation. The Omnibus Budget Reconciliation Act of 1981 (OBRA) permits states to apply for waivers from federal and state laws that have heretofore blocked reforms in the financing mechanism.

States are responding to pressure from cutbacks in federal assistance (reduced matching contribution rates, as well as the fallout of AFDC eligibility restrictions), sharply rising program costs, and diminished states revenues as a result of the recent recession.

The initial reaction of the states in 1981 to the increased financial burden was to stiffen the eligibility criteria by lowering income standards or by letting inflation cut into existing standards. Additionally, about 30 states limited the scope of health services covered under Medicaid. Other states continued to pay physicians very low fees for office visits, thereby discouraging their participation in the voluntary program. Penny-wise and pound-foolish, these states have ended up paying for other, more costly care—such as emergency-room care.

By 1982, however, states realized that these changes would do little to control their Medicaid costs. Using the increased flexibility accorded them by Congress, about 30 states began to design long-term structural changes in Medicaid which offer more accessible health care for less money.[22]

Some states have begun to steer Medicaid patients toward economy-minded health care providers and to cut profligate providers from the program entirely. Other states are attempting to be more prudent in their purchasing of the various laboratory services and medical devices that they pay for under Medicaid. States are also introducing less costly health coverage for their own employees, and channeling some patients requiring long-term care into non-institutional settings.

Federal Pay

Since 1970 federal pay adjustments for white-collar civilian (GS) employees have been based on an annual comparability survey. This survey, the National Survey of Professional, Administrative, Technical, and Clerical Pay (PATC), needs to be improved by (1) broadening the coverage of the survey; (2) making the survey more representative of the full range of government jobs; and, (3) making some allowance for the differences in pay practices between the public and private sectors.

The criteria for the minimum size of firms included in the survey impart a significant upward bias to the PATC survey results. The exclusion of both state and local government workers and employees in nonprofit organizations eliminates an estimated 30 percent of the nonfederal white-collar workers. Indeed, only one federal job in four is accounted for by employment in PATC

---

22. Rosemary Gibson, "Quiet Revolutions in Medicaid," in Jack A. Meyer, ed., *Market Reforms in Health Care* (Washington, D.C.: American Enterprise Institute, 1983), pp. 75–102.

survey jobs. Altogether, the PATC survey excludes an estimated 75 percent
of nonfederal workers from the control group to which federal employees are
compared.

Another key defect of the PATC comparability survey is its exclusion
of employee benefits from the calculation. Studies by two government agencies indicate that GS employees receive significantly more compensation in
the form of employee benefits than private-sector employees.

Pension benefits comprise the largest single source of difference between
federal and private-sector workers. Federal employees enjoy higher retirement
benefits, earlier retirement with full pension, more liberal eligibility criteria
for disability benefits (though lower disability payments), and more generous
cost-of-living escalators.

Meaningful reform in federal pay would need to address these issues and
redesign the PATC survey to correct the upward biases that build higher costs
into the federal pay structure. The Reagan administration has broken new
ground in proposing to deal with one major issue raised here—retirement
benefits. Prior administrations had attempted to contain federal pay costs
largely through proposing an annual increment lower than the PATC-deter-
mined amount (and hoping that Congress would not override it). The other
issues have yet to be attacked, though changes along the lines outlined here
have been proposed by federal agencies such as the General Accounting Office
and by several commissions and panels.

I now turn to those areas where some basic changes in program design
have been achieved since 1981.

Employment and Training

The Job Training Partnership Act of 1982 (JTPA) marks a new course
in federal job-training programs. Compared to the CETA program, JTPA
offers some clear differences in strategy, in the relationship among levels of
government (as well as between the public and the private sectors), and in
the total amount of funding. JTPA consolidated federal job training assistance
to states into a block grant, with each state retaining some flexibility as to
the training needs that require the most emphasis. It also greatly strengthened
the role of private-sector employers in working with states to gear the training
to actual demand in the labor market. At the urging of the administration,
Congress dropped the public service employment (PSE) component of the
CETA program in 1981, except for the continuation of a summer youth
program.

The private-sector input occurs through Private Industry Councils (PICs)
that were established under Title VII of the CETA program. These local PICs

are in widely varying stages of development around the nation, with some still in the planning and discussion phase, while others are actively involved in directing local training programs.

Another significant change from the CETA program is the requirement that 70 percent of the JTPA funding for job training must be used for training. Previously, an estimated 18 percent of the total money was used for training, with the rest spent on stipends (44 percent), administration (20 percent), and support services (18 percent).[23] Stipends for trainees have been largely eliminated.

Finally, the JTPA money is quite tightly targeted, as eligibility for the program (apart from a small untargeted set-aside) is concentrated on adults in the AFDC program and youth in low-income households. JTPA also authorizes new matching grants to states for assisting dislocated workers. The administration has asked for $240 million for these grants in FY 1984.

While increased targeting in federal training activities has been a gradual and welcome change over the past several years, the restriction of funds for adults to the AFDC recipients continues and augments the bias in federal policy against nondependent, low-income households. It would have seemed preferable to target funds to an income group without regard to welfare benefit recipiency. Moreover, the removal of stipends means that working poor and near-poor households are less likely than those on public assistance to be able to afford the training.

Housing

Traditional social programs have often been designed to favor *providers* of services as much as (or even at the expense of) *recipients* of services. Thus, in housing programs, the interests of home builders and bankers were reflected in the bias toward new construction inherent in federal housing policy for more than four decades. Instead of directly assisting people with inadequate resources, the federal government has funneled money to local housing authorities for public housing projects and to builders through mortgage-subsidy programs.

This preference for new construction over existing housing has been costly, as is reflected in recent estimates of the Housing and Urban Development (HUD) subsidy under the two approaches. In the Section 8 housing program federal subsidies are nearly twice as high for new construction as

---

23. Marc Bendick, Jr., "Employment, Training, and Economic Development," in Palmer and Sawhill, *The Reagan Experiment,* p. 26.

for existing housing for tenants of similar income. Rents are about 50 percent higher for the newly constructed units—reflecting both government ineffi- ciency and, in some cases, higher quality—than for existing housing.[24] With the tenant's contribution the same in both cases, the government subsidy must be twice as large. For example, John Weicher reports rents of about $360 and $240 per month in new construction and existing housing under the Section 8 program in 1981. With tenants paying about $110 per month for both types of housing, the government must pay $250 per month on behalf of residents in newly constructed units, about twice as much as the required $130 per month needed to bridge the gap for residents of existing housing. This means that under a given budget ceiling, many more households could be served under a program utilizing existing housing than a program that subsidizes new units.

The Reagan administration has shifted the bias of housing subsidies from new construction toward a greater emphasis on existing housing. The pro- portion of new construction in total assistance commitments fell from 63 percent in 1980 to an estimated 35 percent in 1982.[25] This shift will produce savings for years to come.

Minor Changes

Many programs have been changed in ways that deliver temporary sav- ings, but no real change in the long-term spending path or basic design. For example, the administration has proposed six-month freezes in cost-of-living adjustment payments for programs such as Social Security and SSI. The administration has also frozen spending increases for community development and social service programs (day care, Meals-on-Wheels, Action, foster care, etc.) in nominal terms by its recommendations for level funding of these block grants for a period of several years. In the case of community development, this was a change in the funding pattern for a group of activities already under a block grant since 1974. In the case of social service programs and federal aid to elementary and secondary education, the administration created new block grants by consolidating (and freezing) funds previously allocated under separate programs.

---

24. John C. Weicher, "Housing Lower-Income Families and Individuals," in Jack A. Meyer, ed., *Meeting Human Needs: Toward a New Public Philosophy* (Washington, D.C.: American Enterprise Institute, 1982), p. 340.

25. Raymond J. Struyk, John A. Tuccillo, and James P. Zais, "Housing and Community Development," in Palmer and Sawhill, *The Reagan Experiment*, p. 398.

Concluding Remarks

The first two years of the Reagan administration were characterized by an unwarranted emphasis on cutting spending for low-income programs coupled with insufficient attention to the built-in cost escalation in much larger programs providing benefits to all economic groups. At the same time, program reforms were largely concentrated in the areas of program decentralization and improved management. Despite the advantages of both these developments, the potential savings are not nearly large enough to reconcile the policy conflicts emerging from a substantial national defense buildup, large tax cuts, and a ''business-as-usual'' attitude toward non-means-tested social programs.

During the past year we have seen some hopeful signs of a more equitable approach to resolving this policy dilemma. Several new thrusts and proposals have been put forward in an effort to decelerate the growth path of the major, non-means-tested social programs, while cuts in low-income programs have eased somewhat. Some of these initiatives go beyond one-time savings and entail major program reforms promising a lower outlay path in the future. Other initiatives, however, (such as the six-month freezing of the cost-of-living adjustment), entail only a temporary savings.

In short, the administration still needs more balance in its program of fiscal restraint. And it needs to concentrate on more systemic, basic reforms and fewer Band-Aids. In part, policy conflicts could be eased by a relaxation or postponement of the commitments to increase the nation's defense capability or to reduce inflation. A retreat from these objectives, however, would bring other problems and conflicts to the foreground. The reader can decide how much emphasis or priority these different objectives deserve. My main point is that they cannot all be achieved simultaneously in a brief period of time and that the resultant trade-offs must be soberly addressed.

COMMENTS

Michael C. Barth

Given that one has to cut several tens of billions of dollars from the social welfare budget, how should one do it? To answer this question, one must set forth criteria of fairness and efficiency. The latter is considered elsewhere in this volume; by and large Meyer addresses only the fairness issue.

My criteria, though hardly novel, are (1) horizontal equity—treat equally circumstanced people equally, and (2) vertical equity—treat differently circumstanced people differently, but somehow in rough proportion to the difference.

These criteria are easy to mouth, but difficult to implement. What two people are equally circumstanced—two welfare mothers with the same income but different amounts of time at work? An elderly couple and a childless couple of twenty-five, each without income? How different is a person working full time, at the minimum wage, from a person working half time—enough so the former does not "deserve" any help from the public to pay medical bills?

To investigate the fairness of budget cuts, one can look across programs and within programs.

Looking first *across programs*, the Reagan administration has spent little effort to achieve equity. Meyer clearly shows that the Reagan administration continued and exacerbated a fundamental inequity by skewing the distribution of benefits even further in favor of the elderly. (This inequity was not, of course, invented by the Reagan administration and, indeed, the president did propose a Social Security cut in 1981.) Most Americans, I believe, would applaud David Stockman's 1980 distinction between valid *claims* and valid *claimants*. Yet when budget-cutting time came, the Reagan administration considered the latter.

The question of equity *within particular programs* is one for a welfare technician. If you must cut, how do you do it? There are basically two ways to do so: alter parameters (tax rates, basic program benefits, or eligibility

65

ceilings) or change rules (accounting periods, filing units, work requirements, and so forth).

From a vertical equity viewpoint, one should decide what population is to be helped and then spread the money fairly—that is, give more to the poorest. Take Food Stamps, for example. If I had to cut a few billion dollars, I might first raise the tax rate to 40 percent, then cut the work expense deduction, and then lengthen the accounting period (changes that would anger both those who favor greater income redistribution and those who favor stronger monetary work incentives).

Program redesign is also very important in achieving equity, but it is virtually impossible to achieve, as both Presidents Nixon and Carter learned. In the realm of program redesign, some suggest long accounting periods and broad filing units. But there are good reasons not to make such changes if one believes in providing assistance when it is needed and in providing incentives for larger family units to provide aid in time of trouble.

As the foregoing discussion suggests, the many goals of welfare are in such conflict that I find it hard to say one way to cut within a program is manifestly better than another. On grounds of equity the least poor should be cut first. By and large, the Reagan cuts did this (although raising tax rates reduces vertical equity). Given this problem, it is difficult to criticize what the Reagan administration did, at least on narrow technical grounds. It is hard to cut the least poor first without reducing both the degree of vertical equity and work incentives.

There is, however, a solution: one can opt for further categorization of the poor. I do not necessarily favor this, and I am not sure it can be implemented administratively. But, one could conceive of a world with a high-benefit, high-tax-rate program for those for whom work incentives are of no concern and a low-tax-rate, low-benefit (or no-benefit) program for those for whom work incentives are of concern. (Food Stamps used to be seen in the latter role.) Such a system would allow for some equity and some efficiency, but would not be administratively efficient. It might, however, be the worst of all possible worlds: defining a welfare world from which escape would be virtually impossible, not just extremely difficult, as it is now.

So where does this leave us? Looking *across programs*, the Reagan cuts have been manifestly unfair. *Within programs*, the Reagan administration hit the easy targets first and undertook no systematic attempt to restructure programs to achieve both more equity and more efficiency.

I close with a few general remarks. The data Meyer used largely do not reflect the Reagan administration goals, only the results. It is an ex post evaluation. Perhaps an ex ante evaluation (that is, asking what Reagan intended to do) would have been more to the point. In this regard, I believe that Meyer could have made a stronger case by citing data reflecting Reagan's intentions than the data he assembled with regard to the low-income population. But, the proposed Social Security cuts would have made the picture look fairer across programs. No one has yet totaled up the results on the basis of Reagan's intended budget.

The nation has apparently reached a rough consensus that the share of national output to go through the federal fisc should remain about where it is now. Therefore, for a time at least, I see relatively little to argue about regarding transfer policy (aside from a redistribution from the elderly to the nonelderly). The poor and near-poor cannot expect much help in the next few years (whatever happens in next year's election). Thus, the programs that help them are best left alone for now—not because they are perfect, but because likely changes do not seem manifestly better than the current structure.

IS THE SAFETY NET STILL INTACT?

Timothy M. Smeeding

This paper assesses the effect of the Reagan administration's domestic policies on the social safety net. This task requires that we define the social safety net, as it developed during the 1970s and as it stood when President Reagan took office, and then assess changes in that net since that time. Because the major effects of the administration's policies have only recently begun to be felt, a complete assessment of these outcomes cannot be thoroughly determined at this time. Moreover, while the administration's social policy objectives were substantially fulfilled in the 1982 budget, its 1983 proposals proved less acceptable to Congress, while its current (1984) proposals are not very likely to be adopted as put forth in the FY 1984 budget, if they are adopted at all. Finally, objective analysis of this administration's policies has been confounded by the continuing recession and its effects on both the number of people falling onto (or through) the social safety net, and the federal and state government responsiveness to such changes. Within this context, however, this paper attempts to review the available evidence and to assess the changes in both the depth (generosity) and breadth (size) of the social safety net.

In general, a safety net provides protection against unforeseen income loss due to a decline in earned income. This definition can encompass a wide

Lee Bawden provided countless helpful suggestions, themes, and fresh data at all stages of this paper. G. William Hoagland provided several useful comments on an earlier draft, as did Henry Aaron and Mary Jo Bane. Among countless others, Marilyn Moon, Herb Liebman, Jack Schmulowitz, Wendell Primus, Joe Bonelli, Maurice MacDonald, Barbara Leyser, Gene Hofeling, Demetra Nightingale, and Carol Werner provided the latest facts and figures on safety net program parameters. High-quality research assistance was provided by Michael Hansen and Susan White, while Rosalie Webb typed and retyped.

range of public and private efforts, including benefits provided by employers, private charities, and extended family members as well as those provided by the public sector. Another differentiation is that between social insurance, what the administration calls the *social contract*, and means-tested benefits which encompass the last line of defense in society's safety net. For those who are categorically eligible (aged, disabled, single-parent families), combinations of means-tested benefits provide greater protection than any single program. On the other hand, for many who are categorically ineligible for means-tested benefits (unemployed males, two-parent families), the social contract programs provide the last line of defense. For the long-term jobless in many states, only the Food Stamp program now stands between the social contract benefits (such as unemployment insurance) and economic disaster.

In this paper we will concentrate on those programs that constitute the last line of defense in the social welfare safety net; this includes most means-tested benefits, as well as unemployment insurance. The administration and its critics have paid the most attention to these programs. Given the administration's objectives in this area, this paper will describe both proposed and enacted changes and attempt to assess their effects.

The administration's basic social safety net philosophy, as revealed in speeches and policy proposals, is to keep the safety net intact for the truly needy—those who have no other source of income. This statement is, however, only a hazy generalization. Programs included in the safety net change from one administration statement or speech to another. Those regarded as truly needy vary from "the poverty-stricken" and "all those with true need" to a more specific clientele, for example, "the disabled and the elderly with no other means of support."[1]

The administration began in 1981 to shrink safety net programs by reducing benefit rates and restricting eligibility criteria, as well as proposing to reduce basic benefits, particularly for those who benefit from two or more programs. This paper concludes, however, that means-tested safety net programs for the truly needy having no other income remain basically intact. This conclusion is subject to many qualifications. First, benefit levels for individual programs (e.g., Aid to Families with Dependent Children (AFDC)) and combined programs (e.g., AFDC and Food Stamps) have been declining since about 1975 in real terms. This trend has been reversed only in the case of Supplemental Security Income (SSI) benefits. Moreover, Congress has maintained benefits for the truly needy in opposition to the administration's

---

1. See President Reagan's State of the Union Message of January 1982 (*Vital Speeches of the Day*, February 15, 1982), and February 1981 (*Vital Speeches of the Day*, vol. 47, no. 1, March 15, 1981: p. 323).

policy suggestions. If the administration's budget proposals had been adopted, virtually all of the truly needy would have faced substantial real and even nominal benefit reductions. The effect of cutbacks in programs on truly needy two-parent families who are not eligible for many means-tested programs cannot be accurately determined at this time; however, increased poverty among these families gives some indication of their growing unmet needs.

While the administration has enacted several creditable money-saving changes in program management (e.g., prorating of monthly benefits and stronger child support enforcement actions), most of the structural problems with the safety net that became apparent during the 1970s still remain. Many of the problems have worsened as the administration appears to embrace only policy changes that reduce federal expenditures or program enrollments. Thus there has been little in the way of program expansion or reform, only retrenchment.

This paper reaches these conclusions in four steps. Section II explores the concept of the safety net and specific safety net programs. Section III traces changes in program outlays and numbers of beneficiaries from 1970 through 1981, setting the stage for the current administration's program. Section III also looks at the legislative development of the major cash safety net programs (AFDC and SSI) and their interaction with other in-kind safety net programs (Food Stamps, public housing, and Low Income Energy Assistance). Program growth is traced both in terms of legislated benefit generosity (program guarantees) and the effect of 1970s legislation on a package of benefits for a prototypal beneficiary. Section IV assembles the currently available evidence to evaluate how the administration has both affected and attempted to affect the depth and breadth of the safety net. Finally, Section V considers the effect of safety net program changes on traditional two-parent families with employment problems. Section VI includes a summary and some brief conclusions.

The Safety Net

The Safety Net Broadly Defined

Economic well-being is measured by available resources relative to needs. Besides money, income and assets, resources can include formal and informal contingent claims on resources in the event of such economic misfortunes as involuntary unemployment, disability, or desertion. These contingent claims and the institutional relationships which support them constitute an individual's (or family's) safety net.

Although the modern welfare state offers widespread public and private institutional arrangements for ensuring economic security, not all citizens have adequate protection against economic misfortunes. Some people have numerous sources and substantial levels of both private and public (social contract) protection in the event of financial setbacks. Others (e.g., single mothers with young children) typically have little protection against such contingencies and must either rely on means-tested social programs or on informal family support or charity in case of misfortune.

Sources of economic security and stability (sources of contingent income) can take several forms. The public sector, employers, private charity, the family, and private insurance and savings are alternative means of providing economic protection against such events as retirement, unanticipated death, and medical calamity.[2] This protection can be rendered in cash (e.g., Social Security benefits) or in kind (e.g., a family sharing its home with a needy relative).

The public sector evolved into an important factor in the safety net during the 1970s in two respects. First, the government acts as a provider or intermediator of social insurance benefits, as well as the regulator of formal employer-employee income protection mechanisms (e.g., the Pension Benefit Guarantee Corporation). Second, the government serves as a last resort safety net by providing means-tested programs for those who receive no help or inadequate help from other resources. For example, the government provides Supplementary Security Income (SSI) to the elderly whose Social Security and other income sources do not provide a basic level of support, and issues Food Stamps and Earned Income Tax Credits (EITC) for those with chronic or temporary low earnings.

The Social Safety Net as Defined by the Reagan Administration

The Reagan administration's notion of the public-sector role in the safety net is somewhat different and more limited than that which developed during the 1970s. First of all, with respect to means-tested benefits—the bottom tier in the social safety net—the administration has rejected the notion that the federal government should assist all low-income or poor familes regardless of their circumstances. Instead, it argues that the government should only help the truly needy, which it defines as "unfortunate persons who, through no fault of their own, have nothing but public funds to turn to in order to

---

2. Robert S. Lampman and Timothy Smeeding, "Interfamily Transfers as Alternatives to Government Transfers to Persons," *Review of Income and Wealth*, March 1983.

secure a minimal standard of living."[3] This definition would limit the public sector role in the safety net which had emerged since the 1960s in two important ways. First, low income alone would not make one eligible for aid; for instance, one would have to be unable to work *and* have a sufficiently low income in order to qualify for AFDC. Second, all other alternatives— employers, families, and private charity—would have to be exhausted before the public sector intervenes. President Reagan's frequent calls for churches and private charities to help those in need, his recent policy suggestions for a larger private employer role in employment and training assistance and in day-care provision, and recent initiatives to force adult progeny to help support their parents who are institutionalized at public expense typify this shift in direction.[4]

Beyond exhorting other intermediaries to pitch in and pick up the slack, formal implementation of Reagan's "last line of defense" philosophy involves tightening two traditional sorting devices: categorical eligibility rules and means-testing. These tend to limit those eligible for last resort safety net benefits to the poor, elderly, blind, and disabled who cannot work (or are presumed unable to work) and, in effect, to female-headed families with small children for whom work is most difficult.

The next higher tier of the safety net involves the social insurance system, the so-called *social contract*. Roughly 80 percent of all cash and in-kind transfers are social insurance rather than means-tested benefits. The administration has largely preserved these social insurance benefits, particularly for the elderly and for veterans. It has proposed some cuts, however, for the disabled and for federal government retirees. After President Reagan's aborted attempt at reducing Social Security benefits for early retirees and new SSI beneficiaries in 1981, social insurance benefits for the current elderly have remained largely intact. The most significant changes in the social insurance system to date have been (1) the reduction (and failure to extend) federal unemployment benefits to various types of workers, and (2) passage of the 1983 Social Security amendments.

While these particular benefit reductions involve the social insurance system, means-tested programs have also been affected. Thus, for those who fall through the upper tier of the safety net (e.g., from loss of unemployment insurance), the chances of being caught in the bottom tier have also been reduced. For instance, the number of states with an AFDC for two-parent

---

3. Robert B. Carlson and Kevin R. Hopkins, "Whose Responsibility is Social Responsibility?" *Public Welfare*, vol. 39, no. 4 (Fall 1981), pp. 9–17.

4. For instance, the 1982 Job Partnership Training Act typifies this reliance on private-sector involvement.

families (AFDC-UP) program shrank from 28 to 25 between 1980 and 1982.[5] In March 1982, only 37 percent of the unemployed lived in states with AFDC-UP programs. In addition, both the benefit level of the Food Stamp program and its minimum income qualification levels were tightened to make it harder for the long-term unemployed to qualify.

Some programs are omitted from our analysis because (1) they have not been subject to heavy budgetary activity (e.g., veterans' benefits, workers' compensation), (2) they do not clearly fall into our concept of the safety net (e.g., military and government employee pensions), or (3) they cannot be properly evaluated because of the uncertain impact of budgetary actions at this time (e.g., Medicare and Medicaid). With these limitations in mind, we turn to changes in the social safety net during the 1970s as a context for assessing changes enacted under the current administration.

Changes in the Safety Net during the 1970s

As a prelude for examining the breadth and generosity of safety net benefits, we first turn to trends in overall expenditures in these programs. Table 1 shows federal government outlays and total outlays for major cash and in-kind income support programs for 1970, 1975, 1980, and 1981. We have classified them as either social insurance (i.e., the upper tier of the safety net) or as means-tested benefits (i.e., the bottom tier of the net). Not all programs are singled out; rather, we focus only on those programs that seem to most clearly reflect the types of safety net benefits that the administration's policies have addressed.

Overall Spending

Table 1 shows the expansion of safety net programs during the 1970s.[6] Major social insurance programs, particularly Old Age, Survivors, and

---

5. U.S. Congress, House, Ways and Means Committee, *Background Material and Data on Major Programs Within the Jurisdiction of the Committee on Ways and Means*, 98th Cong. 1st sess., February 8, 1983, p. 27.

6. We refer to the period FY 1970 through FY 1981 as the 1970s because the majority of the impact of the Reagan administration's social policies did not affect the safety net until after FY 1981. A similar time frame is chosen for the detailed analysis of AFDC, SSI, and other programs below. Constant dollars are in all cases computed using the Consumer Price Index. Reliance on alternative price indices (e.g., the Personal Consumption Expenditure deflator) would produce slightly different absolute percentage changes in outlays. However, such changes do not affect the basic results or relative trends shown in table 1 or in any of the tables which follow.

TABLE 1

OUTLAYS FOR MAJOR INCOME SUPPORT PROGRAMS
(In Billions of Constant Dollars)

	1970		1975		1980		1981		Federal Change	
	Federal	*Total*	*Federal*	*Total*	*Federal*	*Total*	*Federal*	*Total*	*Actual*	*Percentage*
Social Insurance Programs										
OASDI	$68.2	$68.2	$105.4	$105.4	$134.8	$134.8	$144.9	$144.9	$76.7	112.5
Medicare	15.2	15.2	23.0	23.0	38.3	38.3	42.5	42.5	27.3	179.6
Unemployment Compensation	7.7	7.7	21.0	21.0	18.5	18.5	18.2	18.2	10.5	136.4
Means-Tested Programs										
AFDC	5.1	9.2	8.5	13.7	8.8	13.9	9.6	14.2	4.5	88.2
SSI[a]	—	4.1	7.5	9.2	7.0	8.6	7.2	8.6	−0.3[d]	−4.0
Food Stamps[b]	2.0	2.0	7.2	7.2	10.0	10.0	11.3	11.3	9.3	465.0
Child Nutrition[c]	1.5	1.9	3.3	3.9	4.7	5.3	4.4	4.8	2.9	193.3
Housing Assistance	2.8	2.8	3.3	3.3	4.9	4.9	5.7	5.7	2.9	103.6
EITC	—	—	—	—	1.4	1.4	1.3	1.3	−0.1[d]	−7.1
LIEA	—	—	—	—	1.7	1.7	1.8	1.8	0.1[e]	5.9
Title XX	—	—	3.1	NA	3.1	NA	2.6	NA	−0.5[d]	−16.1
Medicaid	5.8	10.9	10.4	19.0	15.3	25.4	16.8	30.4	11.0	189.7
BEOG/Pell Grants	0.6	0.6	0.3	0.3	2.2	2.2	2.5	2.5	1.9	316.7
CETA[f]	2.4	2.4	4.8	4.8	3.6	3.6	3.7	3.7	1.3	54.2

SOURCE: Office of Management and Budget, *Budget of the United States Government and Appendices* (Washington, D.C.: Government Printing Office), various years.

a. Before its inception in 1974, SSI was preceded by three state-administered programs—Old Age Assistance, Aid to the Blind, and Aid to the Permanently and Totally Disabled.
b. Includes aid to Puerto Rico, and before 1975, the Surplus Commodities Food Distribution Program.
c. Includes WIC, Special Milk, and other Minor programs.
d. 1975–1981 change.
e. 1980–1981 change.
f. Includes expenditures under Manpower Development and Training Act and Economic Opportunities Act prior to 1975 when CETA began.

Disability Insurance (OASDI) and Medicare, were greatly expanded both in real dollar and in percentage terms. Major means-tested benefits other than Food Stamps and child nutrition (e.g., AFDC) grew less rapidly in percentage terms and far less in real dollar outlays. All of the overall growth in AFDC outlays took place between 1970 and 1975, with real dollar benefits constant since that time. Federal government SSI outlays actually declined in real terms between 1975 and 1981, mainly due to declining enrollments which are attributed to the increased generosity of OASDI benefits over this period. Social service outlays (Title XX) also declined during the 1970s. While the Earned Income Tax Credit (EITC) provided income tax relief for low-wage workers with children, the major program growth in means-tested benefits took place in the area of in-kind programs. Food Stamps, an in-kind negative income tax, filled major voids in the bottom tier safety net system due to its noncategorical nature and its nationwide benefit standards. In 1979, for instance, basic Food Stamp benefits exceeded AFDC benefits in seven southern states, even though Food Stamps are reduced by the receipt of AFDC.[7] Child nutrition benefits also expanded greatly as the high social benefits of adequate child feeding and proper prenatal diet in such programs as the Special Supplementary Feeding Program for Women, Infants, and Children (WIC) became evident. Federal aid to higher education in the form of Basic Educational Opportunity Grants (BEOG) (later named Pell grants) expanded college opportunities for lower- and middle-income youth. Federal job and training initiatives were largely consolidated and expanded under the Comprehensive Employment and Training Act (CETA). A national Low Income Energy Assistance (LIEA) program was begun in FY 1981, replacing the temporary energy crisis assistance program which had operated under the Community Services Administration since 1978. Medical benefits grew the fastest, with overall real outlays for Medicare and Medicaid tripling during the 1970–1981 period. While this growth both instigated, and fell prey to, rapid medical price increases, the quality and quantity of medical care available to the poor and the elderly was greatly expanded.

In sum, by the time Ronald Reagan took office in 1981, America had experienced a decade of substantial increases in expenditures for safety net programs. Social insurance benefits had increased most substantially, with real OASDI outlays doubling. In the means-tested benefit arena, new and revamped initiatives in the areas of food and nutrition, energy assistance, and health care outlays grew most rapidly, particularly since 1975. Traditional cash welfare programs such as AFDC experienced a significant but smaller

---

7. Unpublished data from the Department of Health and Human Services. These states were Mississippi, South Carolina, Texas, Tennessee, Georgia, Alabama, and Louisiana.

dollar outlay growth prior to 1975, with outlays since then (for both AFDC and SSI) remaining relatively constant in real terms.

The Breadth of Safety Net Programs

While the figures in table 1 indicate the growth in overall benefits during the 1970s, program coverage also changed considerably. Table 2 presents several indicators of the number of people served by selected means-tested programs throughout the 1970s.[8] These figures indicate some surprising trends. Growth in the number of recipients of the traditional cash transfer programs was not as large as popularly believed. The number of beneficiaries covered by AFDC, SSI, and General Assistance increased by only 13.2 percent, just slightly more than the 11.5 percent increase in the U.S. population between 1970 and 1981. Program enrollments for AFDC and SSI peaked in mid-decade and have remained fairly constant since then. The major program expansion during this period was in the SSI disability rolls, which more than doubled. In fact, the increase in SSI disability beneficiaries was nearly twice as great as the increase in AFDC enrollments from 1970 to 1981. These figures do not support the explosion in the number of welfare recipients commonly believed to have occurred during the 1970s.

Concentrating on the number of *families* receiving AFDC benefits provides only a slightly different picture. Because average AFDC family size declined from four persons to three between 1969 and 1979, the AFDC caseload increased 42 percent by 1981.[9] The large majority of that growth took place by 1975. Of the overall growth of 1.076 million AFDC cases between 1970 and 1981, 93 percent were added by 1975. Since that time there has been almost no growth in the AFDC program in terms of family caseload.

The remainder of table 2 shows the expansion of the rolls for in-kind transfer programs in the bottom tier of the safety net during the 1970s. In particular, Food Stamp program enrollments increased over this period to the point where 5 million more persons were served by Food Stamps in an average month during 1981 than were served by all traditional cash assistance programs combined. New initiatives for energy assistance (LIEA) and refundable Earned Income Tax Credits (EITC) helped millions of additional low-income households cope with the problems of rising energy prices and rapidly increasing payroll taxes. The

---

8. Figures cannot be added because of multiple recipiency, particularly for Food Stamps, LIEA, AFDC, and SSI. Ideally one would like to measure the breadth of safety net programs by investigating changes in program eligibility rather than changes in actual enrollments. But owing largely to lack of data, this type of comparison is not currently possible.

9. U.S. Congress, House, Ways and Means Committee, Background Material, February 1983.

TABLE 2

RECIPIENCY OF MEANS-TESTED INCOME TRANSFER BENEFITS

Program/Units	Number of Recipients (in Thousands)				Change: 1970–1981	
	1970	1975	1980	1981	Actual Number	Percentage Change[h]
Cash Transfers						
SSI (Total Persons)[a]	3,098[g]	4,314	4,142	4,019	921	29.7
Aged	2,082	2,307	1,801	1,678	−404	−19.4
Blind	81	74	78	79	−2	−2.5
Disabled	935	1,933	2,256	2,262	1,727	184.7
AFDC and AFDC-UP						
(Total Persons)[a]	9,660	11,383	11,101	10,607	947	9.8
General Assistance:						
(Total Persons)[a]	1,056	977	986	1,008[b]	−48	−4.5
Total Persons	13,814	16,674	16,229	15,634	1,820	13.2
AFDC and AFDC-UP						
(Total Families)[a]	2,553	3,553	3,843	3,629	1,076	42.1
AFDC	2,396	3,421	3,650	3,409	1,013	42.3
AFDC-UP	157	132	193	220	63	40.1
In-Kind Transfers						
Food Stamps (Persons)[c]	10,434[j]	17,063	19,401	20,626	10,192	97.7
Medicaid (Persons)[d]	15,501	22,413	21,604	22,073	6,572	42.4
Earned Income Tax						
Credit (Families)[e]	—	6,215	6,954	6,703	488	7.9[i]
Low Income Energy Assistance (Households)[f]	—	—	—	7,073	NA	NA

SOURCES: *Social Security Bulletin*, April 1983; Office of Family Assistance, and Office of Research and Statistics, Social Security Administration; "Background Material and Data on Major Programs Within the Jurisdiction of the Committee on Ways and Means," U.S. House of Representatives Committee on Ways and Means, February 8, 1983; Health Care Financing Review, Summer 1983.

a.   December caseloads.
b.   October 1981 estimate.
c.   Average monthly number receiving benefits over the fiscal year.
d.   Unduplicated number receiving benefits over the fiscal year.
e.   Calendar-year figures.
f.   Fiscal year 1981 number of beneficiaries.
g.   Based on Old Age Assistance, Aid to the Blind, and Aid to the Permanently and Totally Disabled prior to inception of SSI on January 1, 1974.
h. $(1981-1970) \div 1975 \times .100$.
i. $(1981-1975) \div 1975 \times .100$.
j.   Includes participation in the Surplus Commodities Food Distribution Program in 1970.

Medicaid program expanded only until 1975; since then the number of recipients has held constant. Table 2 shows that, excluding Food Stamps and new initiatives undertaken after 1975 (e.g., LIEA and EITC), the number of recipients of major means-tested benefits peaked in mid-decade and have remained nearly constant since that time. Even the number of Food Stamp recipients increased only a modest 21 percent from 1975 to 1981.

Benefit Generosity

While table 2 helps document the increased *breadth* of the safety net programs during the 1970s, measuring changes in the *generosity* of the safety net is more difficult. Analysis of total expenditures or average expenditures per person or per recipient unit is inadequate since these figures represent not only legislated changes in benefit levels (the political intent), but also changes in the numbers and types of recipients and their degree of self-sufficiency. For instance, average AFDC benefits are affected by changes in the average size, composition, and income of eligible families, as well as by legislated changes in maximum benefit levels, eligibility standards, income disregards, and benefit reduction rates.

One method of separating legislative intent (i.e., the generosity of the safety net) from actual program outlays is to look at maximum benefits that are payable to families with no other income. In fact, insofar as the truly needy are those who have no other source of income, maximum benefit levels (guarantee levels) most accurately reflect the generosity of the safety net.

AFDC. Table 3 shows the median and overall average maximum AFDC benefits available to a family of four persons on AFDC from July 1970 through July 1981 in constant 1981 dollars. The variance between states in AFDC benefit generosity is shown by comparing the average maximum benefit in the five highest and lowest states (as ranked by their 1975 benefit level). Increasingly, these maximum benefit levels are the actual benefits paid to AFDC families. While in 1969 only 56 percent of AFDC families reported no income other than AFDC, making them eligible for the maximum benefit, 81 percent of AFDC families had no other income in March 1979, the latest available figures.[10]

Median AFDC benefits fell steadily in real terms, at an average rate of 3.7 percent per year, from 1970 through 1981, ending up 33.6 percent below the comparable 1970 level. Thus, in July 1981 the real median maximum benefit was $178.00 per month lower than it was in July 1970. The national average maximum AFDC benefit decreased similarly. In both cases, the most precipitous

---

10. U.S. Congress, House, Ways and Means Committee, Background Material, February 1983.

TABLE 3

MAXIMUM AFDC BENEFITS AND ACTUAL BENEFIT OUTLAYS
(In Constant 1981 Dollars)

Year (July)	Median	Average, Ten Highest States	Average, Ten Lowest States[c]	National Average	Total Outlays (in Billions of Dollars)
1970	526.93	682.67	273.54	508.20	11.365
1972	519.57	708.26	257.17	504.35	15.020
1974	505.54	688.19	242.44	479.70	14.607
1975	445.95	681.93	228.89	469.17	15.559
1976	458.47	622.94	218.85	463.07	16.198
1978	461.65	643.52	226.08	436.57	14.964
1979	426.07	614.41	218.42	421.18	13.871
1980	388.52	580.91	199.12	390.43	13.769
1981	349.00	518.30	185.20	354.35	12.459
Percentage Change 1970–1981[a]	−33.6	−24.1	−32.3	−30.3	9.6
Average Annual Percentage Change 1970–1981[b]	−3.7	−2.5	−3.5	−3.2	0.8

SOURCE: U.S. Department of Health and Human Services, "AFDC Standards for Basic Needs," various years; "Annual Statistical Supplement, 1981" *Social Security Bulletin* (Washington, D.C.: Government Printing Office, 1982).

NOTES: These figures reflect the maximum monthly benefits for four-person families.
a. (1981–1970) ÷ 1970 x .100.
b. Average annual percentage change compounded over the period.
c. Highest and lowest states based on 1975 benefit levels.

declines occurred in the second half of the decade. Interestingly, the ten states with the highest guarantees in 1975 maintained real benefits to a greater extent than did those at the lower end of the scale relative to their original benefit levels in 1970. Those states that were more generous with benefit increases experienced a slower decline in real maximum benefits (2.5 percent per year) than did either the least generous states (where real benefits declined by 3.5 percent per year) or the average state (a decline of 3.2 percent per year). By this measure, interstate differences in AFDC increased slightly over the 1970s.

The final column of table 3 indicates that while total real AFDC outlays increased by 9.6 percent from 1970 to 1981, outlays have declined steadily since 1976. Thus, the AFDC portion of the safety net and overall program outlays for AFDC were falling before Reagan's presidency began.[11]

---

11. It should, of course, be recognized that decisions regarding basic AFDC benefit levels are a state responsibility, despite joint federal-state financing provisions.

SSI. Federal Supplemental Security Income (SSI) benefit levels for the aged, and expenditures for its state-specific precursor, Old Age Assistance, also grew during the 1970s.[12] Table 4 presents three different maximum SSI benefit levels for single elderly individuals: the federal minimum guarantee (column 1); the average maximum supplemental benefit for those states that supplement the federal minimum (column 2); the average maximum supplemental benefit for the five states with the highest supplements in 1974, when SSI began (column 3); and, finally, total federal and state guarantee levels for states providing supplements (columns 4 and 5). We present all three sets of maximum benefits because 47 percent of all SSI elderly live in states that have optional supplements, and 33.5 percent of all beneficiaries live in the highest five supplementing states. Changes in real benefits are calculated for both the overall 1970–1981 period and for the 1974–1981 period when SSI was in force. An identical table for aged couples living alone is presented as appendix table A.1.

As one would expect, given the annual cost-of-living adjustments in the federal minimum SSI benefit, the federal benefit floor has pretty much stayed constant in real terms since 1974.[13] However, optional state supplements fell in real terms by up to 30 percent between 1974 and 1981 despite the 1976 Social Security amendments which required supplementing states to "pass through" all federal minimum-benefit increases to SSI recipients. Supplements fell more for single recipients than for couples, and fell faster in the average supplementing state than in the highest five. Combining federal guarantees with maximum state supplements, we find that overall real SSI guarantees for the low-income aged have declined only slightly since 1974 and have actually increased in real terms since 1970.

Changes in total benefit outlays lead us to a different conclusion. The figures in column 6 show a substantial decline in the real value of SSI benefits whether measured from 1974 or from 1970. Most likely this decline in SSI benefits reflects higher pre-SSI incomes of the low-income elderly. Increases in Social Security benefits, for example, reduce SSI benefits dollar for dollar above a $20 per month disregard for the 70 percent of elderly SSI beneficiaries who participate in both programs.

---

12. We concentrate on the elderly because they are those most identified with the SSI program. Moreover, for purposes of table 4, the various states have different supplemental amounts for the blind and disabled than for the aged, thus confusing the comparison of maximum benefit across beneficiary types.

13. The small real benefit decline of 1.7 percent shown in table 4 owes primarily to timing differences between the CPI deflator used to adjust the nominal values in table 4 as compared to the SSI cost-of-living adjustment formula.

TABLE 4

MAXIMUM SSI BENEFITS FOR SINGLE, ELDERLY PERSONS AND ACTUAL BENEFIT OUTLAYS

(In Constant 1981 Dollars)

	Federal Minimum Guarantee (1)	Average Maximum State Supplements		Average Maximum Federal and State Benefit Levels		Total Outlays (In Billions of Dollars) (6)
		All States Paying Optional Supplements[b] (2)	Five Highest Supplementing States[c] (3)	All States Paying Optional Supplements[b] (4) = (1) + (2)	Five Highest Supplementing States[c] (5) = (1) + (3)	
1970[a]	NA	NA	NA	307.43	436.52	4.362
1972[a]	NA	NA	NA	307.43	436.52	4.080
1974	269.37	85.76	176.38	355.13	445.76	4.618
1976	268.05	74.60	173.61	342.65	441.66	4.007
1978	264.16	73.42	178.33	337.57	442.48	3.393
1980	262.69	65.03	166.89	327.73	429.58	3.018
1981	264.70	60.28	151.98	324.98	416.68	2.775
Percentage Change[d] 1970–1981	NA	NA	NA	8.1	14.1	−36.4
Average Annual Percentage Change[e] 1970–1981	NA	NA	NA	0.7	1.2	−4.0

Percentage Change[f] 1974–1981	−1.7	−29.7	−17.8	−8.5	−6.5	−39.9
Average Annual Percentage Change[e] 1974–1981	−0.2	−4.9	−2.1	−1.3	−1.0	−7.0

SOURCE: Office of Operations, Policy and Procedures, Social Security Administration.

a. 1970 and 1972 figures refer to state-specific Old Age Assistance programs which preceded SSI.
b. Includes only those states with *optional* benefits in excess of the federal minimum benefit. States with mandatory supplements are not included.
c. Includes the highest five supplementary states in 1974: New York, California, Wisconsin, Pennsylvania, and Massachusetts.
d. (1981–1970) ÷ 1970 × .100.
e. Reflects compounding over the period.
f. (1981–1974) ÷ 1974 × .100.

NA = not available.

Other Individual Program Changes. While AFDC and SSI form the traditional safety net for needy single parents and the elderly and disabled, respectively, several other safety net programs experienced changes in their basic benefit levels and program coverage during the 1970s. Perhaps most important, the Food Stamp program grew quite rapidly. In 1970 counties had the option of offering either the Food Stamp program or the Surplus Commodities Food Distribution program, and benefit standards varied across the country. In counties offering Food Stamps, eligible families paid cash for a coupon allotment of Food Stamps based on family size. The difference between the amount of cash they paid (the purchase requirement) and the face value of the coupon allotment made up the food transfer (the bonus value). Congress enacted national Food Stamp standards and benefits in 1971, and required all counties to offer the Food Stamp program after July 1, 1974. In 1973, Congress mandated that Food Stamp coupon allotments and income eligibility be adjusted annually to reflect changes in food prices. Finally, and perhaps most significantly, Congress rescinded the purchase requirement as of January 1, 1979, thereby allowing families to collect only the bonus value of stamps with no out-of-pocket cash outlay. These changes, coupled with the notable absence of categorical eligibility criteria, help explain why average monthly enrollment in the Food Stamp program increased from some 4 million persons in 1970 to over 20 million by 1981. Since 1973, the maximum allotment has been adjusted annually (by the CPI at first, by the price of food later), so the benefit has remained fairly constant in real terms. The maximum benefit for a four-person household was $233 per month in 1981.

Though benefits never exceeded $500 per year in either program, the Low Income Energy Assistance (LIEA) and Earned Income Tax Credit (EITC) programs were created during the latter half of the 1970s. Low-income public housing programs also proliferated, with the total number of units under various programs increasing from 1.1 million in 1970 to almost 2.7 million by 1981.[14]

Perhaps the most significant increases in safety net benefit levels during the 1970s came not from the changes in individual program benefits, but from the increasing number of families who simultaneously benefited from two or

---

14. Congressional Budget Office, "The Long-Term Costs of Public Housing Programs," Background Paper (Washington, D.C.: Government Printing Office, 1979). The value of public housing subsidies is determined by the differences between the market rent of the public housing program and the amount of tenant rent, which was capped at 25 percent of net income during this period. Owing to changes in market rents, tenant incomes, and allowable deductions over this period, it is difficult to determine how, in general, the basic value of these benefits changed during the 1970–1980 period. However, such changes have been calculated for a typical beneficiary in table 6.

more programs. We now turn to this aspect of the generosity of the safety net.

Multiple Benefits

The foregoing analysis indicates that the breadth of traditional cash benefit payments has expanded only slightly, while benefit generosity in real terms has declined substantially in the AFDC program and slightly in the SSI program. These figures do not, however, take into account benefits from the new or rapidly expanding programs of the 1970s mentioned above—in particular, Food Stamps, Low Income Energy Assistance (LIEA), and public housing. The majority of families receiving AFDC or SSI payments also benefited from at least two of these three programs by the end of the 1970s. Thus we should consider them in reaching any conclusions about the breadth or generosity of the safety net during the 1970s.

AFDC, Food Stamps, and LIEA. Some argue that states increasingly came to view increased Food Stamp benefits as a substitute for higher AFDC outlays during the latter 1970s.[15] Over 75 percent of all AFDC families received Food Stamps in 1979.[16] While average AFDC benefits accounted for 77.5 percent of combined AFDC and Food Stamp benefits in 1970, this ratio declined to 68.7 percent by 1980.[17] Thus we must look at the *combined* value of AFDC and Food Stamp guarantee levels during the 1970s. It is not enough to look at AFDC alone.

Beginning in 1981, the LIEA program has provided an average monthly grant (or utility bill payment) of $17 per year. In all states, AFDC families are categorically eligible for LIEA aid. While benefits varied widely from state to state, and joint benefit recipiency often depended on being enrolled in AFDC during the winter months, we have prorated the annual benefit evenly across the twelve months.

Table 5 shows that decreases in real AFDC maximum benefits were only modestly offset by Food Stamp guarantee increases, even though the latter have been indexed since 1973. The median AFDC benefit fell by 3.5 percent per year between 1970 and 1981 (table 3), and combined AFDC and Food

15. See C. Hulten et al., "Historical Trends in AFDC, Medicaid, and Food Stamp Benefits to AFDC Recipients: 1968–1980," Report to U.S. Department of Health and Human Services, (mimeographed) July 1982. (Washington, D.C.: The Urban Institute, 1982).

16. Maurice MacDonald, "Multiple Benefits and Income Adequacy for Food Stamp Participation and Nonparticipant Households," University of Wisconsin (mimeographed), February 1983; T.M. Smeeding, "Alternative Methods of Valuing Selected In-Kind Transfers and Measuring Their Effect on Poverty," U.S. Department of Commerce, Bureau of the Census, Technical Paper #50, March 1982.

17. Hulten et al., "Historical Trends."

TABLE 5

MULTIPLE BENEFIT GUARANTEES FOR AFDC RECIPIENTS
(In Constant 1981 Dollars)

Year (July)	AFDC[a]	AFDC and Food Stamps	AFDC, Food Stamps, and LIEA
1970	527	679	679
1975	446	630	630
1980	389	554	554
1981	349	530	547
Percentage Change[b] 1970–1981	−33.6	−21.7	−19.2
Average Annual Percentage Change[c] 1970–1981	−3.7	−2.2	−1.9

SOURCES AND BASES OF CALCULATIONS: AFDC benefits are taken from table 3. Food Stamp benefits are calculated according to program rules and regulations in force at the time. For July 1975, total itemized deductions for medical expense, shelter, school tuition, etc. were assumed to be $62, which is the average September 1975 deduction for families reporting gross incomes of $264, the median AFDC benefit. This amount is independently reached using a regression formula based on household size and age of head of household. (G.W. Hoagland, "The Food Stamp Program: Income or Food Supplementation?" Congressional Budget Office, January 1977). For 1970, these 1975 expenses were deflated by the CPI to arrive at total deduction. By 1980, the Food Stamp progam had adopted a standard deduction with an excess shelter expense and/or child-care allowance, the only variable deduction. In 1979, 75 percent of all Food Stamp families claimed the shelter deduction, and 19 percent of all such units claimed the maximum. Families with no shelter deduction would receive $34.50 less in stamps. Based on conversations with Food Stamp officials, the calculations in this table assume excess shelter deductions of $80 in 1980 and $90 in 1981. With the full shelter deduction, benefits would have been about $10.50 larger in 1980 and $7.50 larger in 1981. LIEA payments are equal to average annual benefits per automatic recipient household in FY 1981 divided by 12. (D. Rigby and C. Ponce, "Low Income Energy Assistance Program" *Social Security Bulletin*, January 1983; unpublished data, U.S. Department of Health and Human Services, Office of Energy Assistance, estimates for FY 1981).

    a. Reflects median AFDC monthly benefits for family of four.
    b. $(1981–1970) \div 1970 \times .100$.
    c. Reflects compounding over the period.

Stamp benefits fell by 2.2 percent per year. Food Stamps therefore offset only about one-third of the decline in AFDC benefits. Even with the $17 LIEA benefit in 1981, combined real maximum benefits from all three programs fell by 1.9 percent per year throughout the 1970s. Food Stamps and AFDC benefits combined were 87.5 percent of the official government poverty threshold in 1970, but had fallen to 70.7 percent by 1981, even adding in the LIEA benefit.

SSI, OASI, Food Stamps, and Public Housing. The typical elderly SSI recipient also receives multiple benefits. Virtually all SSI recipients not living in public housing receive LIEA, and 70 percent also benefit from OASI. Twenty-three percent of all elderly renters and 37 percent of poor elderly renters lived in publicly owned or subsidized housing projects in 1981. Eighty-seven percent of poor elderly public housing tenants are single persons living alone. Almost 44 percent of SSI families receive Food Stamps as well.[18] In table 6 we show two typical SSI families: one receiving OASI, Food Stamps, and LIEA; and a second receiving OASI, Food Stamps, and living in public housing. It presents their basic benefit guarantees from 1974, when SSI began, until 1981. Public housing benefits are measured by their market value, the difference between the private market rental value of the housing unit and the rent the tenants pay. The value of these benefits can change if either the market value of comparable housing changes or the rental price for public housing changes.

For those SSI elderly who live in nonsupplementing states, the combination of SSI, Social Security, and Food Stamps fairly well kept up with inflation from 1974 to 1981, declining by about 1 percent per year over this period.[19] Adding LIEA payments, the market value of the total package in 1981 was very close to the combined 1974 real benefit level.[20] The final column of table 6 shows that the real subsidy value of public housing declined slightly from 1974 to 1981, bringing this benefit package to a level 14.6 percent below its 1974 value.

SSI recipients in supplementing states (see table 6, panel B) fared worse, owing mainly to the decline in the real value of SSI supplements during this period. The largest difference was in the SSI, Social Security, Food Stamps, and public housing benefit package which declined 18.2 percent, or 2.8 percent per year, between 1974 and 1981.

Non-Elderly Two-Parent Families

Changes in the breadth and depth of the safety net during the 1970s for two-parent families, childless couples, and single individuals are more

---

18. These and preceding estimates were taken from U.S. Department of Commerce, Bureau of the Census, "Characteristics of Households and Persons Receiving Selected Noncash Benefits: 1981," *Current Population Reports*, series P-60, no. 136, January 1983, tables 8 and 21.

19. Again, the differences noted between 1974 and 1981 largely reflect differences in cost-of-living adjustment periods and formulas for SSI and Food Stamps.

20. In 1980 the energy assistance program was termed "energy crisis assistance" and was administered under the Community Services Administration budget. The low-income elderly were generally included in this program. In 1981, it was superseded by LIEA.

TABLE 6

MULTIPLE BENEFIT GUARANTEES FOR SSI RECIPIENTS
(In Constant 1981 Dollars)

Year (July)	SSI and Social Security (SS)	SSI, SS, and Food Stamps	SSI, SS, Food Stamps, and LIEA	SSI, SS, Food Stamps, and Public Housing
Federal Minimum				
1974	306	346	346	487
1980	285	320	329	416
1981	285	322	339	416
Percentage Change[a]				
1974–1981	−6.9	−6.9	−1.0	−14.6
Average Annual Percentage Change[b]				
1974–1981	−1.0	−1.0	−0.3	−2.2
Average for States Paying Optional Supplements				
1974	391	415	415	566
1980	350	365	374	466
1981	345	364	381	463
Percentage Change[a]				
1974–1981	−11.8	−12.3	−8.2	−18.2
Average Annual Percentage Change[b]				
1974–1981	−1.8	−1.9	−1.2	−2.8

SOURCES AND BASES: SSI guarantees are taken from table 4, columns (1) and (4), plus the $20 Social Security disregard which 70 percent of all SSI elderly qualify for. In calculating Food Stamp deductions for July 1974, average total deductions for single individuals and for those with monthly incomes in the appropriate income range were $48 in September 1975. Deflated to July 1974 figures, these deductions were assumed to be $44. In 1980 (1981) the standard deduction of $75 ($85) plus a shelter allowance of $80 ($90) was assumed. LIEA payments averaged $17 per automatic recipient in 1981.

The market value of public housing subsidies, the difference between the market rent of the unit and the tenant's payment, for single elderly in the top panel averaged $83 per month in 1979 and $70 per month in 1972 (T. Smeeding, "Alternative Methods for Valuing Selected In-Kind Transfer Benefits and Measuring Their Effect on Poverty," Technical Paper #50, U.S. Bureau of the Census, March 1982). These were adjusted to 1981 and 1974, respectively, using the CPI rental housing component deflator.

For 1981, the 1980 average market rent of $164 (the subsidy value of $87 plus the tenant's rent of 30 percent of income) was increased by the CPI rental housing deflator, and 30 percent of SSI income was assumed to be paid in rent. The difference between these amounts, $92, was the market value of the housing for the tenants. Subsidies in the bottom panel were calculated in the same way.

a.   Reflects monthly payments to single, elderly persons. (1981−1974) ÷ 1974 × .100.
b.   Reflects compounding.

difficult to characterize. While unemployment compensation benefits generally kept up with wage growth during the 1970s, the Aid to Families with Dependent Children-Unemployed Parent (AFDC-UP) program for two-parent families never expanded beyond a 220,000-family caseload and was never available in more than twenty-eight states during the 1970s. For eligible families living in states offering AFDC-UP benefits, the maximum benefits were essentially the same as those shown for AFDC recipients in tables 3 and 5. In the other states, Food Stamps provided the only public assistance other than unemployment compensation to such families. However, two additional efforts in behalf of these nontraditional needy families and individuals bear mention.

First, during the 1975–1976 recession Congress added to the federal-state unemployment insurance system an Extended Benefits (EB) program for workers who remained unemployed longer than the state's maximum benefit duration (usually about twenty-six weeks). The Extended Benefits program was triggered whenever the insured unemployment rate reached 4.5 percent on a nationwide basis. A temporary Federal Supplemental Benefit (FSB) program further lengthened the maximum duration of unemployed benefits. Altogether, the long-term unemployed could receive benefits for up to sixty-five weeks through these three programs. As a result of these changes over 75 percent of the unemployed collected monthly unemployment insurance benefits from March 1975 through March 1976 at the height of the recession (up from 49.5 percent in 1974).[21] Second, the Comprehensive Employment and Training Act (CETA) of 1973 consolidated and expanded federal efforts for job training and job creation. In its heyday during the Carter administration, CETA provided up to two million training or job slots. After 1978, the CETA program was more specifically targeted at the long-term unemployed and disadvantaged (as opposed to the cyclically unemployed).[22,23]

The Nixon and Carter administrations proposed other substantial safety net initiatives for the noncategorically needy which were not passed by Congress. Both Nixon's Family Assistance Plan and Carter's Social Welfare Reform Amendments of 1979 would have effectively expanded means-tested AFDC-UP cash benefit guarantees to all two-parent families with children

---

21. Unpublished data from the Division of Actuarial Services, U.S. Department of Labor, Employment and Training Administration.

22. Laurie J. Bassi, "CETA—Has It Worked?" Research Report (Washington, D.C.: The Urban Institute, 1982).

23. The extent to which CETA actually expanded jobs, as opposed to merely substituting federal money for state and local job funding, is in some doubt. See D.H. Saks, "Jobs and Training," chapter 6, in J. Pechman, ed., *Setting National Priorities: The 1984 Budget* (Washington, D.C.: Brookings Institution, 1983).

and would have established a national minimum benefit similar to the SSI program. In addition, the Carter administration's Program for Better Jobs and Income (PBJI) initative in 1977 would have guaranteed temporary public-sector jobs (paying the minimum wage) to the noncategorically eligible needy who could not find jobs on their own (rather than extending them AFDC-UP benefits). Congress defeated this effort, but the notion of extending the safety net to include guaranteed jobs to those who had none is noteworthy.

Summary

Our investigation of the breadth and generosity of the safety net during the 1970s yields the following conclusions:

1. The number of beneficiaries of individual programs exhibited two distinct characteristics. While overall traditional cash assistance enrollments increased only modestly over the entire 1970-1981 period, the number of beneficiaries served by programs with radically changed eligibility criteria and scope (such as Food Stamps) and new programs (such as LIEA) increased tremendously. Most of the enrollment growth in all of these programs (except for LIEA) either slowed noticeably or came to a halt in 1975; AFDC, SSI, and Medicaid programs all experienced declining enrollments after that date.

2. While average benefits per recipient kept even with inflation, AFDC benefit guarantees for those with no other income declined in real terms. The federal SSI guarantee kept up with prices, but state supplements did not.

3. Decreases in real AFDC benefits were not offset by increased Food Stamps or LIEA benefits for the typical AFDC family who received benefits from all three programs. SSI recipients fared slightly better. Those receiving Food Stamps and LIEA received combined guarantees that just about kept even with inflation between 1974 and 1981. Those living in public housing and in states whose optional supplements failed to keep up with prices suffered a fairly substantial (18 percent) decrease in real benefit guarantee value over this period.

4. The safety net for needy two-parent families was not nearly so strong or broad as that available to single parents and the elderly. However, the growth of Food Stamps, the EITC, extended unemployment benefits, and the CETA program did help many truly needy two-parent units during the 1970s. Proposals for a national minimum income and job guarantees for two-parent families were not adopted.

Other than the Food Stamp and LIEA programs, the breadth of the safety net was not growing very rapidly, and the degree of protection afforded by the safety net was declining in real terms even before Ronald Reagan took office in January 1981. We now turn to his administration's impacts on the social safety net.

The Safety Net under the Reagan Administration

The Reagan administration took immediate steps to reduce safety net program expenditures, mainly by reducing benefits for those with other sources of income and by instituting administrative reforms. Many of these administrative reforms contributed to reduce program outlays without affecting the generosity of the safety net for those without other means of support. However, the administration later made additional proposals affecting program generosity for all beneficiaries. In this section we again concentrate mainly on those programs that were discussed in the previous section.

Changes in Expected Outlays: Legislative Action vs. Economic Changes

Before we begin to investigate specific changes in the safety net, the general scope and magnitude of cutbacks in the safety net programs under President Reagan can be derived from the estimates in table 7. Here we have employed several Congressional Budget Office reports to separate expected cumulative changes in program outlays for fiscal years 1982 through 1985 into two components: (1) those changes due to legislative action between January 1981 and July 1983; and (2) those changes due to revisions in economic, demographic, and other technical assumptions between April 1981 and February 1983. While it is not possible to separate cumulative changes into those affecting the breadth, generosity, or administrative efficiency of program outlays, table 7 does separate the effects on outlays of legislative action under the Reagan administration from those primarily attributable to changing economic conditions brought about by the 1981–1983 recession.

For instance, consider outlays for unemployment insurance. In 1981 the Reagan administration expected to spend $77.2 billion over the 1982–1985 period based on economic assumptions in force in early 1981. However, the recession was worse than expected and unemployment rose significantly above that projected. Based on events in 1981 and 1982 and on revised forecasts of unemployment made in February 1983, the administration now expects to spend a total of $105.4 billion on unemployment compensation programs

TABLE 7

CUMULATIVE CHANGES IN INCOME SUPPORT PROGRAM OUTLAYS
(In Billions of Current Dollars)

	Total Expected Federal Outlays 1982–1985		Changes in Total Expected Outlays			Percentage Change in Outlays[f]		
	Based on February 1983 Baseline[a]	Based on 1981 Baseline[b]	Total[c]	Due to Legislative Action[d]	Due to Economic and Technical Changes[e]	Total	Due to Legislative Action	Due to Economic and Technical Changes
Social Insurance Programs								
OASDI	695.2	734.0	-38.8	-24.1	-14.7	-5.3	-3.3	-2.0
Medicare	248.7	237.5	11.2	-13.2	24.4	4.7	-5.6	10.3
Unemployment Compensation	105.4	77.2	28.3	-7.8	36.0	36.5	-10.1	46.6
Total Outlays	1049.3	1048.7	0.7	-45.1	45.7	0.0	-4.3	4.3
Means-Tested Programs								
AFDC[g]	32.9	36.3	-3.4	-4.7	1.3	-9.4	-13.0	3.6
SSI	33.3	35.0	-1.7	1.4	-3.1	-4.9	4.0	-8.9
Food Stamps	48.3	51.1	-2.8	-7.0	4.2	-5.5	-13.7	8.2
Child Nutrition[h]	17.8	22.8	-5.0	-5.2	0.2	-21.9	-22.8	0.9
Housing Assistance[i]	38.3	41.0	-2.7	-1.8	-0.9	-6.6	-4.4	-2.2
EITC	4.5	4.0	0.5	0.0	0.5	12.5	0.0	12.5
LIEA	7.9	10.9	-3.0	-0.7	-2.3	-27.5	-6.4	-21.1
Social Services[j]	10.3	13.0	-2.7	-2.9	0.2	-20.8	-22.3	1.5
Medicaid	82.4	81.9	0.5	-3.9	4.4	0.6	-4.8	5.4
Pell/Self-Help Grants	13.7	15.6	-1.9	-2.1	0.2	-12.2	-13.5	1.3
CETA (PSE)	0.1	17.3	-17.2	-17.0	-0.2	-99.4	-98.3	-1.1
Total Outlays	289.5	328.9	-39.4	-43.9	4.5	-12.0	-13.4	1.4

SOURCE: U.S. Congressional Budget Office, various publications.

a. The 1983 baseline projections were developed using an updated CBO economic forecast and extrapolation based on February 1983 economic assumptions and actual expenditures for FY 1982.

b. The 1981 baseline projects were developed in the spring of 1981 based on congressional actions through the end of the 96th Congress. The 1981 baseline projections utilized the economic assumptions of the first budget resolution for fiscal year 1982.

c. Total outlay changes are the difference between the 1981 and 1983 baseline estimates.

d. The estimated outlay changes resulting from the actions of the 97th and 98th Congress (January 1981 to July 31, 1983). These legislative changes are estimated using 1983 economic assumptions and estimating techniques.

e. These reflect estimated outlay changes due to revisions in economic, demographic, and technical assumptions based on changes in economic activity experienced between 1981 and February 1983.

f. Calculated as a percent of 1981 baseline estimates.

g. Includes Child Support Enforcement.

h. Includes the National School Lunch Program, National School Breakfast Program, Childcare Feeding Program, Special Milk Program, Summer Feeding Program, Special Supplementary Feeding Program for Women, Infants, and Children (WIC), and the Commodity Supplementary Feeding Program (CSFP).

i. Includes both subsidized housing program and public housing operating subsidies.

j. Social Services expenditures are in the form of a block grant to the states; formerly these expenditures were under Title XX of the Social Security Act.

during this three-year period. This represents a $28.3 billion increase over the earlier estimates. However, without the legislative changes affecting un-employment insurance provisions between January 1981 and July 1983, the revised forecasts of outlay for unemployment would have been an additional $36.0 billion. Thus legislative changes affecting unemployment compensation reduced actual and expected outlays over this period by $7.8 billion or 10.1 percent of the 1981 baseline estimate.

The Reagan administration expects to spend $38.8 billion (5.3 percent) less on Social Security (OASDI) over the 1982–1985 period due to (1) lower-than-expected inflation (which affects outlays via the OASDI cost-of-living escalator), (2) other economic changes which save $14.7 billion, and (3) legislative actions (primarily the 1983 Social Security amendments) which save $24.1 billion.

Meanwhile, Medicare will cost $11.2 billion more than was anticipated, despite a savings of $13.2 billion due primarily to the phase-in of prospective reimbursement, which was begun on October 1, 1983. Underestimating the increased cost of medical care (primarily the escalating cost of hospitalization) also led budget analysts to underestimate total outlays by $24.4 billion in 1981 as compared to current estimates.

Together, these three programs—unemployment insurance, Social Se-curity, and Medicare—are expected to cost as much this year as they did in 1981 in nominal terms, with total expected outlays differing by only about $0.7 billion. However, such a comparison masks the economy-induced net increase of $45.7 billion in outlays which was virtually cancelled by the $45.1 billion worth of legislated program reductions.

While cuts in social insurance benefits affect the needy, the means-tested safety net programs (the lower part of table 7) are our major focus. Means-tested programs were cut an average of 13.4 percent; outlays are expected to be 12 percent less in 1982 because of a rise in outlays of 1.4 percent due to a change in economic conditions. Other than the SSI program (where Congress increased benefits by $1.4 billion) and the EITC (which Congress left alone), Congress reduced means-tested benefits anywhere from 4.8 percent (Medi-caid) to 98.3 percent (CETA). The only programs expected to have higher nominal expenditures for fiscal years 1982–1985 than in 1981, when Reagan came into office, are the EITC (due to economic changes induced by the recession) and Medicaid (due to the rapidly rising cost of medical care). The recession would have caused increased outlays for means-tested programs had program parameters remained unchanged by legislation. Yet the Reagan administration engineered overall spending reductions in most of these pro-grams. For instance, Food Stamp outlays will be $2.8 billion less for 1982 through 1985 than they were expected to be when Reagan took office—the

$7.0 billion (13.7 percent) legislated reduction exceeding the $4.2 billion
recession-induced increase in expected outlays. Outlays for AFDC, child
nutrition, social services, and Pell grants follow a similar pattern. Owing
mainly to reduced energy prices and lower AFDC and SSI enrollments, LIEA
outlays will decline by $3.0 billion over this period.

Table 7 does not take into account potential changes to the administration's FY 1984 budget when it is acted on by Congress. For instance, the
administration has requested an additional $2.3 billion reduction in Food
Stamp outlays for fiscal years 1984 and 1985.[24] It has also proposed a one-
third reduction in LIEA outlays and a 60 percent reduction in Pell expenditures
for 1984 as compared to 1981. Except for the recent increase in SSI outlays
designed to compensate for a delay in the SSI cost-of-living increase of the
Federal Supplemental Benefit (unemployment compensation) program, the
administration has again generally proposed further cutbacks in safety net
program outlays for FY 1984.

While table 7 illustrates the administration's success in legislating benefit
reductions in safety net programs, it does not indicate how these changes
have affected recipients. For example, some changes may affect program
eligibility and coverage (the breadth of the safety net) while others may affect
basic benefit levels for those with no other source of income (the generosity
of the safety net). These types of changes most interest us and occupy the
bulk of this section of the paper. Expenditure reductions may also be due to
gains in administrative efficiency or intraprogram equity, which would have
little effect on the truly needy, but potentially large effects on program waste.
Savings resulting from changes to monthly reporting, retrospective accounting, prorating of monthly benefits, and penalizing states for benefit errors
have already improved the efficiency by which benefits are targeted to those
in need, but it is difficult to estimate how much of the legislated benefit
reductions in table 7 can be attributed to these initiatives.

Separating legislative program changes that improve program equity or
efficiency from those that affect only the generosity or breadth of the safety
net program is difficult. For instance, prior to January 1983, parents or
relatives living together could apply for Food Stamps as independent units.
Today, relatives living together may file as independent eating units only
under more stringent conditions. This may be viewed either as an improvement
in intraprogram equity or as a capricious change that limits the generosity or
breadth of the safety net.

---

24. U.S. Congressional Budget Office, "An Analysis of the President's Budgetary Proposals for FY 1984," February 1983, p. 110.

Recent U.S. Department of Agriculture data suggest that 15–30 percent of legislated Food Stamp benefit reductions could be regarded as primarily improving program efficiency or equity. Such estimates for other programs are not available.

Changes in Program Coverage

Only partial data exist comparing numbers of safety net program beneficiaries from 1981 to 1983. Observed changes in numbers of recipients caused by changes in program structure are indistinguishable from changes caused by general economic conditions. Simultaneous changes in eligibility criteria for a given program make it hard to evaluate the effect on enrollments of a given change. For instance, the AFDC program changed to a 100 percent benefit reduction rate on earnings after four months; changed to retrospective (from prospective) income accounting; changed the nominal resource or asset ceiling to a maximum of $1,000; and made other less important adjustments to eligibility rules. All these changes shrank the pool of families eligible for AFDC at the same time that general economic conditions were rapidly deteriorating and increasing that pool.

Social Security Administration figures show that SSI caseloads declined from 4.0 million in December 1981 (table 2) to 3.8 million in December 1982. Elderly SSI recipients fell to 1.5 million in December 1982, an all-time low. The 1970s trend towards increasing caseloads in the SSI disability program, which peaked in 1980 and 1981, began to reverse itself as eligibility criteria and tougher reviews of disabling conditions for current recipients helped program participation decline from 2.26 to 2.23 million between December 1981 and December 1982. The April 1983 AFDC caseload was 10.7 million persons, slightly above the December 1981 figure of 10.6 million, while the number of AFDC families stayed about constant at 3.6 million.[25] Finally, Food Stamp enrollments reached a new peak enrollment of 22.2 million persons in February 1983, an increase of 1.5 million since FY 1981.

From these meager data little can be concluded. Probably the enrollment-reducing effects of program restrictions largely cancelled the enrollment-increasing effects of the recession for such programs as AFDC and Food Stamps. For instance, program changes terminated an estimated 1 million Food Stamp recipients in FY 1982.[26] If so, the 1.5 million net increase in

---

25. Unpublished data from the U.S. Department of Health and Human Services, courtesy of Herb Liebman, Office of Family Assistance.

26. R. Greenstein and J. Bickerman, "Effects of the Administration's Budget, Tax, and Military Policies on Low-Income Americans," Center on Budget and Policy Priorities, February 1983.

enrollments represents a 2.5 million gross increase in program enrollment and 1.0 million decrease due to program changes. Another missing piece of information is how changes in program enrollments are distributed among persons who would otherwise receive benefits. Most cutbacks in enrollment presumably affected those with some other income who were near the program break-even level before the legislated changes, but this may not always be the case. For instance, a single disability test determines eligibility for Social Security Disability Insurance (and concomitantly Medicare) and SSI disability benefits (and concomitantly Medicaid). Thus persons who fail to pass a single disability recertification test can be simultaneously disqualified from four benefit programs.

Changes in Benefit Generosity

The effects of legislated program changes in AFDC and SSI maximum benefit levels during 1982 and 1983 relative to their 1981 levels are shown in table 8. In general, AFDC benefits continued to decline at roughly the same annual rate as during the 1970s. The AFDC guarantee in the median-benefit state fell at an annual rate of 2.4 percent between July 1981 and July 1983, as compared to an annual rate of 3.7 percent from 1970 to 1981. The average guarantee in the high-, low-, and average-benefit states fell at a 2.3–3.1 annual rate. Thus AFDC guarantees continued to decrease in real terms both due to federal benefit changes and due to fiscal pressure on the states. While the Reagan administration argues that the lessening of inflation has greatly benefited the poor, increased fiscal pressure on the states due to the current recession has worked in the opposite direction. For instance, between July 1982 and July 1983, thirty-four states kept their nominal AFDC benefits at the same level, only fifteen states increased benefits, and two states reduced their basic benefits by an average of $45 per month.[27] The nominal median state's maximum benefit did not change at all while the nominal average state's amount increased by only 1.3 percent. Thus, despite the lessening of inflation, real median and average benefits declined by 3.7 and 2.4 percent, respectively, over this period.

Table 8, panel B, shows that federal SSI benefit levels expanded by 4.5 percent in real terms from FY 1981 to FY 1983. While average optional state supplements continued to decline in real terms from 1981 to 1982, they increased slightly in real terms for the five highest-paying states. Overall benefit levels, including federal minimum benefits plus supplements, grew

---

27. These data were provided by the Center on Social Welfare Policy and Law. The states which reduced their nominal AFDC guarantees were Nevada (by $52), and Utah (by $37).

TABLE 8
(Panel A)

MAXIMUM AFDC AND SSI BENEFITS UNDER THE REAGAN ADMINISTRATION
(In Constant 1981 Dollars)

AFDC (Family of Four)				
Year (July)	Median	Average Ten Highest States	Average Ten Lowest States	National Average
1981	349.00	578.30	185.20	354.35
1982	347.50	498.77	179.70	342.95
1983	334.53	497.73	176.45	334.55
Percentage Change				
1981–1982	– 0.4	– 3.8	– 3.0	– 3.2
1982–1983	– 3.7	– 0.2	– 1.8	– 2.4
1981–1983	– 4.1	– 4.0	– 4.7	– 5.6
Average Annual Percentage Change				
1970–1981	– 3.7	– 2.5	– 3.5	– 3.2
1981–1983	– 2.4	– 2.3	– 2.8	– 3.1

(Panel B)

SSI (Single Individual)	Federal Minimum Guarantee (1)	Average Maximum State Supplements		Total Average Federal and State Benefit Levels	
		All States Paying Optional Supplements (2)	Five Highest Supplementing States (3)	All States Paying Optional Supplements (4) = (1) + (2)	Five Highest Supplementing States (5) = (1) + (3)
1981	264.70	60.28	151.98	324.98	416.68
1982	268.46	58.40	153.01	326.86	421.47
1983	276.63	NA	NA	NA	NA
Percentage Change					
1981–1982	1.4	–3.1	0.7	0.6	1.1
1982–1983	3.0	NA	NA	NA	NA
1981–1983	4.5	NA	NA	NA	NA
Average Annual Percentage Change					
1974–1981	–0.3	–4.9	–2.1	–1.3	–1.0
1981–1983	2.1	NA	NA	NA	NA

SOURCES: Calculated in the same way as tables 3 and 4, but using more recent data. The 1983 AFDC figures were provided by the Center on Social Welfare Policy and Law.

NA = not available.

in real terms by 0.6 percent over this period, as opposed to the 1.3 percent per year decrease from 1974 to 1981. While the level of state supplements is not yet known for 1983, the Social Security amendments passed by Congress in April 1983 stipulate a federal increase of $20 for single individuals (and $30 for couples) effective July 1, 1983. The administration recommended a similar increase in the OASDI disregard for July 1983 in lieu of the cost-of-living increase that was postponed until January 1, 1984.

The actual amendments worked more in favor of SSI recipients than the administration's proposal in two ways. First, the $20 and $30 increases were made in actual benefit guarantees rather than in OASDI disregards alone. There would be no difference in effect for the 70 percent of SSI elderly (and 50 percent of all SSI beneficiaries) who also receive OASI; changes in either the disregard or the guarantee mean increased benefits of that amount for these beneficiaries. But, by increasing the guarantee, those SSI recipients who do not receive OASDI payments also benefited from the change. Overall, these SSI recipients are poorer than those who also qualify for OASI.[28]

Secondly, the postponed cost-of-living increase would have raised nominal federal minimum guarantees by only about $11 per month. Thus, real minimum SSI benefits increased by about 3 percent this July. Since states may or may not increase their optional supplements, only the federal minimum benefit guarantee is presented for July 1983. Similar changes for couples are shown in Appendix table A.2.

Multiple Benefits: Actual Changes

As argued previously, one cannot view the AFDC and SSI programs in isolation from other programs that benefit the same needy individuals. Table 9 updates the multiple program benefit guarantee levels shown in tables 5 and 6 from July 1981 to July 1983. Basically, combined AFDC, Food Stamp, and LIEA program changes over the 1981–1983 period have continued the downward trend in benefits that began in about 1975, declining an average of 1.5 percent per year. However, all of these decreases occurred from 1981 to 1982. Owing primarily to the lagged (and therefore high) cost-of-living increase in Food Stamp benefit levels of October 1982, combined real guarantee levels from all three programs increased by one dollar from July 1982 to July 1983.

At the very least, these combined benefits have not fared any worse under this administration than during the 1970s.

---

28. Richard V. Burkhauser and Timothy M. Smeeding, "The Net Effect of the Social Security System on the Poor," *Public Policy*, Summer 1981.

Combined federal minimum SSI, Food Stamps, Social Security (SS), and LIEA benefits increased slightly in real terms between 1981 and 1983; the July 1983 increase in SSI guarantees reversed the 1974–1981 and 1981–1982 decreases. Adding public housing benefits (and subtracting LIEA) results in a very small decline in real benefits, much smaller than the 1974–1981 average annual decline. Assuming no decline in the real value of optional supplement levels for states exercising these options, real maximum benefits for SSI, OASI, and Food Stamp recipients rose from 1981 to 1983, again largely owing to the significant increase in SSI benefits as of July 1, 1983. Adding in LIEA or public housing, real benefits declined from 1981–1983, but by a much smaller amount than the average 1974–1981 decline.

On the whole, real AFDC and SSI maximum benefit levels, as well as combined benefit levels for SSI and AFDC recipients receiving benefits from more than one program, performed *better* from 1981 to 1983 than during the 1970s. Why, then, the great outcry that the safety net has been violated? One explanation is that for everyone except the truly needy with no other income, benefits were substantially reduced or eligibility was terminated. However, the administration never defined these other "working poor" as being truly needy. In fact, these cuts reflect another of the guiding principles of the administration's social benefit policies: reduce eligibility levels and benefits for low-income families with earnings. One may disagree with this philosophy, favoring instead the principle of providing a helping hand to the working poor, but at least judged by the administration's own principles, the changes it effected were desirable.

Does this mean that the Reagan administration tried to preserve the safety net for the truly needy as it defines them? Before agreeing, remember that table 9 reflects policy changes enacted by Congress and were not in all cases the wishes of the administration. For instance, in 1981 the administration recommended that the $20 OASI disregard for *new* SSI recipients be rescinded after July 1, 1982 (contrary to the Greenspan Commission recommendation that the disregard be increased by $20–$30). Congress went its own way and increased the federal guarantee (not the disregard) by $20. What then would have happened to the safety net if the administration's 1982, 1983, and 1984 budgets and other policy changes were adopted exactly as it proposed them?

Proposed Changes in Safety Net Programs

While the administration has proposed much legislation in the safety net arena, basic restructuring of the welfare system has been minimal. However, it has proposed several changes in program structure that would reduce benefits to those participating in more than one means-tested transfer program.

TABLE 9

MULTIPLE BENEFIT GUARANTEES UNDER THE REAGAN ADMINISTRATION
(In Constant 1981 Dollars)

AFDC (Family of Four)

Year (July)	AFDC and Food Stamps	LIEA Only	AFDC, Food Stamps, and LIEA
1981	530	17	547
1982[a]	515	14	529
1983[a]	515	15	530
Percentage Change			
1981–1982[b]	− 2.8	− 17.6	− 3.3
1982–1983	0.0	7.1	0.2
Average Annual Percentage Change			
1981–1983	− 1.4	− 6.1	− 1.5
1970–1981[c]	− 2.2	NA	− 1.9

SSI (Single Individuals)

	SSI and Social Security (SS)	SSI, SS, and Food Stamps	SSI, SS, Food Stamps, and LIEA	SSI, SS Food Stamps, and Public Housing
Federal Minimum				
1981	285	322	339	416
1982[d]	287	317	331	415
1983[d]	295	325	340	415
Percentage Change[b]				
1981–1982	0.7	1.6	− 2.4	− 0.2
1982–1983	2.3	2.5	2.7	0.0
Average Annual Percentage Change[b]				
1981–1983	− 1.7	0.5	0.2	− 0.1
1974–1981[e]	− 1.0	− 1.0	− 0.3	− 2.2
Average for States Paying Optional Supplements				
1981	345	364	381	463
1982[e]	346	359	373	457
1983[f]	351	364	379	460
Percentage Change[b]				
1981–1982	0.3	− 1.4	− 2.0	− 1.3
1982–1983	1.4	1.4	1.6	0.7
Average Annual Percentage Change[b]				
1981–1983	0.9	0.0	− 0.3	− 0.3
1974–1981	− 1.8	− 1.9	− 1.2	− 2.8

Multiple Benefits: Proposed Changes. Table 10 recomputes the benefit combinations in table 9 based on the hypothetical scenario that the administration's objectives, as put forth in budget documents and formal policy proposals, were fully achieved. For FY 1982 and FY 1983, the administration proposed the following substantive changes for AFDC, SSI, and related program benefit guarantees:

1. It proposed adoption of the Helms Amendment to reduce Food Stamp benefits for families with children receiving free school lunch benefits. Two-thirds of the affected families and 71 percent of the children losing benefits had cash incomes below the federal poverty line in 1979. Sixty percent of these children were in families that also received AFDC.[29]

2. It proposed a 30 percent reduction in LIEA funding (to $1.3 billion) in FY 1982 with outlays to be frozen at this level through FY 1984. This proposal was reinitiated in both the FY 1983 and FY 1984 budgets.

3. It proposed the inclusion of LIEA grants in AFDC countable income (and in Food Stamp countable income) with no offset or disregard. In effect, this change would have reduced other benefits by the amount of the LIEA grant. It has been proposed again for 1984.

---

29. Timothy M. Smeeding, "Policy Options for Food Stamp Budget Reductions," Testimony prepared for the U.S. Senate, Committee on Agriculture, April 2, 1981.

Notes to table 9

a. Based on national median AFDC benefits plus Food Stamps allowing for an $85 standard deduction and a $95 excess shelter allowance. LIEA national average annual benefits of $181 are divided by 12. The 1983 figures were calculated in the same way but were based on FY 1983 outlays for LIEA and July 1983 Food Stamp benefit rules. No increases in standard deductions or excess shelter allowances were allowed since these allowances are frozen until October 1983.

b. Percentage change and average annual percentage change are as described previously (see, for example, tables 5 and 6).

c. From table 5.

d. Based on federal minimum SSI benefits plus Food Stamps allowing for an $85 standard deduction and a $95 excess shelter allowance. LIEA national average annual benefits of $181 are divided by 12. Public housing benefits are based on a 25 percent of gross income tenant rent and a market rental value for the unit which increased from 1981 to 1983 by the actual or expected increase in the rental housing component of the CPI. July 1983 figures were calculated in the same way, but allowing for the $20 increase in the SSI guarantee instead of the normal indexation (which was postponed until 1984) as provided by the 1983 amendments to the Social Security Act.

e. From table 7.

f. Calculated as in note "d" above, but based on Social Security Administration reports of annual median supplements and assuming no change in the real value of optional supplements between July 1982 and July 1983, and an increase in the excess shelter allowance to $100. The standard deduction was frozen at $85 until October 1983.

TABLE 10

MULTIPLE BENEFIT GUARANTEES ASSUMING THAT CONGRESS ADOPTED THE
ENTIRE ADMINISTRATION PACKAGE
(In Constant 1981 Dollars)

Year (July)	AFDC and Food Stamps Only	LIEA Only	AFDC, Food Stamps, and LIEA
1981	530	17	547
1982[a]	492	10	502
1983[b]	493	11	504
Percentage Change[c]			
1981–1982	−7.2	−41.2	−8.2
1982–1983	0.2	10.0	0.4
Average Annual			
Percentage Change			
1981–1983 (Proposed)	−3.6	−19.6	−4.0
1981–1983 (Actual)	−1.4	−6.1	−1.5
1970–1981	−2.2	NA	−1.9
Constant-Dollar			
Benefit Changes			
1981–1983 (Proposed)	−37	−6	−43
1981–1983 (Actual)	−15	−2	−17

SSI (Single Individuals)

	SSI and Social Security (SS)	SSI, SS, and Food Stamps	SSI, SS, Food Stamps, and LIEA	SSI, SS, Food Stamps, and Public Housing
Federal Minimum				
1981	285	322	339	416
1982[d]	287	317	328	387
1983[e]	295	318	329	372
Percentage Change[c]				
1981–1982	0.7	−1.5	−3.2	−7.0
1982–1983	2.8	0.3	0.3	−3.9
Average Annual				
Percentage Change[c]				
1981–1983 (Proposed)	1.7	−0.6	−1.7	−5.4
1981–1983 (Actual)	1.7	0.5	0.2	−0.1
1974–1981	−1.0	−1.0	−0.3	−2.1
Constant-Dollar				
Benefit Changes				
1981–1983 (Proposed)	10	−4	−10	−44
1981–1983 (Actual)	10	3	1	−1
Average for States Paying Optional Supplements				
1981	345	364	381	463
1982[d]	346	359	369	435
1983[e]	351	351	362	409

TABLE 10 (*continued*)

SSI (Single Individuals)				
	SSI and Social Security (SS)	SSI, SS, and Food Stamps	SSI, SS, Food Stamps, and LIEA	SSI, SS, Food Stamps, and Public Housing
Percentage Change[c]				
1981–1982	0.3	− 1.4	− 3.2	− 6.0
1982–1983	1.4	− 2.2	− 1.9	− 6.0
Average Annual				
Percentage Change[c]				
1981–1983 (Proposed)	0.9	− 1.8	− 2.5	− 6.0
1981–1983 (Actual)	0.9	0.0	− 0.3	− 0.3
1974–1981	− 1.8	− 1.9	− 1.2	− 2.8
Constant-Dollar				
Benefit Change				
1981–1983 (Proposed)	6	− 13	− 19	− 54
1981–1983 (Actual)	6	0	− 2	− 3

a.　Estimates based on adoption of:
　　1.　The Helms Amendment, which reduces Food Stamp benefits an average of $24.00 per month for families with children receiving free school lunch.
　　2.　Thirty percent reduction in LIEA from FY 1981 as requested in the FY 1982 (1983 and 1984) budgets.
　　b.　Estimates based on adoption of:
　　1.　Continued funding of LIEA at 30 percent below FY 1981 levels.
　　2.　A $12 reduction in AFDC benefits from counting the LIEA grants in the AFDC benefit calculations with no disregard.
　　3.　Increased benefit reduction rate in the Food Stamp program from 0.30 to 0.35.
Both proposed and actual FY 1983 Food Stamp calculations reflect the delayed cost-of-living adjustment in allowable deductions.
　　c.　Percentage change and annual percent change are as previously defined (see table 6, for example).
　　d.　Estimates based on adoption of:
　　1.　Thirty percent reduction in LIEA from FY 1981 levels as requested in the FY 1982 budget.
　　2.　An increase in public housing rent rates from 25 to 30 percent of income.
Benefit changes are estimated in the same way for states with optional supplements, only using the higher basic SSI benefit.
The administration proposal to eliminate the $20 per month SS disregard in the SSI program for *new* SSI beneficiaries in FY 1983 was not simulated. If so, benefits would decrease by another $8 to $12 below those shown here.
　　e.　Estimates based on adoption of:
　　1.　Continued funding of LIEA at 70 percent of FY 1981 level.
　　2.　Increasing the Food Stamp tax rate to 0.35 percent of net income (with delayed cost-of-living adjustments in nominal deduction limits).
　　3.　Inclusion of Food Stamp benefits as income for determining public housing rent.
　　4.　A deduction of $23 in allowable rent for public housing units.
　　5.　The proposed increase in the public housing tax rate from 25 to 30 percent of income.
Benefit changes are estimated in the same way for states with optional supplements, only using the higher-basis SSI guarantee.

4. It proposed increasing the Food Stamp benefit reduction rate from 30 to 35 percent.

5. It proposed an immediate increase in public housing rents from 25 to 30 percent of income (Congress actually passed a four-year phase-in of increases), inclusion of Food Stamp benefits as income in determining public housing rent, and a reduction averaging $23 per month in the maximum allowable market rent paid to public housing tenants.[30]

6. It proposed an option for states to count Food Stamp benefits as income in determining AFDC benefit levels to the extent that the bonus value of the stamps exceeded that part of the state's AFDC needs standard allocated for food.

7. It proposed mandatory state copayments for Medicaid which would reduce real income by increasing medical expenses for low-income families needing health care.

8. It proposed to eliminate the OASI $20-per-month disregard for *new* SSI beneficiaries after January 1, 1983.

Table 10 shows the effect on the safety net of the first five of these proposals (which Congress did not pass) along with the last three (which were actually adopted). Proposal 6 was passed as part of the FY 1982 budget, but no state has implemented it. It could reduce the maximum AFDC grant by as much as a third in southern states with low needs standards—a particularly severe reduction in benefits in light of evidence that states substituted Food Stamp benefit increases for AFDC benefit increases during the 1970s.[31] While all AFDC beneficiaries (and most SSI beneficiaries) are automatically eligible for Medicaid, the effect of the Medicaid copayments (proposal 7 above) cannot be determined without estimates of the size and number of copayments a typical family would make in an average month.

Table 10 shows that from 1981 to 1983 the changes proposed by the Reagan administration in multiple benefit packages would have caused sizable benefit decreases. Altogether the real combined AFDC, Food Stamp, and LIEA benefit guarantees would have dropped from 1981 to 1983 by 4.0 percent per year, almost three times the actual annual real benefit reduction

---

30. James Zais, R. Struyk, and T. Thibodeau, *Housing Assistance for Older Americans: The Reagan Prescription* (Washington, D.C.: The Urban Institute Press, 1982), tables 6-8, p. 116.

31. Hulten et al., "Historical Trends."

rate over this period (1.5 percent), and more than twice the 1970–1981 annual rate of decline (1.9 percent).[32]

SSI benefit combinations would have been similarly affected. While the administration proposed no changes for existing elderly beneficiaries of SSI and OASI combined payments, its proposed changes in Food Stamps, LIEA, and public housing benefits would have wiped out any real benefit gains from 1981 to 1983 resulting from the recently adopted Social Security amendments. If the Reagan administration proposals had been adopted, combined OASI, Food Stamp, and LIEA benefit levels would have declined by an average of 1.7 percent per year from 1981 to 1983, in contrast to the minimal 0.2 percent average gain actually observed over this period (and in contrast to the average 0.3 percent real annual benefit decline of the 1970s). The elderly living in public housing would have suffered still larger benefit decreases between 1981 and 1983. A single elderly SSI recipient of OASI and Food Stamp benefits and living in public housing, would have experienced a real benefit decrease of $44 per month, a 10.6 percent decline. In states with optional supplements, assuming the real value of these supplements remained unchanged from 1982 to 1983, the real benefit losses would have been even larger.

If the administration proposals to eliminate the OASI disregard had been adopted, new SSI beneficiaries would have been further affected beginning in 1983. Combined SSI and OASI benefits would have been $20 per month lower, and combined benefit packages $8–$12 per month lower than those shown in table 10.

In conclusion, if the Reagan administration had had its way with changes in means-tested benefit programs, the benefit generosity in the safety net would have shrunk at a much faster rate than in the 1970s. Congressional action was responsible for preserving, or at least slowing, the deterioration of the safety net over the past two years.

Interstate Benefit Differences. In the opinion of many, one of the most serious problems in the safety net involves the wide variance between states in both the breadth and depth (generosity) of the safety net programs. The administration began in 1981 by proposing that responsibility for the AFDC and Food Stamp programs be delegated to the states. State officials and policy analysts alike were dismayed by these "fiscal federalism" plans, and they have been put on the back burner.

---

32. According to the U.S. House Ways and Means Committee, February 1983, table 12, 80.6 percent of AFDC households have no reported income other than AFDC and thus would qualify for maximum benefits. Of these, 75 percent also receive Food Stamps and virtually 100 percent LIEA or public housing.

If providing an adequate bottom tier to the safety net is seen as a national responsibility, the facts in table 11 are a national embarrassment. Here we compare several characteristics of the safety net in the poorest and the least poor states (based on 1980 census figures).[33] We also provide summary comparisons of totals and averages at the bottom of the table. Almost a third (32.6 percent) of the U.S. poor live in the poorest thirteen states, while only about 13 percent live in the eleven richest states.

The means-tested cash public assistance systems vary considerably between these groups of states. For instance, overall benefit generosity, again measured by AFDC guarantee levels for four-person families, differs significantly. The lowest group had average guarantees that were only 58 percent of the national average, while the highest averaged 116 percent of the national mean. In 1980, twenty-seven states had AFDC-UP programs; this included only one from the poorest group as compared to seven from the least poor group. Similarly, twenty-six states provided optional supplements to basic federal SSI recipients in July 1980. Only two of the thirteen poorest states offered optional supplements, while eight of the eleven least poor states offered such benefits. While the number of persons receiving cash assistance is not the same as the number of poor people in a state, table 11 does provide some summary information on the breadth of the safety net. As one might expect, the poorest states offer the narrowest benefits.

Medicaid benefit generosity and coverage (again based on total recipients as a percentage of state poor) provide another measure of the depth and breadth of the safety net in each state. Again, benefits and coverage in the poorest states are far below the national average, while the least poor states are above or close to the average.

The Food Stamp program is a national program that is administered by the states. Differences in Food Stamp participation rates (number of recipients as a percentage of persons estimated to be eligible) provide additional information on the effectiveness of the state social service systems in reaching the needy. Again, participation rates are lower in the poorer states. Because of the low cash benefits in the poorest states, higher benefits from Food Stamps are available to eligible participants. One would expect, then, that participation

---

33. The table shows the thirteen poorest but only the eleven least poor states. The twelfth and thirteenth least poor states are Alaska and Hawaii whose AFDC, Food Stamp, and other benefit levels differ so greatly due to cost-of-living differences that a more accurate comparison is possible by leaving them out of these calculations. If they are included, they only add to the credibility of the arguments made below.

rates would be higher, not lower, in such areas.[34] However, local attitudes towards welfare programs including Food Stamps influence outreach efforts and cause more stringent enforcement of eligibility rules. Thus the lower participation rates in the poorer (mainly southern) states may reflect regional attitudes towards national welfare programs in general.

Finally we consider combined AFDC and Food Stamp guarantee levels and their generosity relative to the official poverty definition. This perspective complements the *average* combined benefit information in tables 5 and 9 by focusing instead on the *variance* in these benefits across the states. While the poorest states offer maximum benefit levels that are only 56 percent of poverty levels on the average, the *least* poor states offer maximum benefits that are 75 percent of the federal poverty line. Ranking states from least generous to most generous on this combined benefits basis, we find eleven of the poorest states in the bottom twelve states nationwide. Moreover, these differences have persisted throughout the 1970s with little change. Figures for 1970 and 1975 reveal the same pattern, with largely the same states at either end of the spectrum.[35]

Clearly, states have significantly different philosophies towards the breadth and generosity of their safety nets. The ability of individual states to revamp programs has been at least partially thwarted by federal involvement and participation. Consequently, one would expect even wider benefit differentials between states had the administration's fiscal federalism plan to turn AFDC and Food Stamps over to the states been adopted.

Previous Republican (Nixon) and Democratic (Carter) administrations alike have argued that the federal government must initiate and maintain a national safety net for the poor.[36] A reasonable national minimum AFDC benefit with optional state supplementation, as typified by the SSI program, would provide a solid safety net for truly needy single parents, while giving states the option to further assist the poor by increasing benefits. The Reagan administration chose instead to pursue a policy of fiscal federalism.

---

34. Richard Coe, "Participation in the Food Stamp Program," G. Duncan and J. Morgan, eds., *Five Thousand American Families*, volume X (Ann Arbor: University of Michigan Press, 1983).

35. See Timothy M. Smeeding, "The Antipoverty Effectiveness of In-Kind Transfers, A 'Good Idea' Gone Too Far?" *Policy Studies Journal*, March 1982.

36. Larry Orr, "Income Transfers as a Public Good: An Application to AFDC," *American Economic Review*, June 1976, pp. 359–371; and Helen F. Ladd and F.J. Doolittle, "Which Level of Government Should Assist the Poor?" *National Tax Journal*, vol. 35, no. 3 (September 1982), pp. 323–336.

TABLE 11

COMPARISON OF THE WELFARE SYSTEM IN THE POOREST AND RICHEST STATES: 1980

| | Poverty | | Cash Public Assistance | | | | Medicaid | | Food Stamps | Combined Maximum AFDC and Food Stamps | |
| | Population (Millions) | Percentage of Population | Maximum AFDC | AFDC-UP Program | Optional SSI | Cash Assistance as Percentage of State Poor | Benefits Per Recipient of State Poor | Recipients as Percentage of State Poor | Participation Rate | Level | Level as Percentage of Poverty Line |
	(1)	(2)	(3)	(4)	(5)	(6)	(7)	(8)	(9)	(10)	(11)
Poorest States											
MS	0.600	24.5 (1)	120	No	No	46.5	687	51.2	44.5	295	47.9
DC	0.115	18.9 (2)	349	Yes	Yes	82.0	1,323	110.4	73.1	431	70.0
AL	0.777	18.9 (3)	187	No	No	43.9	1,137	47.0	46.1	331	53.7
AR	0.417	18.7 (4)	188	No	No	38.5	1,059	53.2	37.4	343	55.7
KY	0.657	18.4 (5)	235	No	No	39.1	722	62.4	51.4	375	60.9
LA	0.684	17.9 (6)	148	No	No	45.3	812	47.4	40.2	315	51.1
NM	0.222	17.4 (7)	267	No	No	35.1	795	39.6	39.9	371	60.2
TN	0.760	17.0 (8)	148	No	No	37.7	1,073	46.6	49.5	315	51.1
GA	0.869	16.4 (9)	173	No	No	42.1	1,074	49.5	35.7	315	51.1
SD	0.107	16.1 (10)	361	No	Yes	26.1	1,571	32.7	25.7	449	72.9
SC	0.479	15.9 (11)	158	No	No	47.8	769	70.4	40.2	298	48.3
TX	2.055	14.8 (12)	140	No	No	27.0	1,426	33.5	29.4	309	50.2
NC	0.827	14.6 (13)	210	No	No	39.7	1,064	45.6	37.8	351	57.0
Least Poor States[a]											
MD	0.409	9.9 (41)	326	Yes	No	61.6	1,022	76.5	55.8	398	64.6
MA	0.547	9.8 (42)	444	Yes	Yes	84.7	1,302	141.7	97.2	488	79.2
IN	0.523	9.8 (42)	315	No	No	37.8	1,727	39.2	43.3	403	65.4
NJ	0.699	9.7 (44)	414	Yes	Yes	76.3	1,118	96.7	58.7	473	76.8
IA	0.266	9.4 (45)	419	Yes	No	48.9	1,292	66.9	42.1	487	79.1
MN	0.370	9.3 (46)	486	Yes	Yes	45.2	1,815	87.8	34.7	508	82.5

	(1)	(2)	(3)	(4)	(5)	(6)	(7)	(8)	(9)	(10)	(11)
NH	0.078	8.7 (47)	392	No	Yes	34.5	1,600	57.7	43.6	453	73.5
CT	0.262	8.7 (47)	553	Yes	Yes	59.8	1,613	82.8	56.1	508	82.5
WI	0.388	8.5 (49)	529	Yes	Yes	71.8	1,614	109.5	42.3	532	86.4
NV	0.067	8.5 (49)	314	No	Yes	27.1	1,800	37.3	25.6	404	65.6
WY	0.037	8.0 (51)	340	No	Yes	23.8	1,273	29.7	36.6	424	68.8
Summary											
National											
Totals	27.526			27/51	26/51						
Average		12.5	354	—	—	52.0	1,148	78.5	46.9	434	68.9
Poorest States											
Total	8.569			1/13	2/13						
Average		17.7	206	—	—	42.4	1,039	53.0	42.4	346	56.2
Least Poor States											
Total	3.646			7/11	8/11						
Average		9.1	412	—	—	52.0	1,471	75.1	48.7	462	75.0

SOURCES BY COLUMN:

(1), (2) U.S. Bureau of the Census, *Characteristics of the U.S. Population from the 1980 Census* (Washington, D.C.: Government Printing Office, 1982).

(3), (4) "AFDC Standards for Basic Needs: July 1980," Office of Policy, Social Security Administration, November 1981.

(5) "SSI for the Aged, Blind, and Disabled; Summary of State Payment Levels, State Supplementation, and Medicaid Decisions," Office of Operation Policy and Procedures, Social Security Administration, Revised January 1, 1981.

(6) Sum of AFDC, SSI, and General Assistance Recipients in December 1980 as a fraction of state poor in column (1); *Social Security Bulletin, Annual Statistical Supplement*, 1981.

(7) Average expenditures per unduplicated recipient for fiscal year 1980; *Health Care Financing Review*, Summary 1983.

(8) Total unduplicated number of recipients for FY 1980 as a percentage of state poor in column (1); *Health Care Financing Review*, Summary 1983.

(9) 1975 participation rates: percentage of all eligible households which receive stamps, *Annual Food Stamp Program Evaluation, Fiscal Year 1978*, prepared for the U.S. House of Representatives Committee on Agriculture, Nutrition, and Forestry, September, 1979.

(10) July 1979 figures, Office of the Assistant Secretary for Planning and Evaluation, U.S. Department of Health and Human Services, unpublished data.

(11) Based on 1979 poverty line for a four-person family of $7,386 or $616 per month; U.S. Bureau of the Census, "*Characteristics of the Poverty Population*," *Current Population Reports*, Series P-60, no. 138. April 1983.

a. We only include eleven states among the least poor because the twelfth and thirteenth poorest states are Alaska and Hawaii, where regional price differences would create an upward bias in AFDC and Food Stamp estimates.

Summary

This section has attempted to separate the Reagan administration's involvement with changes in the social safety net into two parts: proposals that have been implemented and proposals not yet adopted. The following conclusions are offered.

Actual program changes in AFDC and SSI, whether analyzing single programs or for multiple benefits, have either slowed—or at worst have only continued—the decline in the generosity of the means-tested safety net which began in the mid-1970s. The safety net for truly needy single parents and elderly persons with no other income today is not much less generous than it was when Reagan became president.

Had the proposals of the Reagan administration been adopted wholesale, significant decreases in safety net programs for a large majority of the truly needy would have been realized. While the Reagan administration has not proposed *nominal* benefit reductions in individual programs for those with no other income sources, *real* benefits have been reduced (for instance, by postponing scheduled increases in Food Stamp benefits). Moreover, proposed changes in interprogram relationships would have reduced even nominal benefit guarantees for recipients of multiple benefits (e.g., for AFDC and SSI recipients receiving Food Stamps and living in public housing or receiving LIEA benefits). Thus while the administration can claim that on a program-to-program basis, it has not hurt the truly needy, it has made proposals that would have reduced the overall level of safety net support.

The administration's fiscal federalism proposals to transfer the AFDC and Food Stamp programs to the states were not adopted. However, had they been adopted, the already wide interstate variance in safety net benefits under these programs would have probably widened considerably.

Other Programs and Other Perspectives

Many of the administration's proposed changes in safety net programs for groups other than single parents or the low-income elderly do not fit neatly into tabular form. In particular, we cannot ignore policy changes in programs affecting two-parent families (e.g., unemployment insurance, training assistance, and educational assistance).

Unemployment Insurance. In early 1983, roughly 2.1 million persons had been out of work for two months or longer.[37] This was about one-fifth

---

37. D.H. Saks, in Pechmar, ed., *SNP83*.

of the total number of unemployed. At the peak of the 1975–1976 recession, over 75 percent of the unemployed during any given month were covered by some type of unemployment insurance (UI). During 1982, the average number covered by UI in any month was only 45.2 percent; during June and July of 1983, fewer than 40 percent were covered.

Legislative changes in UI program regulations help explain these trends. Most state UI programs currently provide up to twenty-six weeks of benefits; the federal-state Extended Benefit (EB) program can provide an additional thirteen weeks for the unemployed in qualifying states. Finally, the Federal Supplemental Compensation (FSC) program can provide from eight to sixteen additional weeks of benefits in states with particularly high unemployment. In 1975–1976 the EB program was activated for a state when its insured unemployment rate[38] exceeded a certain level, and for the nation as a whole when the national insured unemployment rate exceeded 4.5 percent (on grounds that the long-term unemployed deserved help regardless of the unemployment rate in their own state). But in 1981 Congress raised the state trigger (to 5.0 percent) and eliminated the national trigger. As a result of these and other technical changes, only fourteen states qualified for EB by the end of 1982 whereas all states would have qualified previously. The FSC program also was changed and limited in several ways. Congress reenacted it in mid-1982 for a six-month period (October 1982 to March 1983), and since extended it until March 1985.

The combined effect of these changes has been to reduce the maximum duration of UI, EB, and FSC from sixty-five weeks in 1976 to a maximum of thirty-four to fifty-five weeks (depending on state triggers) in 1983. Altogether, UI expenditures would have been $15 billion higher in FY 1983 if the system had compensated the unemployed in proportion to the levels paid in FY 1976.[39]

Most states limit the extent to which two-parent families whose unemployment benefits have run out can rely on means-tested programs from the lower tier of the safety net. Only twenty-five states now have an AFDC-UP program, and many families who have exhausted UI benefits are not eligible because of the stringent asset test (allowable resource limits of $1,000 excluding the family's home and one $1,500 automobile). Most unemployed also lose their employer-provided health insurance coverage. In states without

38. The insured unemployment rate was then the percentage of those unemployed workers covered by state UI programs and state/federal EB. Those receiving EB were excluded from these calculations by the 1981 amendments.

39. U.S. Congress, House, Committee on Ways and Means, "Background Material on Poverty," 98th Cong. 1st sess., October 17, 1983, p. 101.

AFDC-UP, poor two-parent families cannot automatically qualify for Medicaid; only those who incur large medical expenses can become eligible for Medicaid, and then only in a handful of states. As a result of unemployment, almost 12 million persons have lost health insurance coverage since the recession began.[40] Congress is considering several proposals for emergency health insurance protection for the unemployed, but the administration has made no such proposals.

Food Stamps provide the major source of benefits for families that have lost their UI coverage. But in order to qualify for Food Stamps, most families must have gross incomes of less than 130 percent of the poverty line, incomes net of deductions below the poverty line, and assets other than a house and a car of not more than $1,500. Again, few formerly middle-income families who are now among the long-term unemployed (the "new poor") can meet these resource tests without liquidating virtually all of their assets.

Employment and Training Assistance. For adults in two-parent families, jobs are a preferred alternative to dependence on means-tested transfer programs. During the 1970s the CETA program provided short-term relief in the form of public service employment (PSE). The Reagan administration has eliminated public service employment (see table 7) and work stipends for training programs. CETA has been replaced by a scaled-down job training program (the Job Partnership Training Act of 1982) and *workfare* under which some AFDC and Food Stamp recipients are required to work up to thirty-two hours per week to maintain their benefits.

The administration's efforts to require workfare through Community Work Experience Programs (CWEPs) and mandatory job search for all AFDC and Food Stamp households consisting of an able-bodied adult and no children younger than age three have so far failed, but states and localities can voluntarily initiate such programs. As of February 1983, twenty-five states were either operating or were soon to begin CWEP programs on a limited basis. Predictably, this included nine of the thirteen poorest states in table 11, but only one of the eleven least poor states.[41] In its FY 1984 budget, the administration asked Congress to eliminate the Work Incentive (WIN) training program (which helped place eligible AFDC parents in paying, private-sector jobs) and to substitute the mandatory, nonpaying CWEP program in its stead. In the existing WIN program, special tax credits for employers and Targeted

---

40. Alice Rivlin, "Health Insurance and the Unemployed," Testimony before the House Committee on Energy and Commerce, January 24, 1983.

41. U.S. Congress, House, Committee on Ways and Means, "Description of the Administration's FY 1984 Budget Recommendations Under the Jurisdiction of the Committee on Ways and Means," 98th Cong. 1st sess., March 8, 1983, p. 38.

Jobs Tax Credits (TJTCs) help induce businesses to hire WIN registrants. In CWEP, however, states must supply the temporary jobs for participants. Congress has, however, shown little sympathy for these administration proposals.

In summary, the administration has contracted the safety net for the unemployed by curtailing the EB program and enacting a less generous FSC program than in the milder 1975–1976 recession. Public service employment and training stipends have been eliminated. Eligibility for Food Stamps, Medicaid, AFDC-UP, and other means-tested benefits has been narrowed. These changes have reduced both the breadth and the generosity of the safety net for poor two-parent families. The cutbacks in expenditures for social services (Title XX), educational assistance, and child nutrition programs noted in table 7 have had a more indirect but still measurable effect on both the unemployed and those eligible for means-tested benefits.

Recent Changes in Poverty. One testimony to the inadequacy of the safety net are the recent changes in nationwide poverty rates. Since 1979, poverty rates in the United States have increased from 11.7 to 15.0 percent of the population.[42] Two-parent families with children have been hit hardest. They now account for 40 percent of all poor persons (up from 34 percent in 1979). While poverty rates among single mothers with children have also increased, poverty among the elderly has been reduced.

The increase in poverty among children is largely the result of both the current recession and the various safety net cutbacks. While outlays for WIC and Head Start increased, overall federal benefits for children actually declined in nominal terms during FY 1982.[43] To the administration's credit, it has beefed up child support enforcement efforts. This may significantly lower long-term welfare costs for divorced, deserted, and separated women. But considering that more than 21 percent of all children lived in households with cash incomes below the official poverty line in 1982, compared to 16 percent in 1979, increased poverty among children merits great concern.

In contrast to its treatment of children, the current administration has maintained the safety nets for the elderly. Budget reductions for Social Security have been limited, and the maximum SSI benefit has increased. Although the administration argued, in 1981, for reducing the minimum OASI benefit of $121 per month for all current recipients, Congress agreed only to

---

42. These estimates and those which follow are taken from the U.S. Department of Commerce, Bureau of the Census, "Money Income and Poverty Status of Families and Persons in the United States: 1982," *Current Population Reports*, series P-60, no. 140, July 1983.

43. Alice Rivlin, Testimony before U.S. Congress, Select Committee on Children, Youth, and Families, April 28, 1983.

apply this rule to new retirees after January 1, 1982. From the perspective
of the safety net, this minimum-benefit feature of the OASI system mainly
aids those with multiple retirement benefits, spouses, and others who are not
among the truly needy. For most truly needy, low-income elderly, SSI benefits
would have replaced lost OASI benefits dollar for dollar.[44] Major changes
anticipated in the Medicare program could, however, soon signal the end of
the administration's unflagging support for the elderly.[45]

In summary, the elderly have been least affected by changes in the safety
net. Single-parent families, typically with little income other than safety net
benefits, were somewhat affected (insofar as their poverty rates continue to
increase). Children and adults in two-parent families were most seriously
affected by the combination of a deep recession and holes in the safety net.[46]
By the administration's definition, however, two-parent families without serious health problems are probably not among the truly needy. While safety
net programs have traditionally *not* provided benefits for this group, except
in the face of a serious recession, the current administration has provided
even less help in the midst of the most serious recession since the 1930s.
While not all families with unemployed parents have fallen onto hard times,
the recent increase in poverty among such families is a sign that many have
fallen through the safety net.

Summary and Conclusion

The safety net—as it existed in the 1970s, with gaping holes for two-
parent families and non-aged single individuals and childless couples—is still
largely intact. While the administration attempted to reduce the breadth and
especially the level (generosity) of the safety net, Congress successfully opposed these initiatives except for programs primarily benefiting two-parent
families. Had the administration's proposals been adopted wholesale, even
the truly needy (using the administration's relatively narrow definition) would
have suffered substantial income losses.

To the extent that recent changes in poverty rates can measure the effectiveness of the safety net, the elderly have been well protected and

44. Some 250,000 recipients of the minimum benefit would fail the SSI resources test and,
without spending down their liquid assets, would not quality for SSI.

45. Marilyn Moon, "Changing the Structure of Medicare Benefits: Issues and Options,"
Congressional Budget Office, March 1983.

46. Timothy Smeeding, "Recent Increases in Poverty in the U.S.: What the Official Figures
Fail to Show," Testimony prepared for the U.S. Congress, House Ways and Means Committee,
October 18, 1983.

nonaged single-parent families have not been greatly affected. These are the truly needy as defined by the administration. However, the recent sharp increases in poverty among two-parent families reflect both holes in the pre-1981 safety net and a contraction of this net as proposed by the Reagan administration and enacted by the Congress.

APPENDIX

TABLE A.1

MAXIMUM SSI BENEFITS (FOR ELDERLY COUPLES LIVING ALONE) AND ACTUAL BENEFIT OUTLAYS
(In Constant 1981 Dollars)

| | Federal Minimum Guarantee (1) | Average State Maximum Supplements | | Average Maximum Federal and State Benefit Levels | | Total Outlays (in Billions of Dollars) (6) |
		All States Paying Optional Supplements[b] (2)	Five Highest Supplementing States[c] (3)	All States Paying Optional Supplements[b] (4) = (1) + (2)	Five Highest Supplementing States[c] (5) = (1) + (3)	
1970[a]	NA	NA	NA	450.40	605.62	1.361
1972[b]	NA	NA	NA	448.35	623.48	4.080
1974	404.06	121.77	265.68	525.83	669.74	4.618
1976	402.24	125.65	270.29	527.89	672.52	4.007
1978	396.23	117.29	316.82	513.53	713.05	3.392
1980	394.04	110.66	291.28	504.70	685.32	3.018
1981	397.00	98.45	244.72	495.45	641.72	2.775
Percentage Change 1970–1981[d]	NA	NA	NA	10.0	6.0	–36.4
Average Annual Percentage Change[c] 1981	NA	NA	NA	0.8	0.5	–4.01970–19

Percentage Change^f 1981	−1.8	−19.2	−7.9	−.58	−4.2	−39.9 1974–19
Average Annual Percentage Change^e 1974–1981	−0.3	−3.0	−1.2	−0.8	−0.6	−7.0

SOURCE: Office of Operations, Policy and Procedures, Social Security Administration.

a. 1970 and 1972 figures refer to state-specific Old Age Assistance programs which preceded SSI.
b. Includes only those states with *optional* benefits in excess of the federal minimum benefit. States with mandatory supplements are not included.
c. Includes the five highest supplementary states in 1974: New York, California, Wisconsin, Pennsylvania, and Massachusetts.
d. (1981–1970) ÷ 1970 × .100.
e. Average annual percentage change reflects compounding over the period.
f. (1981–1974) ÷ 1974 × .100.

NA = not available.

TABLE A.2

MAXIMUM SSI BENEFITS (FOR COUPLES LIVING ALONE) AND ACTUAL BENEFIT OUTLAYS
(In Constant 1981 Dollars)

	Federal Minimum Guarantee (1)	Average State Maximum Supplements		Average Maximum Federal and State Benefit Levels	
		All States Paying Optional Supplements[a] (2)	Five Highest Supplementing States[b] (3)	All States Paying Optional Supplements[a] (4) = (1) + (2)	Five Highest Supplementing States[b] (5) = (1) + (3)
1981	397.00	98.45	244.72	295.45	641.72
1982	402.54	95.64	246.23	498.28	648.87
1983	414.91	NA	NA	NA	NA
Percentage Change[c]					
1981–1982	1.4	−2.9	0.6	0.6	1.1
1982–1983	3.0	NA	NA	NA	NA
1981–1983	4.4	NA	NA	NA	NA
Average Annual Percentage Change[d]					
1974–1981	−0.3	−3.0	−1.2	−0.8	−0.6
1981–1983	2.1	NA	NA	NA	NA

a. Includes only those states with *optional* benefits in excess of the federal minimum benefit. States with mandatory supplements are not included.
b. Includes the five highest supplementary states in 1974: New York, California, Wisconsin, Pennsylvania, and Massachusetts.
c. Percentage change is calculated as in table 4.
d. Average annual percentage change reflects compounding over the period.

NA = not available.

COMMENTS

G. William Hoagland

Timothy Smeeding's paper, "Is the Safety Net Still Intact?" provides a wide array of statistics intended to answer this conference's premier question. His answer seems to be that for certain segments of the population, the safety net is still intact but no thanks to the policies proffered by the Reagan administration. While I might conclude similarly, I find some of the analyses Smeeding used to derive the answer to be oblique and indirect at best. In fairness, Smeeding himself states concerns over the available data used in his analysis.

My comments will be limited to three general areas presented in the paper: (1) the definition of the so-called safety net, (2) the breadth and generosity of the safety net during the 1970s, and (3) recent administration and congressional action affecting the safety net.

Definition of the Safety Net

At the outset, I should express my frustration with the terms *safety net*, and *truly needy*. Social policy analysts may be giving more importance to the administration's political shorthand than it deserves. I believe that the term *safety net* developed not out of any consistent or coherent social welfare policy agenda, but more as an afterthought to support general budget reductions in many social welfare programs. And, unfortunately, those programs that failed to make the social safety net hall of fame, failed not because of defined objective criteria but because of strongly focused interest groups, bureaucratic power plays (sustained by those programs longest in existence), and selective bias of individuals within the administration. I contend that the Reagan administration itself has never really agreed on what programs constitute the social safety net.

The paper discussed the difficulty of determining how large the role of government should be in providing economic security to low-income indi-

121

viduals. Smeeding's safety net (broadly defined) consists of two tiers: (1) providers and intermediaries of social insurance benefits and (2) means-tested programs for those who fall through the first tier altogether or receive inadequate help from other safety net intermediaries. Smeeding admits that those federal programs included in his safety net, particularly the second tier, largely evolved in the 1970s. I basically agree with Smeeding's analysis, but find it could be strengthened in three areas.

First, Smeeding downplays the role of nongovernmental safety net intermediaries. While I agree that eleemosynary and private charities cannot, nor should be expected to, fill all the gaps, they do serve an important role here. I find Smeeding's de-emphasis of this informal sector inconsistent with his and Lampman's recent excellent work on interfamily transfers as alternatives to government transfers. That study suggests that interfamily transfers of cash, food, and housing were quantitatively more important than governmental transfers thirty years ago, but are now only half as great.[1]

Second, Smeeding fails to point out that the administration's focus on social safety net programs are not programs that evolved during the 1970s, but those that date back to the 1930s. A 1981 White House publication titled *America's New Beginning: A Program for Economic Recovery* states a commitment to preserve those social safety net programs that were the core income security programs erected in the 1930s and maintained over the subsequent four decades.[2] The administration advanced a list of safety net programs in 1981 that included (1) social insurance benefits to the elderly, (2) basic unemployment benefits, (3) Aid to Families with Dependent Children and Supplemental Security Income (AFDC and SSI), and (4) social obligations to veterans. Two years later, in material supporting the administration's fiscal year 1984 budget, the list grew to include (1) Food Stamps and nutrition programs, (2) Medicaid, (3) low-income housing assistance, (4) the Earned Income Tax Credit, and (5) the low-income energy assistance program. This portrays the administration's schizophrenic mettle in defining a basic social welfare agenda. Moreover, such moving targets render an analysis of the administration's social safety net nearly impossible.

Third, Smeeding failed to highlight a fundamental flaw in the administration's welfare logic—namely, that the vast majority of welfare recipients are not dependent on welfare on a permanent basis. Studies have consistently found that long-term welfare dependency is the exception rather than the rule,

---

1. Robert Lampman and Timothy M. Smeeding, "Interfamily Transfers as Alternatives to Government Transfers to Persons," *The Review of Income and Wealth*, series 29 (March 1983).

2. Office of Management and Budget, *America's New Beginning: A Program for Economic Recovery* (February 1981).

and that our welfare system most often serves as a temporary fallback position for those individuals living at the margin who suffer unexpected setbacks.[3] The administration's "truly needy dependent poor" are a very small subset of the nation's poor—and, as Dick Nathan recently suggested, this group constitutes a residuum probably not aided by any of the current social programs.[4] Therefore, locking social welfare policy into a set of 1930s or even 1970s programs seems a very unprogressive approach to meeting real human needs today.

On the other hand, Smeeding implicitly, and unfairly, criticizes the administration for eliminating public service employment. On this point, I totally disagree. If Smeeding were truly interested in defining the broad parameters of a social safety net, he would have to agree that reducing inflation from the high levels experienced in the 1970s is one critical parameter for substantive job creation. Alfred Kahn, looking back on his experience as the chairman of the Wage and Price Stability Council during the Carter administration, described inflation as "socially divisive, eroding our social contracts, and weakening our social fabric."[5] It is my contention that in the long run, the creation of national wealth (and hence jobs) will be best served by reduced inflation and stable input prices. This should be as much a part of the social safety net agenda as the short-term focus of individual program reductions.

Breadth and Generosity of Safety Net in the 1970s

Smeeding accurately presents the growth in federal outlays for the major human resource programs over the 1970s. He also provides some new, updated statistics on real single-program and multiple-program benefit levels over the decade.

However, a critical element in his analysis is his use of the Consumer Price Index to deflate current benefit levels to constant dollars. If those commodities experiencing rapid inflation in the 1970s, e.g., food, housing, energy costs, and medical costs, are being provided by public programs, then a deflator that includes such items would bias upward the real benefit declines for cash benefits. Smeeding's own analysis points out that real aggregate

---

3. Richard Coe, "Welfare Dependency: Fact or Myth?" *Challenge* (September/October 1982).

4. Richard Nathan, *Wall Street Journal*, June 14, 1983.

5. Alfred E. Kahn, "Liberals Must Face the Facts," *Challenge* (November/December 1981).

benefit payments for Medicaid and Food Stamps (both extensively used by AFDC and SSI participants) increased the fastest of any needs-tested programs over the decade.

Recent Administration and Congressional Action

Smeeding's analysis implies that expenditures for safety net programs have declined in real terms under the Reagan administration. In defense of the administration, it should be noted that FY 1984 spending for the Smeeding social safety net programs will be about $65 billion (current dollars) higher than the 1981 outlay levels. This represents a 7.4 percent annual increase, or a 2.2 percent real increase between 1981 and 1984, which is almost identical to current projections of real growth in the Gross National Product over this same period.

As an update (and in support) of the Smeeding analysis, the recently adopted First Budget Resolution for FY 1984 rejects a number of the administration's spending proposals. Under the resolution, entitlement spending will increase at an annual rate of about 6 percent from FY 1982 to FY 1986, about half the rate of increase during the last five years. While the administration would have reduced entitlement spending from a baseline by $26.9 billion between 1983 and 1986, the resolution decreases entitlement spending by only $400 million over this same period.

Conclusion

The Smeeding paper is a broad, far-reaching analysis of a very difficult analytical issue. Unfortunately, the analysis is limited by data availability. Nonetheless, I generally concur that there has been a slowing of growth in social welfare spending, that the administration's proposals may have at times violated a broadly defined social safety net concept, and that the Congress has at times appropriately balanced social welfare reductions against other competing objectives.

I believe, however, that job creation is a central concern of this administration and should have been given more emphasis. Optimizing short-term job creation through politically popular public works and Comprehensive Employment and Training Act-type jobs is clearly not a major goal. Long-term, stable, and noninflationary job creation remains the cornerstone of the administration's economic policy.

WELFARE DEPENDENCY

Blanche Bernstein

It was the Great Depression of 1930–1933 and the election of Franklin Roosevelt to the presidency that prompted an enormous expansion of programs to help the nation's poor. In those days, the poor were primarily unemployed workers and farmers. In the depths of the depression, the unemployment rate reached an incredible 25 percent of the labor force, and foreclosure of farms was widespread. Also included among the poor in large numbers were elderly persons, families with large numbers of children, widows with children, recent immigrants, and the sick and disabled. Undoubtedly, a disproportionate number of blacks were among the poor; they were not, however, a special concern immersed as they were in the vast sea of misery which affected all sectors of the society. Divorced and separated women with children and unmarried mothers were regarded then as a relatively minor problem.

A vast public works program was undertaken to stimulate the economy, including price supports and assistance with mortgage payments to help the farmers and a multitude of social programs to support those suffering, in President Roosevelt's words, from the "vicissitudes of life."

It took the nation years to recover from the depression. Unemployment was still at a high level in 1940 (14 percent of the labor force), but unemployment insurance was by then in place to mitigate its effects. Social Security payments to the aged were beginning, Aid to Families with Dependent Children (AFDC) was helping widows with children, and other categorical programs assisted elderly, blind, and disabled persons.

In the subsequent four decades, 1940–1979, the economic status of the population improved visibly. Unemployment generally stayed in the 3–7 percent range; increased productivity and the effectiveness of organized labor resulted in higher real wages; and women, especially married women, entered the labor market in increasing numbers. The two-earner family, formerly a rarity, became the rule, and with it, a big jump in family incomes. Medicare and Medicaid were instituted to assist the sick, while Social Security and Supplemental Security Income (SSI) were extended to the disabled. The distribution of food, and subsequently the Food Stamp program, was greatly expanded to add to the resources of those with limited incomes. The level of poverty declined to 11.7 percent by 1979, and in-kind transfers brought almost half of the remaining poor above the poverty level.

Who Are the Poor Today?

It is now fifty years since the beginning of the New Deal. While the decline in poverty is clearly a cause for rejoicing, the change in the composition of the poor and the dependent is a cause for concern.

At the outset, it must be noted that poverty and dependency are not synonymous in the United States. Dependency may be defined as the inability to support oneself and one's family at a standard that society in the nation or each state has agreed on as the minimum acceptable level. Inability to support one's family may stem from the death of the family breadwinner, physical or mental illness or disability, old age, unemployment, or the need to care for young children—in other words, events beyond the control of the individual. The term also infers the lack of other financial resources, including the right to draw from such insurance funds as Social Security, unemployment insurance, or Medicare. The minimum acceptable level of income that would trigger aid has changed over time as the economy has grown, the general standard of living has risen, and society's notion of fairness has led to more generous treatment of dependent groups.

The poverty standard is a national standard developed by the federal government: an income of $9,862 for a family of four at 1982 prices is the current poverty line. In contrast, in the AFDC program, the major cash assistance welfare program in the country, the welfare standard is established by each of the states within the general framework of eligibility rules set by the federal government. The variation in state standards is substantial even when account is taken of Food Stamp benefits which are based on a national standard and which serve to moderate the differences in the cash grant levels. As a result, in some states, welfare recipients may be at or even above the poverty level; in others, they are sometimes significantly below it. Nevertheless, there is substantial overlapping between the poor and the dependent.

In this paper, we shall be discussing both poverty and dependency on welfare payments and Food Stamps.

Unemployment rates exceeded 7 percent in 1980 and 1981 and rose to between 10 and 11 percent in 1982, the highest level since the 1930s. By 1982 the poverty rate had risen to 15 percent, though this figure is about halved when in-kind transfer payments are counted. But the data for New York City, which has an AFDC-UP (Unemployed Parent) program as well as a general assistance (GA) program, show only a modest rise of intact families on welfare with a sharper increase among single individuals.[1] Similarly, welfare caseloads do not indicate any significant increase in dependency among the farm population despite the increased economic hardships they face.

Poverty and dependency among the aged have been declining even more rapidly than among other age groups. From a peak of 2.8 million aged on Old Age Assistance in 1950, the numbers declined to 2.1 million in 1965 and remained at about that level for several years.[2] With the shift to the federally administered SSI program in January 1974, there was first an increase to 2.3 million in December 1975 as many needy aged, who regarded "welfare" as demeaning, accepted the federal program that sounded like Social Security. Since then, the numbers have been declining steadily to 1.5 million by March 1983—despite an increase in the aged population in the country from 16.7 million in 1960 to about 27 million in 1982.

In contrast to the aged, the number of disabled who depend on SSI has risen sharply—from less than 70,000 in 1950 to 935,000 in 1970 to over 2.2 million in March 1983.[3] This reflects an expansion of program coverage more than an expansion in the number of disabled.

Widows and their children, the major target group of the AFDC program when it was established in 1935, have practically disappeared from the welfare caseload. This is due to (1) the increased longevity of men, (2) coverage of widows under the Social Security program based on their husbands' contributions to the Social Security fund, (3) the generally improved economic situation of families, and (4) the increased number of women in the labor force.

Who then are the poor and the dependent in the 1980s? To an overwhelming degree in relation to their proportion of the population, the poor

---

1. New York City, Human Resources Administration, Monthly Statistical Reports, unpublished.

2. U.S. Department of Health and Human Services, Social Security Administration, *Social Security Bulletin*, vol. 46, no. 4, June 1983, table M-19, p. 36, and table M-28, p. 44.

3. Ibid., table M-18, p. 36, and table M-28, p. 44.

and the dependent are families headed by women as a result of divorce, separation, or desertion, or who never married. Also, although the majority of people in poverty and dependent on welfare are white, a disproportionate number of poor and dependent are black or Hispanic.

In considering whether (and how) welfare dependency can be reduced, we must determine why these particular subgroups are poor, whether it is a short- or long-term phenomenon, and whether recent changes legislated under the Reagan administration are likely to reduce welfare dependency.

When and Why the Shift Occurred

Between 1940, when the AFDC program became well established, and 1960, the number of recipients rose from about 1.2 million to 3.1 million (after a dip during the war years). After a fairly rapid postwar readjustment, these were relatively prosperous years; but they were also the years of large-scale migration of blacks from the South to the North and West and of Hispanics from Puerto Rico to the mainland, especially New York City. Migrants are a vulnerable group likely to need help when unemployment, illness, or other catastrophes strike. Family break-ups and out-of-wedlock pregnancies also began rising during these years.

The major explosion in welfare caseloads, however, came in the 1960s, a period of declining unemployment—from 6 percent at the beginning of the decade to 3 percent at the end—of rising real wages, and declining migration from the South and Puerto Rico. The caseload rose from 3 million recipients in 1960 to 9.7 million in 1970 and continued upward to a peak of 11.4 million in 1975. It then tapered off to a low of about 10.4 million in 1978–1979 when it began to rise gradually; by June 1981 it reached a level of 11.1 million, still below its 1975 peak.[4] These welfare recipients are mainly families headed by women. The AFDC-UP program (covering two-parent families with a disabled or unemployed wage earner) operates in only twenty-five states and has never accounted for more than 10 percent of the total AFDC caseload in any state (and in most states, has remained substantially below this level).

The increased dependency of families headed by women cannot be attributed to a lack of welfare programs for the intact family. In states that have both AFDC-UP and general assistance programs (including New York, Pennsylvania, and Michigan), the number of intact families on welfare has not

---

4. Ibid., table M-28, p. 44.

been very large since 1940 and has been decreasing in most of the post-World War II years. Only in the last two years, and in cities particularly hard hit by unemployment—such as Detroit with 16 percent unemployment, and Rochester with over 13 percent—has the number of two-parent families on welfare increased significantly.

The Duration of Dependency

Society's concern about dependency is different for short-term than long-term dependency. Assistance for those suffering from the "vicissitudes of life" is widely acceptable. Doubts arise where dependency appears to be long-term and unrelated to physical or mental illness or other uncontrollable factors. Until recently, most of the data on duration of poverty and welfare dependency were totally inadequate. We now have appropriate data from the Panel Study of Income Dynamics (PSID) done under the aegis of the Survey Research Institute of the University of Michigan. Analysis of the data has been done by members of the institute staff as well as by Mary Jo Bane and David T. Ellwood at the Kennedy School of Government at Harvard University. Much is to be learned from both.

Based on ten years of data, 1969–1978, Coe, Duncan, and Hill at the Survey Research Institute find that only 2 percent of the total population were poor in each of the ten years and only 5.1 percent of the poor were persistently poor, that is, were poor for eight years or more. They concluded that welfare programs are well targeted and do not encourage long-term dependency. They add, however, that "persistent poverty is heavily concentrated among blacks, particularly in families headed by a black woman." They point out that though families headed by black women account for only 4 percent of the population, they constitute 31 percent of the persistently poor. They also note that the gender of the household head is "the strongest predictor of whether a family began to receive welfare.[5]

In a separate article, Coe adds some further insights to the analysis of the data. He points out that at some point during the ten-year period, 25.2 percent of the total population received welfare. Of these, 12.3 percent were short-term (one or two years), 8.5 percent were intermediate (three to seven years), and only 4.4 percent of the population in the country were long-term

---

5. Richard D. Coe, Greg J. Duncan, and Martha S. Hill, "Dynamic Aspects of Poverty and Welfare in the United States," Paper prepared for Conference on Problems of Poverty and Welfare in the United States, Clark University (mimeographed), August 1982 (revised, March 1983) pp. 34–35.

(eight years or more) welfare recipients. In all, 48.8 percent of welfare recipients are short-term, 33.7 percent are intermediate, and 17.5 percent are long-term. Coe notes that the composition of the short-term welfare population closely parallels the composition of the population as a whole, but the long-term welfare population is disproportionately black, constituting only 11.7 percent of the total population but 55.3 percent of the long-term welfare recipients.[6]

Coe and his associates correctly concluded that a large portion of those who become dependent remain so for only a year or two. But two problems exist with the data. First, the data include the elderly receiving SSI benefits, a diminishing as well as a distinctive group. The data might look somewhat less encouraging if the analysis excluded the elderly. Second, the definition of long-term as eight or more years is questionable; even five years might well be considered long-term. Nevertheless, receiving welfare apparently does not lead to long-term dependency for at least half of the people who need it at some point in their lives.

Another way of looking at the issue of the duration of poverty or dependency is to consider, at any point in time, who the poor are and how long they have been poor. The analysis of the PSID data by Bane and Ellwood, an analysis which excludes the elderly poor, concludes that "the distinction between the ever poor (or newly poor) and poor at a point in time is crucial in understanding poverty and shedding light on the question of culture, dependency, and allocation of resources." Their primary finding based on the PSID data for the decade 1969–1978 is "that although many people have short spells of poverty, the few with very long spells account for the bulk of all poverty and represent the bulk of the poor at any point in time."[7] They find that the median duration of poverty for a newly poor person is two years, and that two-thirds of the newly poor will escape poverty by the end of the third year. Nevertheless, 15 percent of the newly poor will remain poor for a long time. According to their estimates, at any particular time, 60 percent of the poor have been poor for more than eight years, while 73 percent have been poor for five or more years. The mean duration of poverty for the long-term poor (those who are poor for eight years or more) is over thirteen years.

In a more recent work focused on families receiving AFDC benefits, Bane and Ellwood find that duration of dependency on AFDC follows a similar pattern. While most AFDC recipients remain on welfare for relatively short

---

6. Richard D. Coe, "Welfare Dependency: Fact or Myth?" *Challenge*, vol. 25, no. 4 (Sept./Oct. 1982), pp. 43–49.

7. Mary Jo Bane and David T. Ellwood, "Slipping Into and Out of Poverty: The Dynamics of Spells," Preliminary Draft, August 1982, pp. 2–3.

periods, 50.2 percent of female heads of families receiving AFDC benefits at any point in time have been on welfare for eight years of more, and 75.6 percent have been on welfare for five years or more.[8]

The difference between the proportion of male- and female-headed households who remain in poverty for eight years or more is less than one might anticipate—58 and 67 percent, respectively. However, when single individuals are excluded from both groups, a much wider difference is apparent. Whereas 59 percent of the children in male-headed households remain in poverty for eight years or more, the figure is 80 percent in female-headed households; the mean duration of poverty for children in female-headed households is sixteen years. For black children in female-headed households, 88 percent have been poor for eight years or more and the mean duration of poverty is more than twenty years. In summarizing the data, Bane and Ellwood conclude that blacks are likely to be poor much longer than whites and "the situation for poor blacks hardly looks dynamic to us, it looks quite chronic."[9]

Bane and Ellwood also provide evidence of specific factors that impel people into and out of poverty. Among male-headed households, 43 percent became poor because of a reduction in the number of hours worked or the level of wages. Among female-headed households, however, the major poverty-inducing factor (accounting for 49 percent of the newly poor) was the transition of women to the status of married or unmarried female head of household. This change in status accounted for an even larger proportion of women who became dependent on welfare—75.6 percent.[10] A much smaller, but still significant, 21 percent of poor female-headed families fell below the poverty line because of reduction in hours worked or in wages, and 22 percent because of other income losses. Only 12.1 percent of female heads of households began receiving welfare because of reduced earnings and 12.2 percent because of other income losses.

The means of escaping poverty are also significant. Two-thirds of male-headed households escape as a result of an increase in hours worked or in wages and an additional 14 percent by increased earnings of the wife or other family members. Among female-headed households, 41 percent escape poverty by increasing hours of work or obtaining higher wages, while 22 percent do so by transition to a male-headed household. The comparable figures for ending dependence on welfare (as opposed to escaping poverty) for female-

8. Mary Jo Bane and David T. Ellwood, "The Dynamics of Dependence: The Routes to Self-Sufficiency," Report prepared by Urban Systems Research and Engineering, Cambridge, Mass., for Assistant Secretary for Planning and Evaluation, Department of Health and Human Service, HHA-100-82-030 table 1, p. 11.

9. Bane and Ellwood, "Slipping Into and Out of Poverty," p. 43.

10. Bane and Ellwood, "The Dynamics of Dependence," table 3, p. 18.

headed households are 52.4 percent by marriage and 31.8 percent through increased earnings though some of the latter group fall back on welfare from time to time.

Finally, the duration of poverty can be analyzed with respect to the factors that caused the poverty. Those in male- or female-headed households who become poor because of a decline in earnings remain poor for the shortest periods of time. Poverty brought on by transition to the status of female head of household leads to somewhat longer-than-average spells of poverty. Children born into poverty spend an average of nine years in poverty and children now poor who were born into poverty will average seventeen years. The prospects for poor black children are even worse; they will remain in poverty for an average of eighteen or twenty-two years, depending on whether they are in male- or female-headed households.

In summary, we have looked at two studies on the duration of poverty and dependency, both based on data from a national sample of households followed for ten years, 1969–1978. Both agree that the majority of households who are poor and receive welfare at some point do not remain on welfare for more than three years, but that a sizable fraction remain longer. Among current welfare recipients, slightly more than half have been on welfare for eight or more years, while three-fourths have been on welfare for at least five years. Blacks are dependent on welfare longer than average, and female-headed black families longer still. Black children in these families remain in poverty the longest of all. Family break-up, or unwed motherhood and loss of jobs or decreased earnings are the major causes of dependency, while marriage and jobs or increased earnings are the major factors in ending dependency.

Testifying in April 1983 before the Select Committee on Children, Youth, and Families, Alice Rivlin, then director of the Congressional Budget Office, presented this dreary scenario: "The number of children living in poverty will probably remain high and may continue to increase, in part because of demographic factors. The Bureau of the Census projects that the number of births per year will continue to rise, resulting in an increase in the number of young children. In addition, the proportion of children living in single parent households is projected to rise to about one-fourth by 1990."[11]

Welfare programs have without doubt helped large numbers of families surmount periods of adversity. It appears that they have also fostered long-term dependency among some recipients.

---

11. Alice M. Rivlin, Prepared Statement before the U.S. Congress, House Select Committee on Children, Youth, and Families, April 28, 1983, p. 9.

The Impact of Welfare Policy and Administration

There is no reason to believe that poor people are either more or less honest than the well-to-do. Nevertheless, beginning in the 1960s, welfare programs have been administered on the assumption that the poor were more honest, an assumption that governed federal as well as state and local procedures. For example, despite the evident contradiction between the decline in unemployment and the rapid rise in welfare caseloads during the 1960s, applications for public assistance were made easier (the self-declaration was introduced in 1967), recertification for continued eligibility was permitted by mail, and home visits to verify applications or recertifications were stopped.

Further, despite mounting evidence of welfare cheating, welfare administrators in many states denied the problem existed.[12] Not until the early 1970s in California and almost the mid-1970s in New York were broad-scale efforts made to deal with the issue of ineligibility and overpayments. New York instituted a series of remedial measures—a more detailed application form subject to verification, a face-to-face recertification procedure, and a series of computer programs to match the welfare payment file against other benefit programs and wage records. These efforts reduced the payment error rate from 25 percent in 1975 to less than 7 percent in 1982.

Beginning in 1975, New York also instituted a semiannual and later a trimestrial (every three months) mail questionnaire. The one-page form asked welfare recipients whether they still needed welfare and if so, to provide updated information on family composition, earnings, etc. In the September 1980 mailing, 1,800 welfare recipients replied that they no longer needed welfare, and 6,750 cases were closed because they did not respond to the questionnaire or the subsequent notice of closing. The results of the mail questionnaire showed that welfare recipients rarely take the initiative to advise the welfare agency that they no longer need welfare (because they have found a job, married or remarried, or whatever). But faced with an official interview, a questionnaire, or a notice asking them to appear and explain evidence of earnings or other benefits, many fail to show up or respond. The agency can then infer that the nonrespondents no longer need welfare.

The loose administration of welfare for more than a decade clearly encouraged unnecessary dependency, at least in the short term (i.e., more families than needed to be were on welfare). Whether long-term dependency was encouraged is not as easy to answer since data are not available on the duration of welfare among those found ineligible.

---

12. Blanche Bernstein, *The Politics of Welfare: The New York City Experience* (Cambridge, Mass.: Abt Books, 1982), pp. 20–30.

As indicated previously, increased earnings from work represent a major escape route from poverty and dependency for both male- and female-headed families. Did the welfare system encourage or discourage welfare families from traveling this route?

During the 1950s, the Congress, other public officials, and the public at large were not too concerned about the relationship between welfare and work. Welfare benefits were generally low, and neither the Food Stamp nor the Medicare programs had been established. Congress adopted only some mild legislation to encourage states to undertake community projects to provide work for mothers receiving AFDC benefits.

But the situation changed in the 1960s and the early 1970s. One must look at this period to understand the impact of welfare policy and administration on the incentive to work and on dependency. During these years many states increased their public assistance grants, Medicare was established, and the Food Stamp program was initiated and then greatly expanded. The total welfare package—including cash grants, Food Stamps, and Medicare—became substantial. During this same period, the unemployment rate went from 6 percent in 1960 to 3–4 percent in 1969–1972.

Despite the plethora of available jobs from skilled to unskilled, welfare administrators made only modest efforts to promote employment for welfare clients.[13] According to welfare administrators, only 2 percent of welfare recipients were employable, a figure arrived at by including children who were on welfare. This myth was demolished in 1973 when a study undertaken by the Rand Institute (commissioned by the New York City Human Resources Administration) revealed that 35–40 percent of the heads of households receiving AFDC benefits were employable and, further, that half of the women had only one or two school-age children and no preschool children.

Welfare administrators in the 1960s also sounded the clarion call against menial labor, emphasizing the importance of education and training. They often overlooked the fact that a job paying $4 to $5 per hour provided a better standard of living than welfare provided to the typical AFDC mother with one or two children (representing half of all welfare families). Moreover, a single person was better off economically working at the minimum wage than remaining on welfare. Suggestions that employable persons on welfare—mainly blacks and Hispanics—should take unskilled jobs were deemed racist. Without denying that education and training are important, the question re-

---

13. Much of this section of the paper is based on my detailed review of events in New York City recounted in *Politics of Welfare*, but many other urban areas were having similar experiences.

mains whether employable welfare recipients should have the right to reject unskilled or semiskilled jobs and remain on welfare.

By 1967, it was becoming increasingly implausible to attribute the continuing increase in the welfare caseload to the unavailability of jobs. Heretofore, the policy, if not the practice, was that AFDC mothers who could work should work. Now Congress decided that a financial incentive was necessary to encourage these women to take jobs. It came up with a formula— the so-called $30-and-a-third disregard of gross earnings in determining welfare grants; deduction for taxes, work expenses, and child care were allowed as well. In effect, Congress was telling AFDC mothers that they need not work unless they obtained more by working than from their welfare grant, to make work "worthwhile."

Despite continued high employment levels, this legislation had little impact; welfare caseloads continued to grow throughout the country. Welfare administrators had little enthusiasm for encouraging AFDC mothers to work. Further, a new obstacle was raised: a shortage of day-care centers. Although there was little evidence that AFDC mothers regarded day-care centers as necessary to permit them to work, the number of publicly funded day-care centers expanded rapidly (though few AFDC mothers used them).

The high cost of day care led to yet another reason that welfare mothers shouldn't be encouraged to work: the expense to society was too great. Of course, this calculation was based on the cost of day care for two children and the incentive payment to mothers for working.

Finally, the conclusion was reached that even the $30-and-a-third disregard was not sufficient incentive to make work attractive to AFDC mothers. The marginal tax rate was too high or, in other words, the difference in net income between working and not working was not sufficiently large to make working worthwhile. Proponents of this view called for lower marginal tax rates on welfare recipients' earnings. They seemed unable to understand that working at unskilled or semiskilled jobs cannot be made financially attractive or "worthwhile" in comparison with a reasonably decent welfare standard at an acceptable cost to society.

In summary, for more than a decade, from 1960 to 1971, when jobs were relatively plentiful, AFDC mothers were not seriously encouraged or expected to work. Instead, it was as if signs were posted saying "Beware of This Road: It May Endanger Your Benefits."

Nor did welfare policy permit a work test for AFDC mothers through workfare programs to determine whether they might be working "off the books" and therefore not discovered through the usual computer checks. Some estimate the underground or informal economy, excluding illicit activities such as the drug trade, to constitute as much as 15 to 25 percent of the total economy, others place it at a lower but still substantial level. The trades that are most commonly plied in the informal economy are house repairs, child care, domestic service, and sidewalk and flea-market vending.[14]

Certainly some people working in the informal economy are also collecting welfare. Experience with workfare programs for individuals on general assistance in New York revealed that 21 percent of those referred for such jobs failed to report for the interview or the work assignment. An even higher percentage, about 35 percent, failed to report for full-time CETA jobs that paid a salary of $7,500 or more a year. Presumably, many of those who were dropped from the welfare rolls because they failed to report for work already had other sources of income.

As with loose administration of the welfare system, the reluctance to impose on AFDC mothers an effective obligation to work or take part in a workfare program fostered dependency in the short run by permitting women who were in fact working in the informal economy to remain on welfare; in the long run, it may have helped dissipate the will to work among those otherwise eligible who could have and should have worked.

The Reagan Changes—Did They Reduce Dependency?

President Reagan proposed changes in welfare policy in 1981 that were largely adopted in the congressional budget reconciliation process. These changes may be analyzed within the framework of four categories: (1) technical procedures to reduce ineligibility and overpayments, (2) cost-saving devices such as postponing indexing for price changes, (3) policy changes that limit the definition of eligibility, and (4) program decisions that affect the need for welfare. Changes in the AFDC program fell into categories 1 and 3.

The major new tools for reducing ineligibility and overpayments in the AFDC program are retrospective budgeting (i.e., determining the welfare grant on the basis of income in the previous month rather than the current one) and monthly reporting of income, changes in family composition, etc. (table 1). Proponents of the new procedures anticipate savings as a result of more timely information, although it is doubtful whether any substantial savings have yet been achieved. Significant savings are anticipated from a new provision requiring prompt repayment of overpayments (of up to 10 percent of the welfare grant), despite any hardship this may impose.

---

14. James D. Smith, "The Measurement of Selected Income Flows in Informal Markets," Report prepared for Internal Revenue Service, contract no. 71R 81-82, December 1982, p. 6.

TABLE 1

EFFECT OF 1981 AMENDMENTS TO AFDC

Category of Change	Estimated Federal Savings in FY 1982 (In Millions of Dollars)	Percentage of Total Estimated Savings
Technical Procedures to Reduce Ineligibility and Overpayments		
Retrospective Budgeting and Monthly Reporting	0	. . .
Adjustments for Overpayments	115	21.1
Policy Changes Limiting Eligibility or Grant Level		
Stepparent Income	154	28.2
Earned Income Disregard (EID)	75	13.7
Four-Month Limit on EID	62	11.4
Dependent Child (under 18 Years)	50	9.2
Pregnant Woman (Third Trimester)	20	3.7
Earned Income Tax Credit	19	3.5
Resource Limit Reduced to $1,000	16	2.9
Sponsor Responsibility for Aliens	15	2.7
Counting Food Stamp Benefits	10	1.8
Lump Sum Payments	5	0.9
Striking Workers	5	0.9
Income Limit (150 Percent of Welfare Standard)	0	. . .
Total	546	100.0

NOTE: The savings estimates were prepared by the Congressional Budget Office and are lower than the estimates made by the Executive Office. The classification of the savings into categories is the author's.

Other amendments will have a significant impact on the determination of AFDC eligibility and the AFDC benefit level. Most significant is the provision requiring stepparents with adequate income to contribute to the support of their stepchildren; previously, stepparents had no such obligation. This change is expected to account for the largest single saving of all the changes (about 28 percent of the total), and represents a more traditional view of a stepparent's role. Another change limiting the income of AFDC recipients to 150 percent of the state's welfare standard on continuing eligibility eliminated many thousands of recipients, despite Congressional Budget Office estimates that it would produce no savings (see table 1).

Amendments limiting dependent children to those under eighteen years of age (down from twenty-one), postponing eligibility of pregnant women to the third trimester of pregnancy, and prohibiting AFDC payments to striking workers and their families together account for 14 percent of the estimated savings under the new rules. But in states that have general assistance programs, the fiscal burden is simply transferred from the federal to the state and local levels and no reduction in dependency is achieved.

The major conceptual change embodied in the 1981 amendments is the abandonment of the notion of providing welfare recipients with a financial incentive to work—the $30-and-a-third disregard. The financial incentive has been reduced in amount and limited in duration to the first four months of consecutive employment; also, it cannot be applied again until twelve months have passed.

Two other important changes are that (1) AFDC mothers will no longer be exempt from workfare programs and (2) employable AFDC mothers whose children are at least three years old (formerly, it was six years old) can be required to participate in workfare programs if adequate child care is available.

Overall, the various amendments adopted in 1981 are estimated to save just over one billion dollars of federal, state, and local welfare funds—or about 7 percent of the welfare expenditure previously anticipated for fiscal year 1982. Of all the changes affecting benefits, four have a significant impact: inclusion of stepparent income (28.2 percent), adjustments for overpayments (21.1 percent), the reduction in the earned income disregard (13.7 percent), and the four-month limitation on the earned income disregard (11.4 percent). In total magnitude of savings, the 1981 amendments can hardly be regarded as a counterrevolution. But the aforementioned changes plus the provision for workfare, which was not expected to realize savings in the first year, do represent a turnaround to more traditional attitudes concerning family responsibility and the head of the family's responsibility to work, as well as a more rigorous adherence to the standard of need established by the states. They can be regarded as reasonable changes reflecting a general consensus of the population.

In 1982 the Reagan administration proposed further restrictions on eligibility for AFDC, but Congress rejected them in the main. The minor cuts that were passed will have little impact. In its proposed FY 1983 budget, the Reagan administration again proposed additional restrictions on eligibility for AFDC—for example, limiting eligibility to mothers with children under sixteen years of age and counting energy assistance as part of income. Of greater potential significance were major proposals for shifting the responsibility for AFDC and Food Stamps to the states in return for federal assumption of complete responsibility for Medicaid and making workfare programs mandatory rather than optional. Again, with minor exceptions, Congress rejected the proposals. The Reagan budget proposals for FY 1984 omit any suggestions for swapping responsibilities among levels of government; but they do again aim to (1) require states to establish workfare programs and to include in this mandate AFDC mothers with children between the ages of three and six, (2) limit AFDC to families with children under sixteen years old, and (3) make various definitional changes that would further restrict eligibility in small ways. Whether any of these proposals will be adopted by Congress remains to be seen.

Before we consider whether and to what degree the 1981 changes in the AFDC program reduced welfare dependency, we need to look at what has happened to the Food Stamp program, the other major means-tested income support program. I have written extensively about the problems experienced with the Food Stamp program.[15] In brief, the government failed to maintain an appropriate balance between two necessary objectives—reasonable access to benefits and program integrity. As a result, actual expenditures greatly exceeded estimates and ineligibility and overpayments reached high levels. The Reagan cuts as revised and approved by the Congress in 1981 were heavier for the Food Stamp program than for AFDC—13.4 percent below the previously anticipated level. Further, as outlined in table 2, the savings stem far less from technical procedures to reduce ineligibility or overpayments or from policy changes, such as prorating benefits from the date of application instead of the beginning of the month in which application was made. Instead, almost half—47 percent—of the savings derive from postponing indexing for price changes, an undisguised cost-cutting device.

Reducing Dependency

In judging the overall impact of the Reagan changes on the level of dependency, one must again distinguish between the short and the long term. Perforce, some reduction in dependency on public assistance and Food Stamps has taken place. Some recipients became ineligible for AFDC because total gross family income exceeded 150 percent of the standard of need. In New York City, 2,726 cases were closed for this reason, slightly under one percent of the city's AFDC caseload. The elimination of the $30-and-a-third disregard as a work incentive after four months resulted in a noticeable drop in welfare caseloads in the first half of 1982. Even in New York City, which had one of the lowest ratios of employed AFDC mothers (less than 6 percent compared to the nationwide average of 15 percent), about 5,700 cases, or about 2 percent of the caseload, were dropped. In the rest of New York state and in other

---

15. Bernstein, *Politics of Welfare*, pp. 101–140.

TABLE 2

EFFECT OF 1981 AMENDMENTS TO FOOD STAMP ACT

Category of Change	Estimated Federal Savings in FY 1982 (In Millions of Dollars)	Percentage of Total Estimated Savings
Technical Procedures to Reduce Ineligibility and Overpayments		
Improved Management (including Elimination of Outreach)	29	1.8
Subtotal	29	1.8
Cost-Saving Devices		
Postponement of Indexing Standard Deductions and Elimination of Excess Shelter Allowance	242	15.1
Three-Month Lag in Indexing Thrifty Food Standard	512	31.8
Subtotal	754	46.9
Policy Changes Limiting Eligibility		
Initiation of Pro Rata Benefits	495	30.8
Reduction in Gross Income Limit to 130 Percent of Poverty Level	110	6.8
Repeal of Enriched Deductions[a]	63	3.9
Definition of Family and Elimination of Boarders	60	3.7
Elimination of Benefits to Strikers	50	3.1
Decrease in Earned Income Deduction from 20 to 18 Percent	48	3.0
Subtotal	826	51.3
Total	1,609	100.0

NOTE: The savings estimates were prepared by the Congressional Budget Office. The classification of the savings is the author's.
a.   These deductions had never come into effect.

states, apparently more cases were closed as a result of the 150-percent rule
than the four-month limitation on the $30-and-a-third work incentive.[16]

Despite the dire predictions from many in the social welfare community,
including the American Public Welfare Association's National Council of

16. Research Triangle Institute, "Final Report: Evaluation of the 1981 AFDC Amendments," Submitted to the Department of Health and Human Services, Social Security Administration, p.13.

State Executives, AFDC mothers did not quit their jobs en masse to remain on welfare when the $30-and-a-third incentive was removed. A national sampling of cases closed in 1982 because of the 150-percent rule and the four-month limit on the earned income disregard and a sampling of cases closed because of employment earnings in 1981 before the Reagan changes showed that about 18 percent of both groups of wage earners were again receiving AFDC benefits one year later. This suggests a "normal" rate of job loss.[17] The results from this national sample are confirmed by a separate study in New York City.[18] In other words, the elimination of the financial incentive did not diminish the work effort of those AFDC mothers who had' been working. This result becomes even more significant in light of the number of years the wage earners in the national survey had been on AFDC: 39 percent, for six years or more; 19 percent, for three to five years; and 35 percent, one to two years.[19]

Some of the changes, however, resulted only in a transfer of dependency from AFDC to general assistance (GA). Thus in New York City about 1,800 members of AFDC households age eighteen and older were shifted to GA. No data are available on the impact of counting part of a stepparent's income or the income of children in determining eligibility, but this change will have some effect.

Retrospective budgeting and monthly reporting may eliminate some ineligibility and reduce overpayments and thus reduce dependency. But most of the potential to be attained from improved integrity of the caseload, other than through workfare programs, had already been achieved by 1981. At best, these two changes may reduce ineligibility by another 2 or 3 percent. More substantial results can be achieved, however, in the Food Stamp program which in 1981 still had a high ineligibility rate.

Finally, if the states take advantage of the 1981 amendment allowing them to establish Community Work Employment Programs (CWEPs) as workfare programs for heads of AFDC families, some decline in caseloads will occur, if for no other reason than that AFDC recipients who are already employed will be uncovered. In seventeen counties in New York State (not including New York City) where CWEP has been established, provisional figures indicate that of AFDC recipients called, 20–30 percent failed to show up for work assignments, with the result that those cases were closed or the

17. Ibid., p. 14.
18. "Impact of Loss of '30-1/3'," Memorandum prepared for the Administrator of the NYC Human Resources Administration, July 6, 1983.
19. Research Triangle Institute, "Evaluation of the 1981 AFDC Amendments," table 4.4, pp. 4–8. Data were not available for 7 percent of the cases.

grants reduced. New York City in early 1983 started a CWEP project limited to AFDC mothers with a child at least seventeen years old. Of the 660 AFDC mothers in this group, only 36.1 percent were determined to be unemployable; among those deemed employable, more than half (51.5 percent) of their cases were closed, or 34.5 percent of the total group of 660. If past experience is any guide, about half of these cases will remain closed for six months or more.

The payoff of workfare in reduced dependency can be substantial. The states have not, however, rushed to take advantage of CWEP for several reasons. First, the federal government—though it shares the cost of the work expenses involved and, of course, benefits from any resulting reduction in caseload—does not contribute to the cost of supplies, equipment, and supervision. State and local budget directors are always loath to incur heavy costs this year for potential savings next year. Second, it takes time to mount a large-scale work program, especially one that provides meaningful work. The payoff will be substantial only if the program's scale is large in relation to the size of the caseload. Otherwise, even if 20–30 percent of those called up refuse the work assignment, the 70–80 percent who accept quickly fill up the available work slots; then only as turnover occurs can the work test be applied to others. A third crucial reason for its nonacceptance is the opposition to workfare by the social welfare community. So, while figures of 20–30 percent sound high, they apply to only a tiny portion of the AFDC caseload; and the number of cases removed from dependency on welfare as a result of workfare has been minuscule so far.

A federal requirement that states establish workfare programs for AFDC mothers would undoubtedly accelerate state action. But the mandate would have to allow a number of years for implementation; states could not possibly set up workfare programs for all employable AFDC mothers in one year. It would require the creation of over 90,000 workfare jobs in New York City alone—excluding the current workfare program of about 9,000 mainly for general assistance clients. Secondly, the federal government would have to contribute to the cost of supplies, equipment, and supervision since most states will resist incurring the initial expenses, even to attain the long-run savings.

In sum, the Reagan changes have reduced dependency, but not much. At the beginning of this section, we stated that the Reagan changes in welfare and Food Stamp policies could be divided into four categories. Yet the fourth category—program changes to reduce the need to apply for welfare—has not been mentioned. The reason is simply that the Reagan changes do not address the important underlying causes of long-term poverty and dependency. Indeed, the substantial cuts imposed on the social service programs, particularly family planning and day care, may arguably create more long-term dependency; and the heavy cuts to employment and training programs certainly do nothing to diminish the potential for long-term dependency. The only significant counterbalancing factor has been the Reagan administration's efforts to strengthen enforcement of the obligation of absent fathers—absent because they are divorced or separated, or were never married—to support their children.

Can We Reduce Dependency?

Reducing dependency by taking away benefits from those who are ineligible for them is all to the good, but it is not enough. Even total success with all the efforts to ferret out welfare cheaters—from computer matching to monthly reporting to workfare—is not likely to cut the welfare rolls by more than about 10 percent. The remaining 90 percent will be, as now, disproportionately concentrated in the black and Hispanic communities and will remain a potent cause of political and social tension. The important task now is to reduce the *need* for welfare—to attack the underlying causes of dependency as they are manifested in the 1980s, not as they were in the 1930s.

Clearly, reduced dependency in the sense of less need for welfare—the sense in which it will be used in the remainder of this chapter—requires as its underpinning an improvement in the economy, a higher level of economic activity, and a substantially lower level of unemployment. But equally clear, the experience of the 1960s indicates that a lower unemployment rate will not automatically reduce dependency. We can hope that the resurgence of the economy which started at the end of 1982 will continue to high levels and stabilize, but we must look beyond that. We must consider what needs to be done through education and training to improve the prospects for independence of families headed by women. And we must look for ways of counteracting the trend toward break-ups and nonformation of families and, above all, teenage pregnancies.

Education and Training

Among the 11 million recipients of AFDC, about 7.6 million are children.Roughly one-third fall into each of these age categories: under six, six to twelve, and twelve to eighteen years old. It is among children on welfare that we find the highest rates of school dropouts, as well as other manifestations of social pathology. To reverse this trend, we must focus on the preschoolers and preteens. We must make available special services to these children and their mothers—tutoring, counseling on study habits, and whatever is required—to insure regular (and successful) attendance at school.

At the same time that we seek to raise the educational attainment of the children on welfare, we must attempt to bring the employable AFDC mothers into the work force. Education and training may be necessary, especially for the 75 percent of AFDC mothers who did not complete high school. It would be a mistake, however, to assume either that all need further education or that no jobs are available that match their limited skills. Too much has been made of the alleged mismatch between available jobs and available skills of AFDC mothers. The U.S. Department of Labor reported in 1981 that the vast majority of job growth in recent decades occurred in generally low-paying businesses and industries and that new jobs in the 1980s will predominantly employ secretaries and stenographers, retail sales workers, building custodians, cashiers, and bookkeepers. A more recent study estimates that in the 1980s, 32 percent of all new jobs created will be in the less skilled categories, compared to 19 percent in the 1970s and 11 percent in the 1960s. The author of that study states by way of illustration that "there will be thirteen times as many jobs for waiters and waitresses as jobs for aeronautical engineers."[20]

One way to reduce dependency, therefore—assuming some decline in the overall unemployment rate—is to enforce the obligation of welfare beneficiaries to work. The American Public Welfare Association stated in a 1981 report that welfare should serve as a backup for those who temporarily cannot work, not as an alternative to work. But this pro-work attitude has not yet permeated the welfare bureaucracy and has not been transmitted forcefully and clearly to the welfare recipients themselves.[21]

It would make good sense to focus this effort, at least in the beginning, on AFDC mothers with only one or two children; they constitute more than half of all cases and, with their children, about one-third of all recipients. These are generally the younger women who are more likely to have some high school education or a diploma and who would find it easier to work and manage their household than women with three or more children.

Yet even when they are working and earning enough not to be dependent on welfare, the average female head of household is unlikely to achieve more than a low standard of independent living. Some will require and should

---

20. Russell W. Rumberger, "The Job Market for College Graduates, 1960–1990," Reported in *The Chronicle of Higher Education* (June 15, 1983), pp. 1, 12.

21. I am indebted to Dr. Larry Mead, New York University, for the several studies he has done that correlate effective communication of expectations to clients with client successes in seeking and finding employment. Mead's studies also highlight variations he found among various WIN offices in New York City in how well the workers articulated appropriate expectations.

receive welfare supplementation to cover the difference between their low earnings and the welfare standard plus allowable work expenses.

It may appear contradictory that I applaud the elimination of the $30-and-a-third disregard as an incentive to work, yet regard as essential the supplementation of low earnings *up to the welfare standard* plus allowable expenses for day care and transportation costs to work. It is not contradictory or inconsistent. The $30-and-a-third disregard turned out to be less an incentive to work than a supplement to bring earnings of welfare recipients substantially above the welfare standard. It was unfair to those in relatively low-income jobs, especially those just above the welfare standard. As previously defined, the state's welfare standard represents society's consensus in that state as to the minimum acceptable standard of living for a family. If a head of the household cannot earn enough to support his or her family at this minimal standard, supplementation should be—and, indeed, can be—provided under existing AFDC regulations. If, as I believe, partial dependency is better than total dependency, we should encourage welfare recipients to work to the extent they are able and can find employment, full time or part time. But no wage earner should have to live at a level below the welfare standard.

The reasons for the relatively dim economic prospects for female heads of households are clear enough: women's wages are lower than men's partly because of different levels of skill and seniority and partly the result of past and present discrimination. Equally important, however, is the fact that it usually takes more than one wage earner per four-person family to reach a reasonably adequate standard of living. Thus a family headed by an employed woman is four times more likely than an intact family to be below the poverty level.[22]

About two-thirds of the AFDC mothers are not employable under current regulations—for example, women with children under three years of age (under six years in New York State where the regulations have not been changed to take advantage of the 1981 amendments)—or because of their own or their children's physical or mental disabilities. Many of these women would not be dependent, however, if a father were in the home. And that brings us to the relationship between the intact family and dependency.

---

22. Janet L. Norwood, *The Female-Earnings Gap: A Review of Employment and Earnings Issues*, U.S. Department of Labor, Bureau of Labor Statistics, Report 673, September 1982.

The Intact Family—The Road to Independence

In general, it takes about 1.3 wage earners per four-person family to achieve the Bureau of Labor Statistics' lower-level standard of living ($15,323 in 1981 prices), 1.7 for the moderate level ($24,407), and 2.0 for the higher level ($38,060). In 1982, only 7.6 percent of two-parent families were in poverty compared to 36.3 percent of female-headed families.[23] Among families with two wage earners, only 4.5 percent of white families, 9.4 percent of black families, and 11.9 percent of Hispanic families were poor.[24] The figures speak for themselves.

The impacts of family breakup or nonformation of families are many. The social and psychological consequences are considerable even where there is enough money; but they are disastrous for those with such limited incomes that the result is welfare for the women and children. The consequences have been especially disastrous for the black community.

The welfare system itself is limited as to how it can foster family stability. It can more effectively enforce child support obligations and workfare and other efforts to encourage entry into the labor force. But what is needed above all is a change in attitude toward family responsibility, despite the availability of the welfare option.

It has not been fashionable to discuss the deterioration of the black family and its impact on social and economic status. The White House Conference on Families and Children in 1980 concerned itself with "the diversity of families" as norms for programs and gave short shrift to the intact family. Little consideration, if any, was directed to possible programs for the prevention of family breakup or the nonformation of families.

Yet, according to an analysis published in 1981, "a fundamental reason for the deterioration of the black/white income ratio between 1970 and 1976 is the substantially faster rate of growth of female-headed families among blacks than among whites. In fact, if the pattern of family composition that existed in 1970 had been present in 1978, the black/white income gap would have narrowed in that period by five percentage points. If one went back to 1960, the gain would have been greater.[25]

Black organizations are well aware of the data, as a perusal of *A Statistical Overview of Black America* published by the National Urban League in

23. U.S. Department of Commerce, Bureau of the Census. "Money Income and Poverty, Status of Families and Persons in the United States: 1982," *Current Population Reports*, Consumer Income Series P-60, no. 140, table B.

24. Ibid., table 18.

25. Steven H. Sandell, *Family Income in the 1970s: The Demographics of Black/White Differences*, Technical Analysis Paper no. 23, U.S. Department of Health and Human Services, December 1981, p. 4, Office of Planning and Evaluation, Office of Income Security Policy.

December 1982 makes clear. But they have tried to discount the family structure explanation of the economic disorder which has befallen blacks by saying, "People are not poor because they are female and household heads; they are poor because they do not have jobs or adequate income." Black leaders, with a few exceptions, have been reluctant to take up the issue of family structure. Only recently has that changed.

Thirty liberal black leaders (known as the Tarrytown group) and members of the Black Leadership Forum issued a pamphlet in June 1983 entitled *A Policy Framework for Racial Justice*. These leaders list the following as the most urgent problems to be tackled to bring poor blacks into the mainstream: progress in the economy, *the condition of the black family* [my emphasis], and educational opportunity. They add that, unless major efforts are made quickly, "the condition of a large portion of the black population will deteriorate beyond the point where any program of intervention can be effective."[26]

The Tarrytown group also points out that despite all the misfortune that afflicted black families for generations, "a remarkable 75 percent of black families included both husband and wife until the 1960s." One may argue about the reasons they give—rapid urbanization and ghettoization—for the subsequent deterioration of black family structure, but one can only agree with their conclusion that "the rapid growth of female headed families can and must be reversed."[27] As they point out, intact black families improved their economic position in the 1970s while female-headed families regressed: "If the increase in female headed families had not occurred, black family income would have increased by 11.3 percent instead of decreasing by 5 percent. Black husband-wife families provide the foundation for a permanent black middle-class."[28]

We need to find new ways to counteract trends toward family instability and to promote the formation of families; we must not simply continue the past pattern of providing more public assistance and social services to shore up female-headed families. Yet reversing the trend of family breakup will not be simple. Past successes in lowering unemployment, improving access to education and training, and reducing discrimination indicate these factors do not automatically lead to family stability.

The Tarrytown group suggests that "black organizations constitute the natural leadership in any effort to restore black families to their historic

26. *A Policy Framework for Racial Justice*, (Washington, D.C.: Joint Center for Political Studies, 1983), p. 2.
27. Ibid., pp. 10–11.
28. Ibid., p. 12.

strength.'' Black leadership is indeed a necessary ingredient; but financial and technical support from government, private foundations, and voluntary social service agencies is also essential for research, development, testing, and expansion of programs likely to achieve the goal. One must hope that such a coalition will be formed and a detailed program of action developed.

The condition of black (and Hispanic) families is clearly intertwined with the major cause today of dependency: teenage motherhood.

Teenage Motherhood—The Road to Dependency

Families headed by teenage mothers are the most vulnerable of all families. Kristen A. Moore and Martha F. Burt of The Urban Institute found that women who were teenagers when their first child was born account for more than half of total AFDC expenditures in the country and comprise an astounding 71 percent of all AFDC mothers under thirty years of age.[29] Teenage mothers under sixteen years of age incur the most long-term disadvantages. They exhibit a high dropout rate from school; have larger families, less opportunity for employment, and lower earnings when they do work; and are more likely to find themselves and their children trapped in long-term poverty with its harmful consequences for health, housing, learning, and social development.

A few figures are necessary to understand the growth and size of the problem of teenage pregnancy, as well as its impact on the well-being of the major ethnic communities. The number of teenage out-of-wedlock births rose from 91,700 in 1960 to 262,500 in 1979. For whites, the comparable figures were 34,000 and 119,700; for blacks, 57,000 and 143,000. If one counts only those under seventeen years of age, the numbers for all races go from 48,300 to 129,500; for whites, from 16,200 to 57,600; and for nonwhites, from 32,000 to 72,100. While out-of-wedlock teenage births have increased more rapidly among whites than among blacks, the rate of 14.9 births to unmarried teenagers per 1,000 white births is still far below the rate of 87.1 for blacks. Some 1.3 million children in this country live with teenage mothers, while an additional 1.6 million children under five years of age live with mothers who were teenagers when they gave birth.[30]

---

29. These as well as most of the other data on teenage pregnancy used in this section are from Kristin A. Moore and Martha F. Burt, *Private Crisis, Public Cost: Policy Perspectives on Teenage Child Bearing* (Washington, D.C.: The Urban Institute Press, 1982).

30. New York State, Temporary Commission to Revise the Social Service Law, *Teenage Motherhood and Public Dependency: New York's Response to the Issue of Adolescent Pregnancy*, Study Report no. 10, March 1983, p. 15.

Perhaps even more revealing than the data on teenage out-of-wedlock births are the trends in teenage sexual activity and its outcome. Between 1971 and 1979, while the number of females aged fifteen to nineteen increased from 9.7 to 10.3 million (a 6 percent rise), the number of sexually active unmarried females almost doubled from 2.5 to 4.7 million; during the same period, the number of married teenage girls declined about 12 percent. Further, the number of teenagers who conceived a child was about double the number who gave birth out-of-wedlock. In other words, about half the conceptions terminated in an abortion or miscarriage, mainly the former.

In part, the increase in teenage births reflects the demographic trend of a teenage population that has been growing since the late 1960s. Now the number of teenagers has begun to decline and will continue to do so for some years. One analyst expects that, as a result of demographic changes, the number of female-headed families will peak sometime during the 1980s. But this expectation will be frustrated if the trend toward increased sexual activity among teenagers continues. Indeed, if the trend is not reversed, we are likely to see a continuation of a substantial level of long-term poverty and welfare dependency in this country, especially among black and other minority families.

What Needs to Be Done

The adverse effect of teenage pregnancy on the economic and social well-being of the teenage mothers and their children is well documented, but what can be done?

Let's start with sex education. According to various estimates, no more than half of all schools, and possibly substantially fewer, offer sex education and most courses are limited in scope. Voluntary social service and some religious organizations offer programs that cover some of the more controversial subjects such as contraception, sexual decision making, values, feelings, etc. But since few of the programs have been evaluated, we are uncertain as to which programs work best with which groups.

Family planning services have expanded over the last several decades and are widely available, although recent cutbacks in federal funding have forced some reduction in services. The main problem, however, is that most young teenagers have an imperfect understanding of the fertility process and are too immature to use contraceptive devices regularly.

Thus we come to the controversial issue of abortion. Federal legislation now prohibits the use of federal Medicaid to pay for abortions except under very limited circumstances. Nevertheless, many states (among them New York) continue to cover the costs of abortion for those who meet the income eligibility requirements. Certainly any move in the populous urban states to eliminate or severely restrict Medicaid funds for abortion could mean almost a doubling of the number of out-of-wedlock births to teenagers, especially those under sixteen years of age. The costs to society and, above all, to the teenagers and their children would be enormous.

Very few services are being provided to teenage mothers to help them cope with their problems—for example, to return to and complete high school, to move into the world of work, to provide proper care for their children, and to reduce the probability of further pregnancies. Although a high proportion of teenage mothers are on public assistance and remain there for long periods of time, public welfare departments do very little for them beyond providing cash grants, Food Stamps, and medical services through Medicaid. If I may quote myself—"It may be hard for those outside the welfare field to believe, but it is true that for more than a decade, since the separation of social services from the provision of public assistance was mandated, local welfare agencies are not required to consider the family's social situation and determine whether and what social services may be needed. The decision whether services are needed is left to the welfare family. The concept does not make much sense for any family on welfare; it is nonsense when the welfare client is an unmarried teenager of fourteen to seventeen. . . . She and her child have serious problems, whether she knows it, or not, and whether she knows what help she may need."[31]

In the last few years a number of foundations have stepped into the vacuum and supported demonstration programs consisting of various packages of services to teenage mothers. Among others, the Manpower Research and Development Corporation, through its Project Redirection, and the Ford and the Rockefeller foundations have established or are evaluating programs designed to help teenage mothers complete at least their high school education, prepare them for jobs, and assist with problems of caring for their child. An interim report issued on the results of Project Redirection after twelve months of operation presents some evidence of success: a comparison of the experimental group obtaining the services and the control group that did not shows that 66 percent of the former and 50 percent of the latter were either enrolled in an education program or had completed high school; 52 percent versus 40 percent worked in at least one job during the period; and only 16.8 percent versus 22.4 percent had a repeat pregnancy during the year—a short period,

---

31. Bernstein, *Politics of Welfare*, p. 152.

however, to test the repetition of pregnancy.[32] The results are statistically significant, though not enormous, and though cost data are not yet available, these types of services will not be cheap. Even if successful, it is questionable whether sufficient funds will ever be available to replicate these programs on a large scale. Moore and Burt state, "Programs to support teenagers through pregnancy and early motherhood are intensive and expensive—taken all together, the difficulty of the options available once a teenager becomes pregnant accentuate the importance of primary prevention."[33]

What, then should we be doing that we are not doing about the teenage pregnancy problem? The first imperative is to change attitudes among teenage girls and boys to discourage early sexual activity. Moore and Burt estimate that postponing childbirth among teenagers *for one year* would result in a 22 percent reduction in the probability of the poor teenager remaining poor.

An encouraging development is the increasing recognition among black spokesmen of the serious consequences of teenage pregnancy to the well-being of the black community. In a signed editorial in the *New York Times* (July 7, 1982), Robert Curvin, a black, says, "An increasing number of unmarried black teenagers are *choosing* poverty by choosing to become mothers." He goes on to say that in addition to sex education (including the social and economic ramifications of parenting), "something else is needed—more emphasis on old values, like it is all right for young people not to have sex." And William Haskins, director of social services and human resources for the National Urban League, writes on the Op-Ed page of the *New York Times* (October 4, 1982) that in the past, black communities have been ambivalent about family planning programs and have even regarded efforts to promote birth control among blacks as genocide. The time has come, he says, for "the black community to seriously confront the issue of teenage pregnancy" and he adds that "black leaders can begin this initiative by making unequivocally clear that it is wrong for teenagers to have babies out-of-wedlock."

And indeed the time has come. The Tarrytown group of black leaders says in *A Policy Framework for Racial Justice*: "Teenagers and young men and women need to be encouraged to pursue training, work, and personal development while they delay pregnancy and family formation." They say further, "For young people, there is a special need for sex education and

---

32. Denise F. Polit, Michael B. Tannen, and Janet R. Kahn (American Institutes for Research in the Behavioral Sciences), *School, Work and Family Planning: Interim Impacts in Project Redirection*, Manpower Demonstration Research Corporation, June 1983, pp. 4–10.
33. Moore and Burt, *Private Crisis, Public Cost*, p. 128.

education about the importance *of delaying sex, pregnancy and marriage"* [my emphasis][34]. The effort to change attitudes must include information on the social and economic consequences of teenage pregnancy, of the better options that are open for those who postpone sexual activity, and how young girls and boys can deal successfully with the current peer pressures to have sex and become pregnant. White, black, and Hispanic leaders must help develop and promote a change in the social climate so that, as Curvin so simply put it, "It is all right for young people not to have sex." This issue cannot be left to the Moral Majority, because the appeal must be based on socioeconomic consequences rather than on morality.

The foundations also must do more to help. To my knowledge only one such project is being carried on with foundation support (Teaching Teens To Say No, located in Cleveland and Atlanta). The foundations need to go beyond their current efforts at family planning and helping teenage mothers by focusing attention on the first stage in the decision making that may lead to teenage pregnancy and encourage teenagers to delay sexual activity.

To summarize, we can reduce dependency if we do the following:

1. We must retain the reasonable changes in the Reagan program— particularly limiting the income disregard to four months, making stepparents financially responsible for their stepchildren, and more effectively enforcing the obligation of AFDC mothers to work (including workfare). At the same time, we must resist further cuts in public assistance, Food Stamps, and social services simply aimed at reducing federal expenditures.

2. We must devote the resources necessary to improve the effectiveness of the educational system with particular attention to children under twelve years of age and expand employment and training opportunities for the young, the unemployed, and the never-employed.

3. We must begin to work creatively to reverse the trend toward family instability and must persuade the young to postpone sexual activity until they have the education and training to cope effectively with life's problems in the world of work and in the home. The problems are complex, but surely some solutions are not beyond the powers of the human brain—and, it now appears, not beyond the political will.

---

34. *A Policy Framework for Racial Justice*, p. 12.

COMMENTS

Barry R. Chiswick

Blanche Bernstein's paper on welfare dependency covers a range of topics, but I will focus my attention on only three: the relationship between welfare and the female-headed family, policies to reduce dependency, and the effect of amnesty for illegal aliens on the number of families on welfare.

Welfare and the Female-Headed Household

Bernstein emphasizes the changing demographic characteristics of the nonaged dependent population over the past forty years, and particularly the last two decades, during which the number of female-headed households on public aid has increased sharply. Some documentation of the extent to which the public aid programs increase poverty and dependency would have been useful. The programs do this in part by subsidizing unmarried women having children and by making marital breakups more economically feasible. Perhaps more important are the disincentives created by public aid for women with children to marry.

Policies to Reduce Dependency

Bernstein discusses various policies to reduce welfare dependency, including (1) more stringent enforcement of existing work requirements, (2) education and training, and (3) family planning.

Work Requirements

Bernstein calls for more stringent enforcement of the work requirement that has been part of the AFDC program since 1972. Increasing stringency,

153

starting with those most able to work (i.e., those women with the fewest young children), would have several benefits. Since there are and will be more job vacancies for low-skilled workers, requiring AFDC recipients to search for work is not unreasonable. Most postschool training in the United States is the informal training received on a job. Since the only way of receiving this training, which increases future earnings and job stability, is by working, the work requirement may have beneficial long-term effects.

Workfare programs may also serve as a bridge between not working and having a regular private-sector or government job. Bernstein emphasizes that workfare programs often uncover ineligible welfare recipients through their failure to report to assigned jobs. The danger, of course, is that workfare jobs may become permanent employment. If so, a growing public sector with outputs of low social value will become part of the *unmeasured* cost of public assistance.

Education and Training

Bernstein considers education and training programs, but wisely focuses this discussion on in-school youth. We need to learn more about increasing the productivity of school for youths from disadvantaged households. Various enrichment programs seem to benefit most those who are from more advantaged households, suggesting an important complementarity between home-produced human capital and schooling. Perhaps the renewed focus on the quality of schooling in the United States will generate insights particularly relevant for the disadvantaged.

Bernstein essentially ignores public job training programs for adults. This is to her credit as our experience with these programs has been very poor. Not surprisingly, high school dropouts who have not benefited from private job training programs, or on-the-job training, have a low pay-off from public training programs. Indeed, the programs are targeted to those least likely to succeed.

Training programs may be more productive, however, for the younger members of the newer groups of structurally unemployed. Much of this training is likely to be undertaken by the private sector.

Family Planning

Bernstein believes that programs designed to keep families together and reduce out-of-wedlock and unwanted pregnancies, particularly among minority teenagers, offer considerable promise. The issue here is not the *number* of births, but the timing of these births. An unmarried fifteen-year-old mother is not likely to complete high school and has substantially reduced chances of enjoying a stable marriage. Childbirth delayed by a decade may result in the same number of children, but the mother has a greater likelihood of completing high school, experiencing a stable marriage, and enjoying adequate family income to prevent dependency.

It is an unlikely coalition that opposes public aid for family planning programs, including sex education, subsidized contraceptive devices, and subsidized abortions. While some want to reduce out-of-wedlock sexual activity, others are concerned with alleged genocide. I prefer to couch the discussion in terms of the quality of life for the children that are born. If teenage and unwanted pregnancies can be reduced, more stable intact family relationships are likely to emerge. This strengthening of the family—economically, socially, and psychologically—will reduce welfare dependency not only in the parent's generation, but in the next generation as well.

The effectiveness, however, of a public approach to family planning is still unproven. Too little information on the relevant behavioral responses has been collected. For example, how many abortions would a public program have to finance to reduce the number of children on AFDC by one? The answer is surely greater than one. An abortion may merely delay by a few months the birth of an AFDC recipient. In addition, publicly financed abortions may simply be substituted for privately financed abortions, or they may lead to less effective use of contraceptive techniques.

I agree with Bernstein that delaying child bearing may be the most effective means of reducing long-term dependency. Early pregnancies, however, are the product of a set of social and economic circumstances that provide incentives for having children.[1] Public financing of family planning programs may turn out to be as ineffective in reducing welfare dependency and welfare costs as are other publicly financed training programs for the long-term dependent population.

Amnesty for Illegal Aliens

Welfare dependency can be influenced by policies that would seemingly have little relation to the welfare system. Indeed, it may well be that the

---

1. Michael cites research showing that those with higher levels of schooling are not only more productive in the market place but also have fewer unwanted pregnancies. Robert T. Michael, "Education and the Derived Demand for Children," in Theodore W. Schultz, ed., *Economics of the Family: Marriage, Children and Human Capital* (National Bureau of Economic Research, 1974), pp. 120–156.

manipulation of nonwelfare policies is the most effective avenue for aiding recipients and reducing welfare dependency. In this regard it is noteworthy that the Reagan administration has indicated its support for legislation that, as a side effect, may have a much greater adverse impact on the low-income population and on welfare dependency than the essentially minor adjustments in various welfare programs that have been the focus of Bernstein's paper. I am referring to the Simpson-Mazzoli Immigration Reform Bill, which would grant amnesty to most of the 3 to 6 million illegal aliens believed to be residing in the United States.

The illegal aliens are believed to be disproportionately low-skilled, non-aged adult males, about half of whom are Mexican nationals. Since unattached nonaged men are generally not able to receive public assistance, how can granting amnesty increase welfare dependency?

Granting amnesty does more than merely ratify the presence of the illegal alien workers. It increases their permanence in the U.S. labor force by enabling them to remain here without fear of deportation, and by enabling them to legally bring their own dependents to the United States. Furthermore, by encouraging the prospect of future amnesty, rather than "wiping the slate clean," an amnesty encourages increased illegal migration. By increasing the labor supply of low-skilled workers, amnesty will depress the wages and employment opportunities of low-skilled native-born workers, particularly youths and members of minority groups. This relative deterioration places on the welfare rolls some families whose labor market opportunities would have otherwise provided for self-sufficiency.

There are also direct impacts of amnesty that need to be considered. The change in legal status may have a sharp impact on the welfare dependency of the former illegal alien population, as they now become eligible for a wide range of welfare programs and can legally bring dependent family members to this country.

Immigration policy should be added to the research agenda of those interested in the nexus between public policy and the causes and consequences of welfare dependency.[2]

---

2. Two recent immigration studies that discuss this nexus in greater detail are Barry R. Chiswick, "Guidelines for the Reform of Immigration Policy" in William Fellner, ed., *Essays in Contemporary Economic Problems* (Washington, D.C.: American Enterprise Institute, 1981), pp. 309–347 and Pastora Cafferty, Barry Chiswick, Andrew Greeley, and Teresa Sullivan, *The Dilemma of American Immigration: Beyond the Golden Door* (New Brunswick: Transaction Books, 1983).

HOW WIDESPREAD ARE INCOME LOSSES IN A RECESSION?

Edward M. Gramlich and Deborah S. Laren

One of the main problems confronting the Reagan administration as it took office in 1981 was inflation. The rate of general price inflation had risen gradually during the 1970s, and in the twelve months just prior to January 1981, consumer prices rose at the alarming rate of 12.4 percent. While there has been a debate in the economics profession about the exact nature and size of the costs of inflation, particularly when it is anticipated, the inflation rate was high enough by 1981 that most Americans wanted it reduced.

Unfortunately, nobody has discovered any very good way to stop inflation. Compulsory wage-price controls generate economic inefficiencies and political disputes; voluntary controls are easily evaded and penalize those who cooperate; and microefficiency measures, such as deregulation, are usually politically difficult and do not have large enough effects to make a dent in the overall rate of inflation. The one tried and true remedy is to follow restrictive monetary and fiscal policies. These will almost certainly work if given enough time. Their problem is that they only work by reducing the demand for output and labor, causing a recession, and imposing large and unwanted income losses on many people.

Whatever the Reagan team believed about the wisdom of various anti-inflation strategies, there is no doubt that the administration wanted to fight inflation. But the Reagan administration did not believe in, and had no plans to use, either compulsory or voluntary wage-price controls. And despite its promises of deregulating various sectors, the Reagan administration must have

We would like to thank Paul Courant and Lee Bawden for helpful comments and Greg Duncan and Peggy Hoad for allowing us early access to some of the Panel Study of Income Dynamics data for 1981.

157

realized that these measures would have little effect on the overall rate of inflation. Some members of Reagan's economic team clearly believed, and argued often in *Wall Street Journal* editorials, that restrictive policies were necessary whatever their impact on unemployment—an impact believed to be only transient. (Indeed, by late 1979, the Carter administration had already put into effect the necessary restrictive measures.) Others no doubt believed that the large tax cuts promised by the administration would unleash a supply-side miracle that just might cure inflation without any painful unemployment.

If anybody seriously believed this, they were soon proven wrong. The new administration continued the restrictive monetary policy measures initiated during the latter part of the Carter administration. These were augmented by cuts in domestic spending, but offset by increases in defense spending and personal and corporate tax cuts. This package was enough to cause a recession that sent the unemployment rate up to 10.8 percent by December 1982—the highest rate experienced in the United States since the 1930s. Unemployment rates were particularly high in some of the older industrial areas in the Great Lakes region, as well as among certain demographic groups—such as nonwhite teenagers. This recession was not entirely in vain; the inflation rate did decline to 2.7 percent by June 1983—but it was very painful to many people.

Economists still don't know precisely how to measure the size and extent of losses from a recession and determine who bears them. The traditional view has been that since unemployment rates are low, a small proportion of the work force is taking most of the losses. But this view was questioned in papers by Hall, Perry, and Holt et al., all of which show how short the mean duration of unemployment is—only about twelve weeks on average during the 1970s.[1] Such short durations may indicate that a large share of the work force is taking smaller losses. Clark and Summers questioned that interpretation by showing that many of the supposed short spells of unemployment are illusory, ended only by job-seekers dropping out of the labor force. Akerlof and Main showed that the same workers may experience many short spells of unemployment that add up to lots of unemployment.[2] But these studies apply only to unemployment rates. Three other questions that arise involve (1) the income levels of those who are laid off

1. Robert E. Hall, "Why Is the Unemployment Rate So High at Full Employment?" *Brookings Papers on Economic Activity*, no. 3 (1970), pp. 369–402; George L. Perry, "Unemployment Flows in the U.S. Labor Market," *Brookings Papers on Economic Activity*, no. 2 (1972), pp. 245–278; Charles C. Holt, C. Duncan MacRae, Stuart O. Schweitzer, and Ralph E. Smith, "Manpower Programs to Reduce Inflation: Manpower Lyrics for Macro Music," Institute Paper 350-28 (Washington, D.C.: The Urban Institute, 1971).

2. Kim B. Clark and Lawrence H. Summers, "Labor Market Dynamics and Unemployment: A Reconsideration," *Brookings Papers on Economic Activity*, no. 1 (1979), pp. 13–60; George A. Akerlof and Brian G. M. Main, "Unemployment Spells and Unemployment Experience," *American Economic Review*, vol. 70, no. 5 (December 1980), pp. 885–893.

in a cycle, (2) the extent to which their income losses are cushioned by increases in work effort on the part of others in the family, and (3) the extent to which these families benefit from public and private transfer payments.

The ideal way to deal with all of these variables would be to take a sample of families with various incomes and race, sex, and age of the primary earner. These families could be observed in years of prosperity and recession, measuring how much cyclical unemployment they experienced, their average income over a long period of time, the degree to which offsetting labor supply adjustments took place within the family, and the extent to which families were able to take advantage of transfer payments to cushion their losses of income. This is exactly what Gramlich did, using the University of Michigan's Panel Study of Income Dynamics (PSID) as the basic data.[3] That study is now out of date since it was conducted in a period when the overall unemployment rate never exceeded 6 percent and before Food Stamps were available nationwide. Hence in this paper, we update that study, in addition taking advantage of the longer time span of observations to use more powerful statistical techniques. The earlier study focused only on what might be called the vertical incidence of the income losses in a recession: how much family incomes declined for families of varying income levels. Here we extend the analysis to show the horizontal incidence as well: how widely burdens are shared within any income class.

The first section of the paper briefly describes the model used to measure cyclical income losses and presents the results on vertical incidence. The next section gives the results on horizontal incidence. A final section of the paper attempts to determine whether our estimates of income losses bear any resemblance to what people actually tell public opinion pollsters about how much they worry about unemployment.

The Vertical Incidence of Income Losses in a Recession

The model we used to calculate income losses in a recession features four blocks of equations. The first determines the probability that the primary earner in a family (the one who earns the most) will experience some unemployment. The second determines the amount of time unemployed for those having some unemployment. The third deals with the cushioning effect of adjustments of labor income within the family: does the primary earner try to work longer hours; do other workers in the family work longer hours?

---

3. Edward M. Gramlich, "The Distributional Effects of Higher Unemployment," *Brookings Papers on Economic Activity*, no. 2 (1974), pp. 293–336.

The fourth determines the cushioning effect of public and private transfers: income and payroll taxes decline when primary earners are laid off, while unemployment insurance payments, public assistance payments, Food Stamps, and private transfers rise. In each case we try to distinguish between factors that explain the general level of the relevant dependent variable and factors activated by the recession. The precise details of these equations and calculations, some of which get fairly complex, are included as an appendix.

The model is fit with PSID data over the fourteen-year period, 1967 to 1980. The PSID initially began by observing 5,000 families. Some dropped out over time and others were added to the sample as new family units were formed from the original families. Since we needed longitudinal data for this study, we confined our attention to those families for whom the primary earner was the same in five or more consecutive years, under age sixty-five, and in the labor force most years. This left a basic sample of 3,124 families who were observed for an average of eleven years. In the case of the tax and transfer equations only, we are interested in the way things are now, not back in 1970, so for these equations we used only the data for one year, 1980 or 1981, whichever was available.

Cyclical impacts on different groups are likely to differ substantially, in a way not easy to deal with by constructing elaborate mathematical functional relationships. Because of the large number of observations, we had the luxury of adopting a simple and very intuitive way of dealing with these differences. We first split the sample into three groups depending on whether the family's primary earner is a white male, nonwhite male, or female (of all races). Then for each family in each year we computed what is known as the family's income-to-needs ratio (Y/N). The numerator of this ratio, Y, is the family's income for that year before taxes and before transfers. The denominator is the poverty needs standard for the family in that year. Hence a Y/N value of 1.0 means that the family's income was just at the poverty level in that year, a value of 2.0 signifies an income level of twice the poverty level, and so forth. We then averaged these annual values of Y/N over the number of years of observations for each family to arrive at what we call the permanent income-to-needs ratio. We subdivided the families in each of the three demographic classes into eight income classes on the basis of their permanent income-to-needs ratio, giving us a total of twenty-four cells. Most of the results are based on this twenty-four-cell classification.[4]

---

4. Doing things this way, while convenient, does introduce a slight simultaneous equations bias. Since average Y/N values will to some extent be a function of average unemployment rates, Y/N values will not be entirely exogenous, as we assume them to be. A more elaborate procedure would have replaced our average Y/N values with average *predicted* Y/N values from some instrumental variable technique.

Primary Earner Unemployment

The first set of results refers to the probability that the primary earner will experience some unemployment. These probabilities, in percentage form, are shown in table 1, assuming the overall unemployment rate equals 6 percent (its average over the fourteen-year period). Note how high these probabilities are. While the overall unemployment rates for the three groups from the aggregate statistics (not the PSID) fall in the 3 to 9 percent range, the probabilities that the primary earners in our study will experience at least some unemployment in an average year are in the 13 to 20 percent range (from twice to four times as high as the aggregate rate). These results indicate that unemployment is more broadly based than is apparent from the overall low rates.

We next observe that unemployment declines as family income rises. For all groups of primary earners, this probability declines at the rate of 15 to 20 percent per class for the first five classes, and more rapidly thereafter. Hence the probability that white male primary earners just above the poverty line (Y/N from 1.0 to 1.5) will experience some unemployment in an average year is more than three times as great as for white males in a high-income bracket (Y/N from 4.0 to 5.0). While this finding is not unexpected, we must caution against thinking that unemployment only befalls low-income families: almost 4 percent of the highest-income white male primary earners experience some unemployment in an average year.

A final comparison worth noting refers to the ratios of unemployment probabilities for each group. It is well known that overall unemployment rates for nonwhite males are higher than those for white males, as can be seen from the bottom row of the table. This is confirmed in the micro data from the PSID when family income is held constant: unemployment probabilities are higher in each income class for nonwhite males. But the other well-known dictum—that female unemployment rates exceed male rates—is not confirmed once the comparison is made for primary earners with average incomes held constant. The unemployment rates for females are lower in each income class than those for white males. The disparity in overall unemployment rates is then mainly due to the fact that average incomes for females are lower, and perhaps also to the fact that females who are not primary earners have higher unemployment probabilities than those who are.

The second block of equations, not shown here, finds that for all three groups the expected number of hours of unemployment depends negatively on family income. Among primary earners who experience unemployment, those with lower permanent incomes stay unemployed longer. When these relationships are combined with those in table 1, they yield what might be

TABLE 1

PROBABILITIES OF THE PRIMARY EARNER HAVING SOME UNEMPLOYMENT
DURING A YEAR

Y/N Class	White Males	Nonwhite Males	Females
	Average for Whole Period (Percentage Points)		
<1	32.3	35.0	26.7
1.0–1.5	27.3	30.0	21.2
1.5–2.0	22.9	25.0	16.7
2.0–2.5	19.5	20.8	13.6
2.5–3.0	16.3	17.0	11.0
3.0–4.0	12.4	12.7	7.4
4.0–5.0	8.2	8.5	4.4
>5	3.8	3.8	1.8
Overall Weighted Average	13.0	19.5	13.4
	(Pooled) Sample Size		
<1	317	1125	1213
1.0–1.5	979	1630	1068
1.5–2.0	1673	1712	869
2.0–2.5	2431	1097	495
2.5–3.0	2878	906	441
3.0–4.0	5012	936	558
4.0–5.0	3268	339	219
>5	3655	234	156
Mean (Weighted) Y/N	3.820	2.697	2.637
Mean Unemployment Rate for Group (Percent)	3.2	6.4	8.5

SOURCE: Panel Study of Income Dynamics data tape.

called sensitivity rates (shown in table 2). The sensitivity rates show for each income bracket the change in the average amount of time spent unemployed when the overall unemployment rate rises from 5.5 to 6.5 percent.[5]

These sensitivity rates are well below unity (the weighted average is about one-half), indicating that a large share of the increase in cyclical unemployment is borne by groups for whom we do not have panel data on unemployment (teenagers, secondary earners, those who dropped out of the

_____

5. Since the sensitivity rates are determined by altering the underlying group unemployment rates and nothing else, they are equivalent to the results of nonstochastic differentiations of the equations. People only lose wage income—nobody gains.

TABLE 2

Sensitivity of Cell Unemployment Rates to Overall
Unemployment Rates

	Marginal Percentage Point Change in Percentage of Worktime Unemployed for Cell for a One Percentage Point Change in Overall Unemployment Rate		
Y/N Class	White Males	Nonwhite Males	Females
< 1	2.655	2.362	0.657
1.0–1.5	1.512	1.472	0.383
1.5–2.0	0.912	0.804	0.176
2.0–2.5	0.576	0.525	0.104
2.5–3.0	0.545	0.309	0.016
3.0–4.0	0.277	0.055	−0.020
4.0–5.0	0.127	0.281	−0.010
> 5	0.111	0.062	0.050
Weighted Average	0.422	0.672	0.162

Source: Panel Study of Income Dynamics data tape.

PSID). The question of how incomplete our overall snapshot of cyclical income losses then becomes is dealt with below. As before, sensitivity rates decline as family income increases for all three groups. Because nonwhite male primary earners who become unemployed generally spend less time unemployed, the sensitivity rates are similar for nonwhite and white males at each income level. Again, the overall sensitivity rate is higher for nonwhites because their incomes are generally lower. The sensitivity rates for female primary earners are lower than those for white males in each income group, enough so that the overall weighted average is also lower.

Family Income Adjustments

The third block of equations analyzes all other adjustments that can take place in a family's labor income in response to the increased cyclical unemployment of the primary earner. In this block there are distinguishable macro and micro effects. The macro effect augments the basic unemployment effect: the earned income of both primary and secondary earners will be reduced when overall unemployment rates rise, through the well-known discouraged worker effect. The micro effect offsets the basic unemployment impact: as the primary earner experiences more unemployment, other family members tend to supply more labor and wage income to cushion the family's income. For this reason business cycles are commonly alleged to be less painful now than when families did not have so many secondary workers. But in our sample, the micro effects are quite weak and are clearly dominated by the macro effects.

Combining these responses with the basic unemployment reactions yields the percentage decline in pretax, pretransfer incomes, shown in column 1 of table 3. The overall weighted average decline, found by combining the averages of the three groups, is 1.3 percent. Thus a single percentage point rise in the overall unemployment rate generates a 1.3 percent decline in wage income, according to our PSID results.

Some years ago Arthur Okun published a famous article that seems at variance with this finding.[6] Because of labor hoarding in a business cycle, Okun found with time-series data that a one percentage point rise in the overall unemployment rate would lead to as much as a 3 percent decline in total income earned. This three-to-one ratio became enshrined as *Okun's Law*. While laws are supposed to remain invariant with time, Okun's Law has not. When Perry reestimated the model a first time, the coefficient fell to 2.8.[7] When Perry reestimated it a second time, it was 2.2.[8] In the appendix, we reestimated the model again, using even more recent time-series data, and found a coefficient of 1.45. All of this is relevant because it permits a more careful investigation of the incompleteness of our PSID-based snapshot of cyclical income losses, the question alluded to above. While it may seem that our PSID results show too small an income drop, as measured by Okun's Law, in fact Okun's Law gives less dramatic results today than in former times; our PSID results are actually rather close to what one would get from a macro-based calculation of Okun's Law. We can account for 87 percent of the drop in aggregate income, closer than would be apparent from the unemployment data because (apparently) some of the changes in employment of teenagers and secondary workers are included in our family labor income variable.

The distributional results are basically as we have described already. Low-income families suffer more than high-income families for each of the demographic groups, with the percentage drops in income averaging from two to four times the percentage drops for high-income families. Controlling

---

6. Arthur M. Okun, "Potential GNP: Its Measurement and Significance," reprinted in Arthur M. Okun, *The Political Economy of Prosperity* (Washington, D.C.: Brookings Institution, 1970), Appendix, pp. 132–145.

7. Perry, "Unemployment Flows."

8. George L. Perry, "Potential Output and Productivity," *Brookings Papers on Economic Activity*, no. 1 (1977), pp. 11–47.

TABLE 3

CHANGES IN INCOME DUE TO A ONE PERCENTAGE POINT RISE IN THE
UNEMPLOYMENT RATE

Y/N	(1) Pretax and Pretransfer Percentage Change	(2) Posttax and Posttransfer Percentage Change	(3) Replacement Rate (Percentage)
Families Where the Primary Earner Is a White Male			
<1	−5.81	−2.56	55.9
1.0–1.5	−2.85	−1.79	37.2
1.5–2.0	−2.13	−1.27	40.4
2.0–2.5	−1.51	−0.96	36.4
2.5–3.0	−1.37	−0.87	36.5
3.0–4.0	−1.00	−0.67	33.0
4.0–5.0	−0.77	−0.53	31.2
>5	−0.65	−0.45	30.8
Weighted Average	−1.23	−0.78	36.6
Families Where the Primary Earner Is a Nonwhite Male			
<1	−5.88	−3.53	40.4
1.0–1.5	−2.81	−1.75	37.7
1.5–2.0	−2.13	−1.34	37.1
2.0–2.5	−1.67	−1.05	37.1
2.5–3.0	−1.40	−0.95	32.1
3.0–4.0	−1.12	−0.76	32.1
4.0–5.0	−1.30	−0.87	33.1
>5	−0.98	−0.68	30.6
Weighted Average	−2.03	−1.29	36.5
Families Where the Primary Earner Is a Female			
<1	−2.17	−1.58	27.2
1.0–1.5	−1.16	−0.93	19.8
1.5–2.0	−0.81	−0.65	19.8
2.0–2.5	−0.71	−0.58	18.3
2.5–3.0	−0.60	−0.47	21.7
3.0–4.0	−0.54	−0.45	16.7
4.0–5.0	−0.52	−0.40	23.1
>5	−0.56	−0.44	21.4
Weighted Average	−0.87	−0.68	21.8

SOURCE: Panel Study of Income Dynamics data tape.

for income levels, we find that nonwhite males suffer the greatest percentage losses, followed by white males and females (in that order).

Taxes and Transfers

The last step is to add in government taxes and transfers. These are the main vehicle by which cyclical income losses, until now focused on particular families, are shared more widely. When income declines as a result of increases in cyclical unemployment, tax payments decline and transfer payments (for Food Stamps, public assistance, unemployment insurance, Social Security for the nonaged, and private transfers) increase. The posttax and posttransfer changes are shown in column 2 of table 3, contrasted to the pretax and pretransfer changes in column 1. These public policy mechanisms are evidently quite effective in cushioning income losses. As one illustration, families below the poverty line that have white male primary earners suffer pretax and pretransfer income declines of 5.8 percent for every percentage point rise in the unemployment rate; the posttax and posttransfer income decline for these families, however, is only 2.6 percent. The difference, in this case 3.2 percent, divided by the pretax and pretransfer income decline of 5.8 percent, is sometimes called the tax-transfer *replacement rate*.

These replacement rates, shown in column 3 of the table, average out to about 35 percent, implying the existence of a reasonably pervasive safety net for those with cyclical income declines. They are lower for families where a female is the primary earner, partly because fewer women are covered by unemployment insurance. In addition, a much larger percentage of families where females are the primary earners have incomes in the range where positive taxes are not paid. Replacement rates for families below the poverty line where a nonwhite male is the primary earner are lower than those of whites, again mainly because of far lower unemployment insurance coverage.

The lesson here is the relatively unsurprising one that cyclical income losses are clearly greater for the poor than the rich. Inflation may hurt the poor, but fighting inflation with high unemployment appears to hurt the poor a great deal more. We also find that at any income level, percentage losses are slightly greater for families of nonwhite than white male earners and greater for families of male primary earners than for families of female primary earners. Regarding public policy, the tax-transfer safety net does succeed in ameliorating the losses, especially for families below the poverty line. But this is all the cushioning there is: the alleged intrafamily cushioning as secondary earners go back to work is almost nonexistent.

The Horizontal Incidence of Income Losses

Until now we have focused on the vertical incidence question: how cyclical income losses are spread across income classes. This information is relevant in assessing the impact of the business cycle on the income distribution. But it is not the only relevant information. The model we used in the previous section determines income losses for each family. Thus we can measure the incidence of large losses within each income class and, from that, the overall percentage of families who take large losses in a cycle. That information, in turn, shows how broadly the cyclical losses are shared in general.

Some of these results are given in table 4. The table illustrates three levels of income loss, all resulting from a one percentage point rise in the overall unemployment rate. We first show the incidence of family income drops of 5 percent or more, a very large reduction in response to a one percentage point rise in the overall unemployment rate. Next we show drops in family income of 2 percent or more, still a significant loss. Finally, we show the incidence of income drops of one percent or more, losses that are roughly in proportion to the aggregate 1.3 percent decline in family income. We intentionally do not try to analyze carefully the small losses, because those would be heavily influenced by the pattern of implied (but not analyzed) tax increases to pay for the degree of cushioning provided by tax reductions or transfer benefit increases dealt with in table 3. All numbers in table 4 are based on the posttax and posttransfer drops in income shown in table 3.

Taking up first the very large losses (5 percent or more), only 1.1 percent of the population in the aggregate suffers losses of this magnitude. But table 4 shows that almost all of the hardest hit families are among the lowest income groups (Y/N classes of 2.0 or less). Surprisingly, the incidence of these very large losses is quite low for families with female primary earners, partly because the pretax and pretransfer decrease in income is moderate for females. The incidence of very large losses is highest for families with nonwhite male primary earners, though it is also surprising that at almost every given income level, the incidence of very large losses is below that for families with white male primary earners.

A larger share of the overall population, 7.4 percent, suffers income losses of 2 percent or more. Again, families with nonwhite male primary earners are hardest hit; the nonwhite male incidence in most income classes is below that for white males; and the incidence of large losses is appreciably less for families with female primary earners..

TABLE 4

PERCENT OF POPULATION TAKING LOSSES DUE TO A ONE PERCENTAGE POINT RISE
IN THE UNEMPLOYMENT RATE

| | Posttax and Posttransfer Income Loss | | |
Y/N Class	Loss Greater than 5 Percent	Loss Greater than 2 Percent	Loss Greater than 1 Percent
Families Where the Primary Earner Is a White Male			
<1	28.7	50.2	65.3
1.0–1.5	8.1	26.7	63.6
1.5–2.0	1.7	17.6	48.4
2.0–2.5	0.4	12.5	18.7
2.5–3.0	0.4	9.9	16.5
3.0–4.0	0.3	3.7	10.7
4.0–5.0	0.0	0.8	6.3
>5	0.1	1.2	4.0
Weighted Average	1.1	7.2	16.2
Families Where the Primary Earner Is a Nonwhite Male			
<1	19.0	43.0	79.4
1.0–1.5	4.8	28.5	56.0
1.5–2.0	1.0	17.9	40.8
2.0–2.5	0.2	7.4	33.4
2.5–3.0	0.5	6.1	21.3
3.0–4.0	0.1	1.0	5.2
4.0–5.0	0.0	0.8	21.1
>5	0.0	0.9	2.4
Weighted Average	2.5	12.4	31.3
Families Where the Primary Earner Is a Female			
<1	3.6	29.2	49.4
1.0–1.5	0.0	10.7	40.2
1.5–2.0	0.0	0.6	13.6
2.0–2.5	0.0	0.3	6.0
2.5–3.0	0.0	0.0	0.0
3.0–4.0	0.0	0.0	2.6
4.0–5.0	0.0	0.0	0.0
>5	0.0	0.8	5.9
Weighted Average	0.4	4.7	14.5
Overall Weighted Average	1.1	7.4	17.3

SOURCE: Panel Study of Income Dynamics data tape.
NOTE: These income loss figures are based on a one percentage point rise in the unemployment rate.

The final column shows the incidence of cyclical income losses of one percent or more, roughly the overall average loss. Now 17.3 percent of the population takes losses on this order. That this share is much less than 50 percent implies that the median income drop across all families is less than one percent, and noticeably less than the mean drop of 1.3 percent. The distribution of losses, in other words, is highly skewed. The pattern is largely the same as before: smaller losses for families with female primary earners at each income level, and roughly equal losses for families with white and nonwhite male primary earners. Given the lower incomes on average, the weighted average loss for families with nonwhite male earners is about twice as high as for the two other groups. Computing the numbers in this way provides new evidence on the old claim of how very bad recessions are for nonwhites.

Since for the most part our results on income losses are based on data from the fourteen-year span of the PSID, 1967 to 1980, we have not tried to simulate the impact of the very high unemployment in 1982 on family incomes. Yet we can make a crude estimate of the share of people that are taking sizable income losses using this last column of table 4. The overall unemployment rate in 1982 was 9.7 percent, four percentage points greater than the 5.7 percent average unemployment rate over our entire data period. Extrapolating our results linearly, our finding that 17.3 percent of the population receives an income loss of one percent or more when the unemployment rate rises by one percentage point implies that about the same share of the population receives an income loss of 4 percent when the overall unemployment rate is four percentage points above its historical average. As the unemployment rate rises, then, the share of the population experiencing noticeable losses begins to rise disproportionately. Small cycles cause localized pain; large ones begin to cause general pain. To anticipate some results shown in the next section, the implication here is that serious recessions will be far more politically unpopular than moderate recessions.

The results of this section then imply that the incidence of cyclical losses, both overall and within most income classes, follows a fairly compact distribution. As long as cycles are of moderate severity, the incidence of income loss is also moderate. A small share of the population, mostly in the lowest income classes, takes significant income losses even then, but most people are spared the burden of the cycle. These calculations on horizontal incidence then essentially confirm the results in the previous section, with an added piece of information. Business cycles are now seen to be especially painful for those with low incomes, mainly because they cause extremely serious income losses for a subset of these groups, without apparently affecting other income groups.

A Look at Some Public Opinion Surveys

In this section we compare our previous estimates of cyclical income losses as based on our PSID model with survey data from the Gallup Poll. Since the 1930s, the Gallup pollsters have periodically asked a random sample of the population to identify the most important problem facing the country. Since the results of these polls have been aggregated, they cannot be analyzed in great detail. But the aggregate results can be used to compare the American people's perception of the unemployment problem to our estimate of the problem, as seen through the PSID.

Table 5 shows the proportion of persons citing unemployment as the nation's most important problem in the October 1982 Gallup survey, by income class.[9] Sixty-one percent of those polled gave this answer, far greater than the share of the population experiencing income losses of 4 percent or more in 1982 (from table 4). This may indicate that the pain threshold is below 4 percent; or it may indicate any number of other differences between an income-based calculation and a survey answer. Moreover, Gallup's answers are fairly constant for all income levels, while our loss calculations

TABLE 5

SHARE OF POPULATION CITING UNEMPLOYMENT AS THE
NATION'S MOST IMPORTANT PROBLEM
GALLUP SURVEY, OCTOBER 1982

Y/N Class	Share Citing Unemployment
<1	60
1.0–1.5	63
1.5–2.0	63
2.0–2.5	61
2.5–3.0	63
3.0–4.0	61
4.0–5.0	59
>5	59
Weighted Average	61

SOURCE: *The Gallup Report*, November 1982.

---

9. *The Gallup Report*, Report no. 206 (November 1982), pp. 22–23. The Gallup numbers were actually given in terms of family money income; we converted them to Y/N classes using updated relationships based on PSID data.

decline noticeably as income rises. At this level, then, the Gallup survey results and ours based on the PSID correspond poorly.

But comparing the results another way, the correspondence is fairly good. This method uses a time-series analysis of the Gallup responses. Our previous hypothesis was that if people express their economic self-interest, we should expect to find not many people opposed to moderate unemployment, but a great many people opposed to high unemployment. Since the Gallup Poll also publishes time-series results extending back to 1948, this hypothesis can readily be tested.[10]

We conducted such a test using regressions borrowed from a previous examination of these data by Gramlich.[11] The dependent variable is the percentage share of the population naming unemployment as the worst problem—a number that has averaged 13 percent for the sixty observations from 1948 to 1982. For the independent variables, in addition to the unemployment rate, we tried various macro variables that might explain other prominent answers. Over the years, an average 29 percent of those polled have answered "inflation" or "the high cost of living," while "dissatisfaction with government" and the "economy in general" have been other common responses.

The key variable in this test is the quadratic term in the unemployment rate. This variable has a positive and significant coefficient in all three equations shown in table 6 (and in many more we ran). This implies that the pain of unemployment, as measured by the share of the population citing unemployment as the answer to the poll, rises disproportionately with cyclical unemployment. In the first equation, for example, a recession that caused the unemployment rate to rise one percentage point above its equilibrium value would raise the share of the population answering unemployment by 4 percent (3.37 + 0.65). A two percentage point recession would raise this share by 9 percent (3.37 · 2 + 0.65 · 4). A four percentage point recession would increase those citing unemployment as the answer by 24 percent (3.37 · 4 + 0.65 · 16). The share rises nonlinearly, at least approximately in keeping with the PSID results shown in table 4. At this level, then, there does appear to be a correspondence between people's perception of their economic risk in a business cycle as reported to the Gallup questioners, and their actual risk, as we estimate it from the PSID.

---

10. The Gallup Poll began asking the question on "the most important problem" in the mid-1930s. But only ordinal rankings of the most frequent responses were published for these years. A variant of the question, phrased differently to reflect the war, was asked from the early- to mid-1940s.

11. Edward M. Gramlich, "Macro Policy Responses to Price Shocks," *Brookings Papers on Economic Activity*, no. 1 (1979), pp. 125–166.

172   THE SOCIAL CONTRACT REVISITED

TABLE 6

TIME-SERIES REGRESSIONS EXPLAINING RESPONSES TO THE QUESTION
"WHAT DO YOU THINK IS THE MOST IMPORTANT PROBLEM FACING THE
COUNTRY TODAY?" FROM THE GALLUP POLL, 1948–1983

Independent Variable	Dependent Variable Is Percentage Share of Population Answering "Unemployment"		
	Coefficient (Absolute Value of t-stat)		
	Equation 1	Equation 2	Equation 3
constant	4.13(2.7)	−44.84(3.5)	−9.65(3.3)
pa-pe	0.02(0.1)	. . .	. . .
pe	−0.27(1.2)	. . .	. . .
p	. . .	−0.46(1.4)	−0.64(2.3)
(U-U*)	3.37(3.1)	3.68(3.6)	3.46(3.5)
(U-U*)^2	0.65(3.5)	0.63(2.5)	0.66(2.6)
rb	. . .	−1.20(1.7)	. . .
rg	. . .	. . .	−2.50(3.5)
G	. . .	2.02(3.7)	. . .
Y	. . .	. . .	0.04(5.3)
R^2	0.80	0.76	0.77
Standard error	6.53	5.82	5.33
Sample size	60	58	57

SOURCES: *Employment and Earnings*, various issues; *Current Population Reports, Labor Force*, series P-57, various; *Economic Report of the President*, various years; *Survey of Current Business*, various issues; George Gallup, *The Gallup Poll: Public Opinion*, various years; Citibank Economic database.

NOTES: p is the rate of inflation in the Consumer Price Index over the year preceding the month of the survey; pa is the inflation rate over the three months prior to the survey; pe is the rate over the two years prior to the survey; U is the adult male unemployment rate in the month of the survey; U^*, equal to 3.1, is the implied natural rate of unemployment; rb is the AA corporate bond yield and rg the long-term government security yield in the month of the survey; G is total government receipts as a percent of GNP in the year of the survey; Y is total personal income less transfers, in billions of 1972 dollars, in the month of the survey.

Implications

In this paper we have tried to estimate from longitudinal panel data the incidence of family income losses over the business cycle. Four main types of relationships are estimated: (1) the incidence of unemployment, (2) the amount of time spent unemployed, (3) the nature of intrafamily cushioning of income losses, and (4) the extent to which the tax-transfer system cushions income losses. All calculations are given for twenty-four cells: families with white male primary earners, nonwhite male primary earners, and female primary earners, with each in turn subdivided into eight income classes.

The main result is probably not very surprising: the business cycle hits low-income classes considerably harder than high-income classes, generating percentage losses in income from two to four times as great. The disparities would be even worse but for a substantial amount of cushioning by the tax-transfer system. However, we found almost no cushioning due to adjustment of labor income within the family. Across groups, families of nonwhite males generally suffer more than families of white males in any income class, while families of females suffer considerably less from income losses due to a cyclical rise in unemployment.

Extending these results to a comparison of horizontal incidence—to see how many families in a given income class actually suffer large income drops—there is good news. As long as cycles do not become too severe, fairly small segments of the population suffer significant losses, including only very small segments outside of the poverty classes. Of course, when cycles begin to get serious, the share of people suffering significant losses begins to rise quickly, a finding we have confirmed both with our computations of estimated income losses and with our separate analysis of public opinion poll results.

The main macroeconomic policy lesson to be learned here is that moderate doses of anti-inflationary medicine, in the form of moderate cycles, appear to be politically feasible since they do not make very many people significantly worse off; serious cycles, on the other hand, are much less politic.

The main distributional policy message is that poor people become a good deal poorer in a recession. While recessions by no means affect only poor people (high-income people become unemployed too), average income losses are much greater for the poor, and the incidence of very large income losses is very much greater. Whatever harm inflation brings to the poor, fighting inflation by bringing on a recession brings a good deal more. Thus, when the country undertakes restrictive policies to combat inflation, as was generally favored in 1981, care must be taken to protect lower-income families who will bear the brunt of the resulting unemployment. The absence of such compensatory policies, indeed, their augmentation by the generally pro-rich pattern of tax and benefit cuts in 1981, thus stands out as one of the regrettable features of early Reagan administration fiscal policies.

APPENDIX

To estimate changes in income induced by cyclical increases in the unemployment rate, we develop and estimate the model outlined here. The basic identity explaining the unemployment of the primary earner is

$$U_{ij} = D_{ij} \cdot P_{ij}, \tag{1}$$

where U_{ij} is the unemployment rate for the primary earner in the ith family in the jth year, defined as the annual hours of unemployment for the earner divided by 2080. D_{ij} is the unemployment rate for those primary earners having some unemployment, defined on the same basis as U_{ij}, and P_{ij} is the probability that the primary earner will experience some unemployment.

All three of the variables in (1) can be expected to change over time with the group unemployment rate for the jth year, U_{gj}, and also cross-sectionally with various measures of the family's status. But for econometric reasons we estimate only the equations for D_{ij} and P_{ij}, leaving U_{ij} to be determined by the identity.

A binary choice equation, determining whether a primary earner will or will not have some unemployment, is used to explain P_{ij}:

$$P_{ij} = P(Y_i/N_i, U_{gj}). \tag{2}$$

Y_i/N_i, the multi-year average of the family's annual income-needs ratio, varies cross-sectionally but not over time. The g subscript for the group unemployment rate denotes the three groupings of primary earners we use: white males, nonwhite males, and females. Each of these group rates are in turn related to the overall unemployment rate (U_j) through simple bridge equations. Using annual data, 1959 through 1981, $\partial U_{gj}/\partial U_j$ for white males is estimated at 0.84, for nonwhite males, 1.96, and for females, 0.99.

Equation (2) is estimated in logit form for each of the three groups. The form of the estimating equation is

$$log(P_{ij}/(1 - P_{ij})) = b_0 + b_1 Y_i/N_i + b_2 U_{gj} + u_{ij}, \tag{3}$$

where the dependent variable is the log of the ratio of the odds that a primary earner will have some unemployment. Both Y_i/N_i and U_{gj} are significant in the estimated equations, with higher incomes predicting lower unemployment probabilities and higher group unemployment rates predicting higher probabilities.[1] The formula for the predicted probabilities of unemployment, derived

---

1. Upon request we will supply the actual estimated equations for (2) and the other equations discussed in the appendix.

from (3), is

$$\hat{P}_{ij} = \frac{e^{(\hat{b}_0 + \hat{b}_1 Y_i/N_i + \hat{b}_2 U_{gj})}}{[1 + e^{(\hat{b}_0 + \hat{b}_1 Y_i/N_i + \hat{b}_2 U_{gj})}]}. \tag{4}$$

An ordinary least squares equation is used to estimate the amount of unemployment experienced by those primary earners who had some unemployment, using the sample of only those earners with some unemployment:

$$D_{ij} = D(Z_{ij}, Y_i/N_i, U_{gj}). \tag{5}$$

The Z_{ij} above refers to a vector of family variables not reflected in Y_i/N_i, as well as to some state program variables. In estimating equation (5) we use mathematical forms that allow the marginal impact of U_{gj} on D_{ij} to differ from its average ratio, thus distinguishing cyclical from frictional levels of unemployment. The dependent variable is scaled by the group rate (D_{ij}/U_{gj}) and the inverse of the group rate $(1/U_{gj})$ appears on the right-hand side of the equation. For each of the three groups the coefficient on $1/U_{gj}$ is positive and significant, meaning that the marginal ratio is less than the average $(\partial D_{ij}/\partial U_{gj} < D_{ij}/U_{gj})$ and the cyclical unemployment elasticity is less than one. Both Y_i/N_i and its squared value are used as independent variables to allow for nonlinear income responses.

These equations allow the incidence of cyclical changes in unemployment to be computed. Cyclical movements in the aggregate unemployment rate (U_j) alter the group rates (U_{gj}), the probabilities that primary earners will become unemployed (P_{ij}), the amount of unemployment experienced (D_{ij}), and, through the identity, the unemployment rates for the primary earners (U_{ij}).

The change in the primary earner's unemployment rate with respect to the change in the aggregrate unemployment rate is then

$$\frac{\partial U_{ij}}{\partial U_j} = P_{ij} \frac{\partial D_{ij}}{\partial U_{gj}} \frac{\partial U_{gj}}{\partial U_j} + D_{ij} \frac{\partial P_{ij}}{\partial U_{gj}} \frac{\partial U_{gj}}{\partial U_j}. \tag{6}$$

Values of the partial derivatives in (6) are derived from our estimated equations. Multiplying our estimated equation (5) by U_{gj} and then taking the derivative yields the estimates of $\partial D_{ij}/\partial U_{gj}$. Coefficients on U_{gj} in the bridge equations give the estimates for $\partial U_{gj}/\partial U_j$. We get $\partial P_{ij}/\partial U_{gj}$ from the logit equations:

$$\frac{\partial P_{ij}}{\partial U_{gj}} = \frac{\hat{b}_2 e^{(\hat{b}_0 + \hat{b}_1 Y_i/N_i + \hat{b}_2 U_{gj})}}{[1 + e^{(\hat{b}_0 + \hat{b}_1 Y_i/N_i + \hat{b}_2 U_{gj})}]^2}. \tag{7}$$

For the remaining terms in (6), P_{ij} and D_{ij}, one might use (a) the actual sample values or (b) the fitted values from the estimated equations. Since we prefer to rely on actual, as opposed to estimated values, we feel a stronger case can be made for using actual P_{ij} and D_{ij}. These are the values we use in the numbers we present in the body of the paper. Using estimated values for P_{ij} and D_{ij} gives similar results, though slightly higher values of $\partial U_{ij}/\partial U_j$.

These changes in the primary earners' unemployment are converted to changes in family income with additional behavioral relationships and identities. The basic employment identity is

$$E_{ij} = L_{ij} - U_{ij}, \tag{8}$$

where E_{ij} is the primary earner's annual hours of employment and L_{ij} the annual hours of labor supply, both again scaled by 2080.

The discouraged worker phenomenon is then represented by the equation:

$$L_{ij} = L(Z_{ij}, U_{ij}, U_{gj}). \tag{9}$$

The partial derivative of L_{ij} with U_{ij} gives the microeconomic discouraged worker effect, under which an individual primary earner's unemployment will deter him or her from trying to find additional work. The partial derivative with U_{gj} gives a macroeconomic discouraged worker impact that could in principle exist for primary earners even if U_{ij} were zero. The macroeconomic discouraged worker effect commonly found in time-series labor supply regressions may mask a micro effect that works in the opposite direction, a hypothesis that cannot be tested unless the equation is estimated in this form.

The next set of equations deals with other members of the family unit. They too will presumably vary hours worked either in response to their own primary earner's unemployment or in response to the general level of labor demand, according to

$$S_{ij}/N_{ij} = S(Z_{ij}, Y_i/N_i, 2080W_{ij}U_{ij}/N_{ij}, U_j), \tag{10}$$

where S_{ij} is the labor income of family members other than the primary earner, N_{ij} is the family's need standard, W_{ij} is the hourly wage rate of that earner, and $2080W_{ij}U_{ij}$ is the lost wage income of the earner due to unemployment. This set is estimated just for the households with secondary earners.

Previous work on family labor supply also indicates macro and micro influences here. The macro discouraged worker effect leads us to suppose that $\partial S_{ij}/\partial U_j$ is negative: higher unemployment hurts the work prospects of all secondary earners. But micro work on the labor supply of secondary workers suggests that $\partial S_{ij}/\partial U_{ij}$ will be positive: higher unemployment of the primary earner encourages other family members to work harder to stabilize family income.

The change in the primary earner's hours employed (scaled by 2080) for a one percentage point change in the unemployment rate is then

$$\frac{\partial E_{ij}}{\partial U_j} = \frac{\partial L_{ij}}{\partial U_{ij}} \frac{\partial U_{ij}}{\partial U_j} + \frac{\partial L_{ij}}{\partial U_{gj}} \frac{\partial U_{gj}}{\partial U_j} - \frac{\partial U_{ij}}{\partial U_j}. \tag{11}$$

This can then be converted to a change in income:

$$\text{percent income lost}_{ij} = \frac{2080(\partial E_{ij}/\partial U_j)(W_i/N_i)}{Y_i/N_i}, \tag{12}$$

where W_i/N_i is a measure of the primary earner's permanent wage divided by the needs standard.

The effect of an increase in the unemployment rate on the income contributed by secondary earners in the household is then

percent change in secondary earnings = (13)

$$\left[\frac{\partial S/N}{\partial U} + \frac{\partial S/N}{\partial (A+LY)/N} \frac{\partial (A+LY)/N}{\partial U} + \frac{\partial S/N}{\partial LW/N} \frac{\partial LW/N}{\partial U} \right.$$

$$\left. + \frac{\partial S/N}{\partial (LW/N)^2} \frac{\partial (LW/N)^2}{\partial LW/N} \frac{\partial LW/N}{\partial U} \right] / \frac{Y}{N}.$$

(Subscripts are omitted here for the sake of brevity.) Here, LW is the primary earner's wages lost through unemployment, and $A + LY$ is the asset income of the family plus the primary earner's labor income (used to capture the income effect of the demand for leisure). The value of (13) for families with no secondary earners is zero. In equation (13) note that

$$\frac{\partial LW/N}{\partial U} = -2080 \frac{\partial E}{\partial U} \frac{W}{N} \text{ and} \tag{14}$$

$$\frac{\partial (A+LY)/N}{\partial U} = -\frac{\partial LW/N}{\partial U}. \tag{15}$$

The addition of (12) and (13) yields the change in the family's pretax and pretransfer income for a one percentage point change in the aggregate unemployment rate. The overall average value of this change in income is -1.26 percent using method (a) discussed above, and -1.35 using method (b).

At this point we can check our estimates with a macro calculation of

Okun's Law. We fit the equation

$$U_m = 0.47 + 0.265YG - 0.036YG_{-1} - 0.129YG_{-2} + 0.85U_{m-1}, \quad (16)$$

where U_m is the unemployment rate for adult males in percentage form (0.9 times the group unemployment rate for white males plus 0.1 times the group rate for nonwhite males) and YG is the GNP gap in percentage form (the difference between potential and actual GNP divided by potential GNP). The steady state solution of this equation is

$$U_m = 3.13 + 0.653YG, \quad (17)$$

and on substituting in our bridge equations for the white and nonwhite adult male unemployment rate in 1981, it is

$$U = 5.8 + 0.687YG. \quad (18)$$

This implies that if YG is zero (full employment), the equilibrium, or natural, rate of unemployment is 5.8 percent. And if real output should drop cyclically by one percent (YG increases by one), the overall unemployment rate would increase by 0.69 percentage points. Conversely, if the overall unemployment rate should increase by one percentage point, real output and/or real income would fall by about 1/0.687, or 1.45 percentage points. The PSID results then explain 1.26/1.45, or 86.9, percent of the aggregate drop in income, a reasonable performance given the rest of measurement errors and other possible imperfections. The same ratio in the earlier article by Gramlich was 80 percent.[2]

The final set of equations involve tax and transfer payments. These equations are used to derive, for each family, the replacement rate (r), the fraction of lost wage income replaced by all taxes and transfers. We distinguish between two components of the replacement rate: that dependent on unemployment-based transfers ($r1$) and that dependent on income-based transfers or taxes ($r2$). The first component is defined, for males, simply as

$$r1_i = \frac{(\text{unemployment compensation} + \text{AFDC-UP})_i}{\text{lost wages}_i}, \quad (19)$$

and, for females, as

$$r1_i = \frac{\text{unemployment compensation}_i}{\text{lost wages}_i}. \quad (20)$$

Those primary earners with no unemployment are assigned a zero value for $r1$.

---

2. Gramlich, "Distributional Effects."

The second component, $r2$, may be thought of as an effective marginal tax-transfer rate. We derive this from a set of equations represented by

$$T_i/N_i = T(Y_i/N_i, Z_i), \tag{21}$$

where T_i stands for taxes and various income-based transfers. Separate regression equations are estimated for each of the following: income plus payroll taxes, Food Stamps, Social Security for the nonaged, AFDC (for females), other government transfers, and private transfers.

Because legislative changes have altered the tax-transfer system, the only relevant data are those from the most recent year of the panel. For the income-based transfer programs we were able to obtain and use 1981 data, while the tax equations are estimated using 1980 data. (The $r1$ component in (19) and (20) is also based on 1980 data.)

The sample for the estimation of each of the equations represented by (21) is restricted to the participants of the given program. The equations are estimated now for just two groups, families with male primary earners and families with female primary earners. Here, we no longer restrict the sample to those who have been interviewed five years or more. The results of these estimations are presented in table A.1.

Using these estimated equations and taking the derivatives of taxes paid and transfers received with respect to income gives

$$r2_i = \Sigma(\partial(T_i/N_i)/\partial(Y_i/N_i)). \tag{22}$$

A family that did not participate in a given program is assigned a zero value for the effective tax-transfer rate for that piece in the above summation.

Finally, then, we can compute the posttax and posttransfer loss of income for a one percentage point increase in the unemployment rate, for each family in each year, as

$$(\text{posttax and posttransfer loss})_{ij} = \tag{23}$$
$$(\text{pretax and pretransfer loss})_{ij} (1 - r2_i) +$$
$$r1_i (\partial U_{ij}/\partial U_j) 2080 (W_i/N_i).$$

TABLE A.1

REGRESSIONS FOR MARGINAL TAX AND TRANSFER RATES

Income and Payroll Taxes:
Male-Headed Families:
$$TX/N = -.400 + .328Y/N - .001(Y/N)^2$$
Female-Headed Families:
$$TX/N = -.036 + .125Y/N + .015(Y/N)^2$$

Food Stamps:
Males:
$$TF/N = .130 - .038Y/N$$
Females:
$$TF/N = .190 - .062Y/N$$

Social Security (Nonaged):
Males:
$$TS/N = .591 - .077Y/N + .009(Y/N)^2$$
Females:
$$TS/N = .674 - .224Y/N + .052(Y/N)^2$$

Other Government Transfers:
Males:
$$TG/N = .285 - .152Y/N + .034(Y/N)^2$$
Females:
$$TG/N = .300 - .195Y/N + .041(Y/N)^2$$

Other Private Transfers:
Males:
$$TP/N = .168 - .005Y/N + .002(Y/N)^2$$
Females:
$$TP/N = .139 + .022Y/N + .003(Y/N)^2$$

AFDC:
Females:
$$TA/N = .117 - .187Y/N$$

SOURCE: Panel Study of Income Dynamics.
NOTES: Some control variables are not shown. The sample for each equation is restricted to recipients of the given program. Tax equations are estimated for 1980, transfer equations for 1981.

COMMENTS

Isabel V. Sawhill

When President Reagan took office in 1981, there was widespread agreement that something needed to be done about inflation. The only sure way to accomplish this was by putting the economy through a recession. The remedy has been quite successful, although the recession cannot be credited for *all* of the decline in inflation. Inflation would have declined anyway because of decreases in the prices of food, energy, and imported goods. Still, there has been substantial progress. So, is the average American family better off? Who has gained and who has lost?

Although economists have difficulty specifying and quantifying the benefits from lower inflation, they seem obvious enough to the average person. If the value of what one's income can buy has been shrinking by 10 percent a year as the result of inflation, and its value stabilizes, one is better off—provided one's income is not reduced in the process. Since most people fail to see any correlation between the income they earn and the prices they pay, they assume that reduced inflation is a good thing. This is true, of course, for those on fixed incomes. Those whose incomes fall less than the rate of inflation also gain. But for every person who comes out ahead, there is more than one loser for the simple reason that recessions reduce total output and total income earned.

Most previous attempts to estimate the losses associated with a recession have been based on aggregate data. A typical approach is to estimate the level of real GNP, or GNP per household, that would have prevailed if the economy had grown along its full-employment growth path. The difference between actual GNP and its full-employment levels can then be taken as a measure of the losses. For example, assuming a full-employment unemployment rate of 5.8 percent and a growth of potential GNP equal to 2.5 percent, the losses in real GNP from the first quarter of 1981 through the fourth quarter of 1982 were $412 billion, the equivalent of $4,940 per household over this period.

The Gramlich-Laren approach has a number of advantages over this aggregative procedure. First, and most importantly, it shows us how the losses

181

were distributed. It turns out that poor families have been hurt more than rich ones, families headed by males more than families headed by females, and families headed by black males the most. (One could make unending demands on the authors to characterize families by attributes other than race, sex, and income level. In case they plan to do further analysis, my favorite candidates would be age of household head, presence of children, and geographic region.) The authors' analysis excludes families where the primary earner was not stable over a five-year period, which may bias the results; a lot of families appear to have been excluded for this reason (over 2,000 out of a total sample of 5,000).

The second advantage of the micro as opposed to the macro approach is that it begins to deal more explicitly with the events and behavior patterns that translate a recession-induced rise in the overall unemployment rate into a loss in family income. Generally, we expect a reduction in demand to cause not only more unemployment, but also a reduction in hours worked, and a change in labor force participation, all of which reduce family income. With respect to the labor force response, Gramlich and Laren find that there is a big "discouraged worker effect" which is only minimally offset by extra work effort on the part of secondary earners in a family.

This does not mean, however, that other earners in a family do not provide an important safety net when the primary earner loses a job. Sixty percent of all families and 79 percent of two-parent families where someone lost a job in 1981 had more than one earner. The availability of a second income surely helps reduce the absolute level of hardship associated with unemployment. But it apparently does little to mitigate the decline in standard of living for the unemployed during a recession. I wish the authors could have done even more decomposing as to the amount of family income losses due to greater unemployment, the amount due to reduced hours, and so forth. Some possible effects, such as discouraging entry into the labor force or the pressure to take lower-paying jobs, are not treated at all.

It would also be interesting to try to reconcile the micro with the macro estimates of loss. The authors' macro estimates of loss imply a much smaller Okun's Law coefficient than any I have seen. Even so, the PSID results explain only about 88 percent of the aggregate drop in income. There must be some reasons for the discrepancy. One likely explanation is that wages tend to grow more rapidly than productivity during a downturn, putting a squeeze on profits and causing retained earnings to absorb a disproportionate share of any drop in GNP. Some further analysis and cataloging of these reasons would be very useful.

Another contribution of the Gramlich-Laren paper is its focus on how well the safety net functions during recessions. They find that taxes and transfers serve to replace about 34 cents for every dollar of recession-induced income loss. The safety net makes the distribution of losses a little more equal across income groups, but does not change the basic conclusions about vertical incidence. I would expect an important impact of these programs to be on horizontal incidence. Unemployment insurance, for example, should limit the number of people with very large losses in income—but the paper doesn't provide the data with which to check out this hypothesis.

Gramlich and Laren calculate replacement rates based on data for either 1980 or 1981. Thus, their estimates don't reflect the changes in tax or transfer programs introduced by the Reagan administration, which didn't go into effect until late 1981. Their data can't document, then, the extent to which the replacement rate has been reduced by these changes. For example, we know that a substantially smaller proportion of the unemployed is receiving unemployment insurance, that fewer states have an AFDC-UP program, and that Food Stamps are harder to get, but I have seen no good estimates of the overall effects of the Reagan program on replacement rates. As a methodological footnote, the replacement rates in the paper are based on regressions estimated for a single year: I worried a little about whether it was appropriate to apply cross-sectional elasticities to infer replacement rates over time. Differences in income at a point in time may generate a different structure of taxes and transfers than changes in income between periods.

After discussing vertical incidence and replacement rates, the paper focuses on horizontal incidence—that is, how the losses associated with a recession are distributed within any particular income group. The major conclusion is that only a small fraction of families suffer income losses of 5 percent or more in a mild recession (that is, one in which the unemployment rate increases by one percentage point) whereas in a severe recession like the one in 1981-1982, many families do. This leads to the hypothesis that serious recessions should be much more unpopular than mild ones, which a look at the Gallup Poll data confirms.

I would like to know the number and composition of families that gained noticeably from the recession because they are living on relatively fixed incomes and benefit from the decline in inflation that usually accompanies a recession. From table 4, one might infer that high-income white families, whether headed by males or females, clearly gain. Only about 5 percent of this group suffers income losses greater than one percent, implying that a majority are probably better off as a result of the administration's economic policies. An explicit tabulation of those with income *gains* of one percent or more in table 4 would be a very nice addition to this paper. In addition, a translation of all of these numbers into absolute dollar gains and losses—using 1982 prices—would also be informative.

Overall, this is a very useful and interesting paper. Despite all of the discussion of cuts in social welfare programs and tax changes, this paper suggests that the impact of economic events has been far more significant.

MACROECONOMIC CONDITIONS, INCOME TRANSFERS, AND THE TREND IN POVERTY

Peter Gottschalk and Sheldon Danziger

Debate about the relative effectiveness of economic growth and social welfare policies in reducing poverty has been a recurring theme in the policy arena and in the academic literature.[1] Lyndon Johnson's War on Poverty adopted the premise that economic growth was not sufficient for alleviating poverty. The 1964 *Economic Report of the President* stated:

> Rising productivity and earnings, improved education, and the structure of social security have permitted many families or their children to escape; but they have left behind many families who have one or more special handicaps. These facts suggest that in the future economic growth alone will provide relatively few escapes from poverty. Policy will have to be more sharply focused on the handicaps that deny the poor fair access to the expanding incomes of a growing economy.[2]

Indeed, Kershaw and Courant cite the perceived declining antipoverty effectiveness of economic growth as the "analytical justification" behind the War on Poverty.[3]

This research was supported in part by funds granted to the Institute for Research on Poverty at the University of Wisconsin by the U.S. Department of Health and Human Services and by a grant from the Alfred P. Sloan Foundation. Sally Davies, Daniel Feaster, Susan Marble, and Lisa Barresi provided valuable assistance. Nancy Rortvedt provided excellent clerical assistance. Lee Bawden, June O'Neill, Eugene Smolensky, and participants at the IRP-ASPE Policy Workshop and at the Urban Institute Conference provided helpful comments.

1. For a review, see Henry Aaron, *Politics and the Professors: The Great Society in Perspective* (Washington, D.C.: Brookings Institution, 1978).

2. U.S. Council of Economic Advisers, *Economic Report of the President, 1964* (Washington, D.C.: Government Printing Office, 1964), p. 72.

3. Joseph Kershaw with Paul Courant, *Government Against Poverty* (Washington, D.C.: Brookings Institution, 1970).

The Reagan administration, on the other hand, emphasizes the dual nature of economic growth. According to the U.S. Office of Management and Budget,

> History teaches us that economic growth is a critical determinant of individual and family well-being. In the decade of the 1970s, the economy failed to perform as well as in the 1960s. . . . As a result, it was in the 1960s rather than in the 1970s that the greater inroads against poverty were made. Clearly, economic growth is vital to promoting the well-being of working families. But it also benefits those who cannot work, because as the wealth of the nation grows, more money is available to help those in need.[4]

By implication, economic growth helps the poor by raising their own market income and by raising the income of the nonpoor sufficiently to accommodate redistribution. The Reagan program reflects this dual approach. The safety net is to remain in place for those who cannot work. Yet transfers to those who do work have been reduced, as they are expected to benefit from the expanded employment opportunities associated with growth.

How sensitive is poverty to increased economic activity? One would think that the experience of the last twenty years might offer an almost ideal social experiment to determine the relative importance of growth in market incomes and income transfers. Rapid economic growth in the late 1960s was followed by periods of slower growth and stagnation. The scope of income transfer programs, especially those targeted at low-income people, also underwent dramatic change. Variation in both of these key independent variables should have allowed researchers to accurately estimate how much poverty reduction was due to growth in market incomes and how much was due to increases in government income transfers.

We begin by reviewing the descriptive data on economic growth, transfers, and poverty. Then we report the results of reestimating some of the standard regression equations that have appeared in the literature. We conclude that although these models can be used to project poverty, they cannot be used to disentangle the effects of growing market incomes from the effects of increased transfers. We project that the recent increase in poverty will not be reversed. Poverty will remain close to current levels for the next several years, given the expected trends in economic growth, unemployment rates, and income transfers.

Finally, we use a conceptual framework that links secular and cyclical changes in macroeconomic activity to the mean and the shape of the income distribution, and hence, to changes in poverty. We apply this framework to

---

4. U.S. Office of Management and Budget, "Means-Tested Individual Benefits," in *Major Themes and Additional Budget Details: FY 1984* (Washington, D.C.: Government Printing Office, 1983), pp. 30–31.

data derived from the *Current Population Surveys* for 1967 through 1982. We find that between 1967 and 1979, growth in mean transfer income was about as important as growth in mean market incomes in reducing poverty for all persons. Since 1979, growth in transfers has not been large enough to offset poverty-increasing declines in mean market incomes. Perhaps most important, over the entire 1967-1982 period, changes in the shape of the income distribution had a large impact in increasing poverty, offsetting some of the positive effects of rising average incomes and increasing transfers.

Time-Series Evidence

Table 1 presents the basic trends for macroeconomic performance, income transfers, and poverty. The rapid economic growth during the early 1960s and the slowdown during the late 1970s and early 1980s are readily apparent in the level of real Gross National Product (GNP) per household (column 1).[5] This slowdown was a result of worsening cyclical conditions coupled with slower growth, net of the cycles. In spite of the rise in unemployment rates (column 2), the economy experienced modest net economic growth during the 1970s. Nonetheless, real GNP per household in 1982 was below the 1971 level. Thus, if economic growth tended to reduce poverty, some decline in poverty might have been expected in the 1970s, though at a slower rate than in the earlier years.

The growth in real cash and in-kind transfers per household (columns 3 and 4), commonly referred to as the social welfare explosion, is well known. The growth rate of in-kind transfers has slowed in recent years, but their absolute levels have continued to increase. Possibly less well known is the fact that real cash transfers per household declined almost 7 percent from 1976 to 1980 (column 3). This is not solely a reflection of increases in the number of households, since cash transfers as a percentage of GNP dropped by 8 percent over the same period. Thus, if increased transfers tended to reduce poverty, declines in official poverty through the mid-1970s and increases in the late 1970s would have been expected.

The trend in the official incidence of poverty for all persons (column 5) can be broken down roughly into three periods. Between 1960 and 1969,

---

5. Aggregate GNP and transfers are divided by the number of households to separate the impacts of economic and demographic change. Dividing by population would also correct for demographic change, but would not account for increases in family needs as households split into smaller units. Since the official poverty thresholds refer to household incomes and represent a set of equivalence scales that accounts for economies of scale associated with larger household size, GNP and transfers per household are more appropriate measures.

TABLE 1

TIME SERIES ON MACROECONOMIC CONDITIONS, INCOME TRANSFERS, AND POVERTY, SELECTED YEARS 1950–1982

Year	Real GNP per Household (1972 dollars) (1)	Unemployment Rate (2)	Real Cash Transfers per Household[a] (1972 dollars) (3)	Real In-Kind Transfers per Household[a] (1972 dollars) (4)	Official Incidence of Poverty (5)	Incidence of Poverty Adjusted for In-Kind Transfers[b] (6)
1950	$10,880	5.3%	$ 365	$ 29	NA	NA
1955	12,490	4.4	460	31	NA	NA
1960	13,060	5.5	664	40	20.2%	NA
1961	13,170	6.7	730	43	21.9	NA
1962	13,810	5.5	770	49	21.0	NA
1963	14,200	5.7	791	54	19.5	NA
1964	14,630	5.2	801	58	19.0	NA
1965	15,350	4.5	816	63	17.3	12.1%
1966	16,010	3.8	878	71	15.7	NA
1967	16,020	3.8	891	150	14.3	NA
1968	16,390	3.6	911	204	12.8	9.9
1969	16,470	3.5	958	231	12.1	NA
1970	16,080	4.9	1,010	242	12.6	9.3
1971	16,170	5.9	1,150	273	12.5	NA
1972	16,710	5.6	1,225	304	11.9	6.2
1973	17,170	4.9	1,272	320	11.1	NA
1974	16,720	5.6	1,263	327	11.2	7.2
1975	16,130	8.5	1,395	386	12.3	NA
1976	16,630	7.7	1,513	427	11.8	6.7
1977	17,070	7.1	1,508	452	11.6	NA

1978	17,440	6.1	1,488	464	11.4	NA
1979	17,580	5.8	1,419	472	11.7	6.1
1980	16,850	7.1	1,414	482	13.0	NA
1981	17,020	7.6	1,458	505	14.0	NA
1982	16,160	9.7	1,475	508	15.0	NA

SOURCES: For GNP, consumer price index, and unemployment rates, *1982 Economic Report of the President*; for cash and in-kind transfers, "Social Welfare Expenditures Under Public Programs in the U.S.," *Social Security Bulletin*, December 1968, December 1972, January 1971, January 1977, November 1981; for official poverty incidence and number of households, U.S. Department of Commerce, Bureau of the Census, "Consumer Income," *Current Population Reports*, series P-60; for adjusted poverty figures, Timothy Smeeding, "Antipoverty Effects of In-Kind Transfers," *Policy Studies Journal*, vol. 10 (1982), pp. 499–521.

a. Transfers are divided by all households, not by recipient households.

b. This series also adjusts census incomes for simulated values of taxes and income underreporting.

NA = not available.

poverty rates plummeted from about 20 to 12 percent. This was followed, until 1979, by a leveling of poverty in the 11 to 12 percent range. The 1979 to 1982 period marked the first sharp increase in poverty over the full thirty-year period. Poverty rose from 11.7 percent in 1979 to 13 percent in 1980, to 14 percent in 1981, and to 15 percent in 1982. To put this increase into perspective, note that poverty increased only from 11.2 to 12.3 percent during the 1974–1975 recession. Clearly, the recent rise in poverty stands in sharp contrast to previous experience.

The incomplete series on poverty that includes in-kind transfers (column 6) shows a steeper decline than the official series for the earlier years and the same leveling during the 1970s. Because no data are available after 1979, we cannot be sure that the in-kind poverty series would show as sharp an increase as the official series.

Table 1 suggests that the early period of sharp poverty reductions (in both measures) was a result of strong economic growth, declining unemployment rates, and large increases in transfers. All three factors seem to have contributed to decreasing poverty. The second period, that of steady poverty rates, seems to be the result of two offsetting factors. The rise in unemployment rates was offset by increases in both cash and in-kind transfers. After 1979, all three factors contributed to increasing official poverty. By 1982 GNP per household had fallen below its 1971 value and unemployment had risen from 5.8 percent to 9.7 percent. This was accompanied by a constant value of real cash transfers per household, despite the generally countercyclical nature of transfers.

These facts suggest that the poor benefit from secular economic growth, lower unemployment rates, and increased transfers. However, simple comparisons of data series are obviously inadequate to determine the relative importance of each of these factors in explaining the changes in poverty.

Before we turn to a review of some multivariate models, we discuss the possible effects of demographic change on the trend in poverty. There has been rapid change in the composition of households (families plus unrelated individuals). Between 1965 and 1981, the number of households grew by about 48 percent, while population grew by only about 18 percent.[6] A wide differential also holds for the poor—poor households increased by 27 percent while poor persons increased by only 15 percent. Types of households with the lowest poverty rates made up a declining proportion of all households. For example, the proportion of families headed by men of working age fell from almost 60 to about 45 percent of all households. On the other hand,

6. All of the data in this paragraph come from computations by the authors from the 1966 *Survey of Economic Opportunity* and the March 1982 *Current Population Survey*.

households headed by nonaged women increased from about 13 to almost 20 percent of all households, and from about 25 percent to about 40 percent of all poor households. Thus, even if poverty rates had remained constant for each demographic group, the aggregate poverty rate would have risen. We address this issue below.

Table 2 highlights the differences in poverty levels and trends for several major demographic groups for the 1967–1979 period. The largest reduction in poverty and the largest impact of in-kind transfers are for elderly persons.[7] Adjusted poverty rates for blacks, Hispanics, and women heading households

TABLE 2

ALTERNATIVE MEASURES OF THE INCIDENCE OF POVERTY

Persons Living In Poverty, by Type of Household Head	*Official Measure 1967* (1)	*Official Measure 1979* (2)	*Money Income Plus In-Kind Transfers at Market Value 1979*[a] (3)
All Persons	14.2%	11.1%	6.4%
White	11.0	8.5	5.2
Black	39.3	30.4	15.1
Hispanic	NA	21.4	12.0
Female Head of Household, No Husband Present	40.6	34.8	17.6
Elderly (65 and Over)	29.5	14.7	4.5

SOURCE: For 1979, U.S. Department of Commerce, Bureau of the Census, *Alternative Methods of Valuing Selected In-Kind Transfer Benefits and Measuring Their Effects on Poverty,* Technical Paper no. 50 (Washington, D.C.: U.S. Government Printing Office, 1982). For 1967, U.S. Department of Commerce, Bureau of the Census, *Money Income and Poverty Status of Families and Persons in the United States: 1982,* series P-60, no. 140 (Washington, D.C.: U.S. Government Printing Office, 1983).

a. In-kind transfers for food, housing, and medical benefits.

NA = not available.

---

7. The poverty rates in column 3 of table 2, available only for 1979, are the lowest adjusted poverty rates in the Census Bureau's technical report (U.S. Bureau of the Census, *Alternative Methods for Valuing Selected In-kind Transfer Benefits and Measuring Their Effects on Poverty,* Technical Paper no. 50 (Washington, D.C.: Government Printing Office, 1982). They value the transfers at market cost and include medical expenditures for institutional care. The poverty rate for all persons in column 3 differs from that shown for 1979 in column 6 of table 1. That time series includes in-kind transfers at their cash equivalent values to recipients and simulates additional adjustments for underreporting of incomes and the payment of federal income and payroll taxes. The authors discuss the Census Bureau report and its implications for the measurement of poverty in Sheldon Danziger and Peter Gottschalk, "The Measurement of Poverty," *American Behavioral Scientist,* vol. 26 (1983), pp. 739–756.

remain above the official rates that existed for whites in 1967, when in-kind transfers were few and consequently had little impact. These data suggest that a disaggregated analysis of poverty trends is in order, a point made by Aaron,[8] but not followed in some of the recent time-series literature. We now turn to the types of regressions that have been estimated by previous researchers.

Uses of Time-Series Regressions

In the tradition of Anderson,[9] Gallaway,[10,11] and Aaron,[12] several recent studies have estimated time-series regressions to obtain the partial effects of growth in GNP and transfers on poverty reduction. The results from these studies are conflicting. For example, Thornton et al. state:

Our findings indicate that the contribution of growth has been overstated, . . . much of the past successes are illusory.[13]

On the other hand, Murray claims that:

The effects of economic growth did indeed trickle down to the lowest economic levels of society. . . . The fortunes of the economy explain recent trends in poverty. But the flip side of this finding is that social welfare expenditures did not have an effect on poverty. Once the effects of GNP are taken into account, increases in social welfare spending do not account for reduction in poverty in the last three decades.[14]

If Thornton et al. are correct, the poor will not be greatly aided by economic expansion. But if Murray is correct, poverty rates should fall back to their 1979 levels after the economic recovery gets underway.

Why do studies obtain such different results? To answer this question, we estimated a large number of time-series regressions similar to those found

---

8. Henry Aaron, "The Foundations of the 'War on Poverty' Reexamined," *American Economic Review*, vol. 57 (1967), pp. 1229–1240.

9. W.H. Locke Anderson, "Trickle-Down: The Relationship between Economic Growth and the Extent of Poverty Among American Families," *Quarterly Journal of Economics*, vol. 78 (1964), pp. 511–524.

10. Lowell E. Gallaway, "The Foundations of the 'War on Poverty,'" *American Economic Review*, vol. 55 (1965), pp. 123–131.

11. Lowell E. Gallaway, "The Foundations of the 'War on Poverty': Reply," *American Economic Review*. vol. 57 (1967) pp. 1241–1243.

12. Aaron, "Foundations of the 'War on Poverty.'"

13. James R. Thornton, Richard J. Agnello, and Charles R. Link, "Poverty and Economic Growth: Trickle Down Peters Out," *Economic Inquiry*, vol. 16 (1978), pp. 385–393.

14. Charles Murray, "The Two Wars Against Poverty," *Public Interest* (Fall 1982), pp. 3–16.

in the literature. These regressions attempt to show how poverty is affected by economic growth, changes in cyclical conditions, and transfer growth. The appendix to this paper gives a sample of the estimated regressions. Our results suggest that previous studies have come to different conclusions because the estimated coefficients are not stable enough to accurately separate the impact of economic growth from the impact of growing transfers and of changes in unemployment.

This is because GNP, unemployment, and transfers change over time in similar ways. Consider a simple, but extreme, case. Suppose that when economic growth is rapid, transfers increase as a result of increased taxpayer generosity. Increased economic growth *and* the resulting increased transfers would reduce poverty. However, it would be difficult to separate the impact of the two factors on poverty, since they would move closely together. In practice transfers, economic growth, and unemployment move in a sufficiently similar manner to make it difficult to accurately separate their impacts.

Despite this drawback, the regression framework is a useful tool for analyzing whether the recent increase in poverty will be reversed as the economy recovers. We need not determine whether future changes in poverty will result from changes in market incomes or in transfers. We need only determine how much the *joint* changes in these variables will reduce poverty.

We use the estimated relationship between the poverty rate and real GNP per household, real cash transfers per household, and unemployment to project poverty for 1983 and 1984. The projections are based on the Office of Management and Budget's July 1983 economic assumptions and the projections of transfers found in the FY 1984 budget (although not all of the proposed changes in transfers in this budget were enacted). Growth in real GNP is projected to rise from −1.7 percent in 1982 to 3.1 percent in 1983. Real cash transfers per household are projected to increase by 6 percent, primarily due to the projected increase in the unemployment rate from 9.5 to 9.9 percent between 1982 and 1983. Between 1983 and 1984, economic growth is projected to increase and unemployment to decrease. However, transfers are projected to decrease, partly as a result of declines in countercyclical transfers but also because of legislated changes in transfers.

Table 3 presents the actual poverty rates for all persons and for selected demographic groups for selected years between 1967 and 1982, and our projections for 1983 and 1984. The poverty rate for all persons is projected to drop from 15.0 percent in 1982 to 14.6 percent in 1983 and to remain at that level in 1984. We project that the recent rise in poverty will not be reversed by the projected economic recovery. It would take either a stronger recovery or sustained increases in income transfers to bring poverty back to the 11 to 12 percent range of the 1970s.

TABLE 3

ACTUAL AND PROJECTED POVERTY RATES (PERCENTAGE) BASED ON OMB
ECONOMIC ASSUMPTIONS AND PROPOSED LEGISLATION

			Poor Persons Living in Households Headed by:					
	All	Elderly	White		Black		Hispanic	
	Persons	Persons	Male	Female	Male	Female	Male	Female
	(1)	(2)	(3)	(4)	(5)	(6)	(7)	(8)
Actual								
1967	14.2	29.5	8.1	33.9	30.0	61.6	NA	NA
1970	12.6	24.5	6.8	31.4	21.7	58.8	NA	NA
1975	12.3	15.3	6.6	28.1	18.2	53.6	20.1	55.6
1979	11.7	15.2	5.9	24.9	16.2	52.2	15.5	48.9
1980	13.0	15.7	6.9	27.1	17.9	53.1	18.5	52.5
1981	14.0	15.3	7.6	28.4	19.4	55.8	18.6	54.0
1982	15.0	14.6	8.7	28.7	20.0	57.4	22.0	57.4
Projections								
1983	14.6	14.2	8.4	27.8	18.5	55.2	19.9	56.2
1984	14.6	13.9	8.3	28.5	19.8	55.4	21.7	54.7

NOTE: The projections are based on regressions with the group-specific poverty rates as the
dependent variables and unemployment, real GNP per household, and real cash transfers
per household as the independent variables. All variables are in logarithmic form. The
regressions are estimated over the period 1966 to 1982 (except for the Hispanic equations
where data are available only after 1971). The projections are corrected for autocorrelation. The regressions are shown in column 3 of table A.1 for all persons and in table
A.3 (see appendix) for all of the demographic groups.

There are large differences both in the 1967–1982 rates and in the
projections among demographic groups. Column 2 of table 3 shows that the
decline in poverty among the elderly is projected to continue. Between 1979
and 1984, poverty among the elderly is projected to decline by 1.3 percentage
points, while it increases by 2.9 points for all persons.

The data for whites, blacks, and Hispanics, classified as to sex of the
head of household, are shown in columns 3 to 8. Poverty rates for all of the
groups are projected to decline from their 1982 levels as the economy recovers.
The sharpest projected drop is for black females, a group which experienced
an unusually large increase in poverty in 1982.

Nonetheless, the rates are projected to remain above those experienced
before the recent rise in unemployment. For example, the poverty rate for
white males is projected to remain well above both the 1979 level of 5.9
percent and above the 1967 rate of 8.1 percent. The other demographic groups
are projected to maintain poverty rates below their 1967 levels but above the
rates they experienced during the 1975 recession.

Projections of poverty using an income definition which includes in-kind transfers are less reliable since the Bureau of the Census has not published a consistent time series on poverty that counts the value of in-kind transfers. In a recent paper[15] we describe a method we use to project the adjusted poverty data presented by Smeeding.[16] These data include corrections for underreporting of income and for counting the value of in-kind benefits. On the basis of these adjustments, we project that poverty increased from 6.1 percent in 1979 to 8.8 percent in 1982 (compared to the unadjusted increase from 11.7 to 15.0 percent during that time). By 1984 adjusted poverty is projected to be 8.2 percent, which is comparable to the levels of the early 1970s.

The regression framework is useful for making short-term projections over periods where transfers and economic growth closely follow their historical patterns. However, this methodology does not answer the broader question of whether poverty can be substantially reduced without continuing the expansion in social welfare spending experienced during the 1960s and 1970s.

Changes in the Demographic Composition of Households

In this and the following section, we use two approaches to judge the relative importance of changes in the demographic composition of households, market incomes, and transfers in reducing poverty over the past fifteen years. The first approach focuses on change in the relative size and poverty rates of specific demographic groups. Since the overall poverty rate is a weighted average of rates for the subgroups, we can calculate what the overall poverty rate would have been if the weights, which reflect demographic composition, had not changed or if demographic-specific poverty rates had remained constant. This decomposition provides a measure of the effect of changes in demographic composition. It also provides a rough indicator of the relative importance of increases in transfers, since poverty rates for groups like the elderly are more likely to reflect changes in transfers than in market incomes. The second approach focuses directly on changes in the levels and distributions of market and transfer incomes. We show how changes in these components of income affected poverty over the last fifteen years.

---

15. Peter Gottschalk and Sheldon Danziger, "Changes in Poverty, 1967–1982: Methodological Issues and Evidence," Institute for Research on Poverty, Discussion Paper no. 737-83.

16. Timothy Smeeding, "The Antipoverty Effects of In-Kind Transfers," *Policy Studies Journal*, vol. 10 (1982), pp. 499–521.

We used published data on official poverty rates for eight demographic groups, defined in terms of the head of household's sex, race, and age (over sixty-five or not) to calculate weighted poverty rates in selected years. Table 4 shows the actual poverty rates for all persons (column 1) and the rates calculated using the 1967 demographic weights for each of the eight groups (columns 2–5). Column 2 shows the poverty rate that would have resulted from actual changes in the group-specific poverty rates if there had been no change in demographic composition since 1967. If this had been the case, poverty would have declined from 14.2 to 13.2 percent between 1967 and 1982. The difference between the rates in columns 1 and 2 increases continuously over the period, reflecting a higher proportion of the population living in households headed by those with above-average poverty rates—i.e., women and blacks. For example, actual poverty rates fell from 14.2 to 11.7 percent

TABLE 4

POVERTY RATES IN SELECTED YEARS—ACTUAL AND SIMULATED VALUES

| | | Simulated Rate If Demographic Composition Had Not Changed Since 1967[a] | | | |
	Actual Rate (1)	All Poverty Rates Change (2)	Only Poverty Rates of Elderly Change[b] (3)	Only Poverty Rates of Non-aged Females Change[b] (4)	Only Poverty Rates of Nonaged Males Change[b] (5)
1967	14.2%	14.2%	14.2%	14.2%	14.2%
1974	11.2	10.3	12.7	13.8	12.1
1979	11.7	10.1	12.8	13.6	12.1
1980	13.0	11.2	12.8	13.8	13.0
1981	14.0	12.2	12.8	14.0	13.7
1982	15.0	13.2	12.7	14.2	14.6
Percentage Point Change Over the Period:[c]					
1967–1979	−2.5	−4.1	−1.4	−0.6	−2.1
1979–1982	+3.3	+3.1	−0.1	+0.6	+2.6
1967–1982	+0.8	−1.0	−1.5	0.0	+0.5

    a.   The simulated values are based on a classification of all persons into one of eight demographic groups. Different classifications produce results that differ only slightly from those shown here.
    b.   Poverty rates for all other demographic groups remain at their 1967 levels.
    c.   Percentage point change over the period is defined as final period poverty rate less initial year rate. By definition the percentage point changes in columns (3), (4), and (5) sum to the change in column (2). Some differences are due to rounding.

between 1967 and 1979, the last year of near full employment. If the weights are held constant, the 1979 poverty rate would have been 10.1 percent.

Most of the increase in poverty since 1979, however, cannot be attributed to demographic change. Actual poverty increased by 3.3 percentage points (column 1), while poverty in the absence of demographic change increased by 3.1 percentage points due to increases in the group-specific rates.

Columns 3, 4, and 5 show how changes in the poverty rates for each demographic group affected the rate for all persons. In each column, we hold the demographic composition and the poverty rates for all but the indicated group at their 1967 values. Column 3 shows that reductions in poverty for the elderly accounted for a 1.4 point decrease in the overall poverty rate between 1967 and 1979 (14.2 compared to 12.8); reductions for nonaged females and nonaged males account for 0.6 points and 2.1 points, respectively. Thus, half of the 4.1 percentage point decline in poverty from 1967 to 1979 reflected a drop in poverty for nonaged males.

The deterioration in macroeconomic conditions since 1979 increased poverty rates for all but the elderly. Poverty would have increased from 10.1 to 13.2 percent if the demographic weights had not changed (column 2). Increased poverty for nonaged males accounted for 2.6 points of the total 3.1 point increase.

This decomposition shows that several factors are quantitatively important in determining whether it will be possible to reduce poverty without large increases in transfers in the future. First, if the demographic composition of the population continues to change as it has, it will continue to exert a small upward pressure on poverty rates. This factor accounted for a 1.8 point increase in the poverty rate between 1967 and 1982. A continuation of this trend implies that the poverty rate will increase by only 0.1 percentage point per year due to demographic changes. Second, cyclical downturns had a major impact on poverty. Between 1979 and 1982, poverty rates, adjusted for demographic shifts, increased by 3.1 points. Third, changes in transfers were quantitatively important since declines in poverty rates among households with an elderly head decreased the overall poverty rate by 1.5 points between 1967 and 1982. This largely reflects the increase in Social Security and Supplemental Security Income benefits received by these households. Fourth, the role of economic growth is limited because those who depend most on market income already have low poverty rates. For example, if poverty rates among households headed by nonaged males had been 3 percent in 1979, instead of 6.5 percent, the poverty rate for all persons would still have been 8.5 percent. Further reductions will have to come from increased incomes for households headed by women, who have up to this point benefited little from economic growth.

Changes in the Level and Distribution of Market Income and Transfer Income

The preceeding analysis has at least two drawbacks. First, we derived inferences about the importance of market versus transfer income by associating changes in poverty among nonaged males with changes in market incomes, and changes among the elderly with changes in transfers. At best, this is a rough approximation. Nonaged males receive some transfers (e.g., unemployment insurance) and the elderly receive some market income. Second, we controlled for changes in the cycle by comparing the data between pairs of years.

We derive an alternative method for measuring the relative importance of increased market versus transfer income by using a model that explicitly focuses on cyclical and secular changes in the levels and distributions of these two sources of income. The details of the methodology can be found in a discussion paper we wrote for the Institute for Research on Poverty.[17] The model proceeds as follows. Poverty can be viewed as changing because shifts in the level and distribution of income alter the proportion of households falling below a fixed real poverty line. These shifts in income can be described by changes in the mean income, the dispersion of income around the mean (i.e., the variance), and the degree to which households are concentrated in the lower tail of the distribution (i.e., skewness). Therefore, changes in the shape, as well as the level, of the distribution can affect poverty. For example, poverty will not decrease when mean income grows if growth is accompanied by increased inequality sufficiently large to offset the poverty-reducing effect of the increased mean.

Since reported census income is composed of market income (e.g., wages, salaries, private pensions, dividends, interest, rents, and income from other private sources) and public cash transfers, we decompose changes in census income into changes in these two types of income. Each of these components varies with the business cycle and follows a long-term trend. During the past fifteen years, although average market incomes decreased and average transfers increased during recessions, the overall secular trend was for both to increase. Inequality of earnings, which affects the shape of the income distribution, increased during recessions and generally grew over time.[18]

---

17. Gottschalk and Danziger, "Changes in Poverty, 1967–1982."
18. Martin Dooley and Peter Gottschalk, "Does the Younger Male Labor Force Mean Greater Earnings Inequality?" *Monthly Labor Review* (November 1982), pp. 42–45.

We decompose the impact of changes in macroeconomic conditions on poverty into components due to changes in mean market incomes, mean transfers, and other factors that affect the shape of the distribution.[19] The March 1968 and 1975 to 1983 *Current Population Surveys* were used to calculate the basic data that describe the distribution of market income and transfers in each year (i.e., the means, variances, covariance, and skewness).

We focus on the effects of changes in mean market income and mean transfer income and group the remaining factors into a residual category. This residual category is further decomposed in our previously cited paper.[20]

Table 5 shows the effects of changes in mean market and transfer income in changing poverty between 1967 and 1979 and between 1979 and 1982. Row 1 shows that while the actual poverty rate for all persons declined by only 2.6 percentage points between 1967 and 1979, increases in mean market income would have reduced poverty by 2.4 points if transfers and factors affecting the shape of the distribution had remained constant. Increases in mean transfers would have reduced poverty by an additional 3.1 points, other factors remaining unchanged. These two poverty-decreasing factors were offset by changes in the shape of the distribution that increased poverty by 2.9 points. Thus, between 1967 and 1979, increases in mean transfers were slightly more important than increases in mean market income in reducing poverty. Changes in the shape of the distribution were as important as either of these factors.

Row 2 decomposes the 3.3 percentage point increase in poverty among all persons between 1979 and 1982. The decline in mean market incomes led to a 0.8 point poverty increase, which was partially offset by a 0.4 point

---

19. Our model is based on the assumption that total income divided by the poverty line has a displaced log-normal distribution (see Charles Metcalf, *An Econometric Model of Income Distributions* (Chicago: Rand-McNally, 1972). We use the income-to-needs ratio (income divided by the poverty line) rather than actual income to correct for differences in family size. We use the terms market income and transfer income for the more cumbersome terms market-income-to-needs ratio and transfer-income-to-needs ratio.

20. Gottschalk and Danziger, "Changes in Poverty, 1967–1982." Changes in the shape of the distribution result from changes in the coefficient of variation (variance/mean^2), the coefficient of skewness (the third moment/mean^3) and changes in higher level moments. For example, column 2 of table 5 reflects the poverty-decreasing effects of increases in mean market income but also the poverty-increasing effects of increases in the variance, and the effects of changes in the covariance and displacement factor, all of which would result from proportional growth in the income of each household. The included changes in the mean and variance would keep the coefficient of variation constant. Column 4 shows the impact of changes in the shape of the distribution that result when the changes in the variance, covariance, and displacement factor differ from what would be consistent with proportional growth in each household's income. Peter Gottschalk, "Transfer Scenarios and Projections of Poverty into the 1980s," *Journal of Human Resources*, vol. 16, pp. 41–60, presents a different decomposition model, but ignores changes in the covariance and the variance of transfers.

TABLE 5

DECOMPOSITION OF CHANGES IN POVERTY RATES

| | | Percentage Point Change in Poverty Associated with Change In: | | |
Household Head	Actual Percentage Point Change in Poverty (1)	Mean Market Income (2)	Mean Transfer Income (3)	All Other Factors (4)
All Persons				
1967–1979	−2.6	−2.4	−3.1	2.9
1979–1982	3.3	0.8	−0.4	2.9
Young Men				
1967–1979	−1.9	−2.5	−0.6	1.2
1979–1982	5.8	3.0	−0.6	3.4
Prime-aged Men				
1967–1979	−1.7	−3.1	−0.8	2.2
1979–1982	3.0	0.8	−0.2	2.4
Elderly Persons				
1967–1979	−12.9	0.5	−19.6	6.2
1979–1982	−0.6	−0.1	−1.8	1.3

SOURCE: Computations from data derived in Peter Gottschalk and Sheldon Danziger, "Changes in Poverty, 1967–1982: Methodological Issues and Evidence," Institute for Research on Poverty, Discussion Paper no. 737-83.

NOTE: The sum of the changes in columns 2, 3, and 4 is equal to the change shown in column 1.

poverty decline due to increased transfers. By far the most important factor, however, was the change in the shape of the distribution, which accounted for a 2.9 point increase in poverty. In other words, if all households had experienced the mean (proportional) changes in market and transfer incomes, poverty would have risen by only 0.4 points, instead of the actual 3.3 point increase.

Because changes in demographic composition have had a significant impact on the trend in poverty, the last six rows of table 5 show disaggregated results for persons in households headed by prime-aged males (ages twenty-five to sixty-four), young males (less than twenty-five years of age), and elderly persons (age sixty-five and over).[21] From 1967 to 1979, growth in

---

21. The displaced log-normal distribution does not adequately describe the shape of the income-to-needs distribution for non-aged female heads of households. As a result, we could not decompose the change in poverty for this group.

mean market income accounted for a 3.1 percentage point drop in poverty for prime-aged males. Growth in mean transfers accounted for only a 0.8 percentage point drop. Changes in the shape of the distribution increased poverty by 2.2 points. The cyclical downturn between 1979 and 1982 reversed the effect of changes in mean market income. Changes in the mean increased poverty by 0.8 percentage points. While growth in mean transfers still reduced poverty, the effect was only 0.2 percentage points. As in the earlier period, changes in the shape of the distribution had a large poverty-increasing impact (2.4 points). In sum, for prime-aged men, growth in mean market incomes was more important than transfer growth, but poverty-increasing changes in the shape of the distribution offset their combined effect.

Cyclical changes are even more important for persons in households headed by men less than twenty-five years old. From 1967 to 1979, growth in mean market income decreased poverty by 2.5 points, while growth in mean transfers accounted for only a 0.6 point drop. Changes in the shape of the distribution increased poverty by 1.2 points. The 1979-1982 downturn in mean market income increased poverty by 3.0 points and changes in the shape caused a 3.4 point increase. These effects more than offset the net gains this group had made from 1967 to 1979.

The largest drop in poverty between 1967 and 1982 (13.5 points) occurred for households headed by elderly persons (males and females). As might be expected, this decline was almost solely a result of growth in mean transfers.

Simulations

The fact that increased unemployment increases poverty by decreasing market income has never been disputed in the literature. The key issue revolves around the relative importance of secular increases in market incomes and transfers in reducing poverty. Our method for controlling for cyclical changes has been to compare poverty in 1967 and 1979, two years of almost full employment, and 1979 and 1982, two years of very different macroeconomic conditions. This is a crude method for separating secular from cyclical change.

We now use simulations to remove the cyclical component and focus solely on secular change. We begin with initial-year values for mean market income, mean transfers, and other parameters describing the shape of the income distribution. We then assume that each household's market income and transfer income-to-needs ratios grew at constant rates (which we specify below). We can then simulate values of poverty which would have been consistent with the assumed equal growth rates for all households had there been no cyclical downturn after 1979. We use 1979 as the base year since it was the last year of close to full employment.

By imposing the constraint that market and transfer incomes grow at constant rates, we eliminate all cyclical changes. Since we further assume that market and transfer incomes of those at the bottom of the distribution grow as fast as those higher in the distribution, the shape of the distribution remains constant over time. This restriction will overstate (or understate) the amount of poverty reduction due to secular growth if growth would actually have been accompanied by increasing (or decreasing) inequality of market or transfer incomes.

Table 6 shows the actual poverty rates in 1979 and 1982 (columns 1 and 2) and the poverty rates that would have existed if the market and transfer

TABLE 6

POVERTY RATES IN 1979 AND 1982: ACTUAL AND SIMULATED VALUES

	Actual Poverty Rates		Simulated 1982 Poverty Rates			
	1979 (1)	1982 (2)	Market Income Grows at Actual Trend; Transfer Incomes at 1979 Levels (3)	Transfers and Market Incomes Grow at Actual Trends (4)	Market Incomes Grow at 2 Percent; Transfers at 1979 Levels (5)	Market Incomes Grow at 3 Percent; Transfers at 1979 Levels (6)
All Persons	11.7	15.0	11.5	11.4	11.0	10.7
Persons in Households Headed by:						
Young Men	12.7	18.5	12.4	12.5	11.5	11.1
Prime-aged Men	6.1	9.1	5.8	5.8	5.5	5.2
Elderly Persons	14.9	14.3	14.9	13.6	14.8	14.8

NOTES: Column 3: Market incomes are assumed to grow at the same proportional rate for all people within the demographic group (0.3, 0.4, 0.7, and 0.1 percent for all persons, young men, prime-aged men, and elderly persons, respectively). These rates are obtained from regressions using the observed log mean market income/needs ratio as the dependent variable and time and unemployment as the independent variables.

Column 4: Market incomes are assumed to grow at the rates indicated above and transfer incomes are assumed to grow at 0.7, -0.9, 0.2, and 1.4 for the four groups. These rates are obtained from similar regressions using log transfer income/needs as dependent variables.

Columns 5 and 6: Market incomes are assumed to grow at 2 percent (column 5) and 3 percent (column 6) for each demographic group.

incomes of all households had grown at the rates specified for columns 3-6. The trend rates reflect the secular growth in each income source for each demographic group over the period 1974 to 1981, after controlling for cyclical conditions.[22] Column 3 shows the poverty rate which would have been observed in 1982 if the market income of each household had grown at the specified rate, while transfers had remained constant in real terms. Comparing columns 1 and 3 shows that between 1979 and 1982 trend growth in market incomes would have reduced poverty by 0.2 points for all persons, 0.3 points for young men, and 0.3 points for prime-aged men. Increases in market income for the elderly would have had a negligible impact. Column 4 shows the poverty rates consistent with secular growth in both market and transfer incomes. A comparison of columns 3 and 4 indicates that trend growth in transfers would have reduced poverty by an additional 0.1 points overall, and 1.3 points for the elderly. Secular growth in transfers would have had a negligible impact on prime-aged men and would actually have increased poverty among young men since they received reduced transfers, once we control for cyclical changes in their transfers.

Columns 5 and 6 show the poverty rates that are consistent with 2 and 3 percent yearly market income growth, holding real transfers constant at their 1979 levels. In this sense, they give an upper bound to the poverty reduction which could have been achieved solely through more rapid growth in market incomes. If market incomes of all households had grown by 2 percent per year (column 5), then poverty for all persons would have declined from 11.7 to 11.0 percent over this period. Poverty rates for young men would have declined from 12.7 to 11.5 percent, slightly above the overall rate. Poverty rates for prime-aged men would have been 5.5 instead of 6.1 percent. As might be expected, the elderly would have been considerably worse off if there had been rapid growth in market incomes but no growth in transfers than they were under the actual expanded transfer system and lower market income growth. Under this scenario, their poverty rates would have decreased only from 14.9 to 14.8 percent.

A comparison of columns 5 and 6 shows the incremental effect of an additional one percentage point increase in the growth rate of market incomes.

---

22. If we had used the full 1967–1981 period to estimate secular growth rates, net of cycle, the rates for both mean market and mean transfer incomes would have been higher. Gottschalk and Danziger, in "Changes in Poverty, 1967–1982," simulate with the trends for all persons of 0.9 percent per year for mean market income and 3.2 for transfers, rather than the 1974–1981 trends of 0.3 and 0.7 that are used here. Simulations with the higher growth rates show a larger percentage point decline in poverty, with a larger proportion of the decline attributable to the growth of transfers. We use the 1974–1981 rates because they are more likely than the higher rates to represent the growth between 1979 and 1982 had there been no cyclical downturn.

For example, if market incomes grew at 3 percent per year, poverty for all persons would have been 10.7 rather than 11.0 percent. A comparison of columns 1 and 6 shows that even with sustained 3 percent real growth in market incomes for all households, it would still take about eleven years to reduce poverty from the 1982 rate of 15.0 percent to its 1979 level, if all other factors, including transfers, remained constant.

We also simulated the effects of secular growth in in-kind transfers on poverty. We used data from an adjusted March 1975 *Current Population Survey* provided by Timothy Smeeding and again assumed that all households experienced the same secular growth rates in market incomes and cash plus in-kind transfers.[23] We assumed that Smeeding's adjustment for underreporting, which affects the 1974 poverty level, would not affect the growth rates of market and cash transfer incomes as adjusted. We increased the growth rates for transfers in the simulations, which include cash and in-kind transfers, to reflect the fact that in-kind transfers grew faster than cash transfers.[24]

Table 7 shows the actual adjusted rates for 1974 and the simulated rates for 1982 for all persons and for the three demographic groups. A comparison of columns 1–3 shows how secular growth in market incomes and mean cash plus in-kind transfers affected poverty. Had mean market incomes followed the 1974–1981 secular trend, poverty for all persons would have declined by 0.3 percentage points (7.1 less 6.8). Growth in cash and in-kind transfers would have reduced poverty by an additional 0.8 points, about three-quarters of the total poverty reduction. A comparison of tables 6 and 7 shows that the inclusion of in-kind transfers and the adjustment for underreporting significantly reduce the level of poverty in any year and increase the relative importance of growth in transfer incomes in reducing poverty.

The relative importance of secular growth in cash plus in-kind transfers varies markedly for the three demographic groups. It is responsible for only 0.1 percentage point of the 0.7 point decline for prime-aged men. Because the secular trend in cash plus in-kind transfers is negative for young men,

---

23. Smeeding, "Antipoverty Effects of In-Kind Transfers," adjusted for income underreporting and the payment of personal income and payroll taxes, as well as for in-kind transfers. About half of the difference between the official and the adjusted poverty rates reflects adjustments for underreporting. The decrease in poverty from underreporting is probably an upper bound, since measurement error would cause some overreporting, a factor not taken into account by Smeeding. The March 1975 *Current Population Survey* was the latest computer tape that Smeeding could make available to us.

24. Data on the log of cash and cash plus in-kind transfers per houshold, shown in table 1, were regressed against time and unemployment. The different growth rates in transfers for each group (see column 4 note, in table 6) were adjusted by the ratio of the two coefficients on the time trends, which was 2.07. Since these regressions were not differentiated by demographic group, the same scaling factor was applied to all groups.

TABLE 7

ADJUSTED POVERTY RATES IN 1974 AND 1982: ACTUAL AND SIMULATED VALUES

		Simulated 1982 Poverty Rates	
	Actual 1974 Rate (1)	*Market Incomes Grow at Trend; Cash and In-Kind Transfers at 1974 Levels* (2)	*Cash and In-Kind Transfers and Market Incomes Grow at Trends* (3)
All Persons	7.1	6.8	6.0
Persons in Households Headed by:			
Young Men	9.7	9.0	9.4
Prime-aged Men	4.6	4.0	3.9
Elderly Persons	4.9	4.9	0.3

NOTES: Market incomes are assumed to grow at 0.3, 0.4, 0.7, and 0.1 percent respectively for the four groups. Cash and in-kind transfers are assumed to grow at 1.5, − 1.9, 0.4, and 2.8 percent, respectively.

more young men would have been in poverty under the assumed scenario than under a scenario where transfers were fixed. As in the other tables, the elderly experience a large reduction in poverty as a result of secular growth in cash plus in-kind transfers.

Summary

At the outset of the War on Poverty, analysts thought that poverty could be eliminated by 1980 if the economy could be kept on a stable growth path and if additional opportunities could be made available to the poor.[25] Poverty obviously has not been eliminated. Income transfers to the poor have grown more rapidly than expected and the economy has not followed a stable growth path.

Our goal in this paper was to determine the relative importance of secular growth, cyclical conditions, and income transfers in reducing poverty. We began by questioning the ability of the regressions that are common in much of the previous literature to determine the relative importance of these three factors. However, we concluded that these regressions could be used for projecting poverty. We then reported the results derived from a model which focuses on the impacts of changes in market and transfer incomes on the

---

25. Robert Lampman, *Ends and Means of Reducing Income Poverty* (Chicago: Markham, 1971).

shape and position of the income distribution. Finally, we provided some simulations that used this framework to control for cyclical changes.

Our major findings are as follows:

1. Poverty is projected to remain above the 1979 rates through the mid-1980s, even if the economy grows according to official predictions.

2. Between 1967 and 1979, increases in mean transfers were roughly as important as increases in mean market incomes in reducing official poverty for all persons. Between 1979 and 1982, declines in mean market incomes were only partially offset by increases in transfers.

3. During both periods, changes in the shape of the income distribution had a large poverty-increasing impact.

4. Experiences differ across demographic groups. For persons living in households headed by young and prime-aged men, changes in cash and in-kind transfer income affect poverty levels less than changes in market incomes. For the elderly, increased transfers account for almost all of the decline in poverty. For all groups, however, changes in the shape of the distribution were quantitatively important.

Our review of the last twenty years makes us pessimistic about the prospects for reducing poverty by economic growth without increased transfer payments. Our simulations show that it would take over a decade to reduce poverty for all persons to the 1979 level if mean market incomes grew at 3 percent per year and all other factors affecting the income distribution remained constant. The prospects for various demographic groups are also not encouraging.

The elderly experienced the largest drop in poverty of any demographic group. They were a sufficiently large group to have a substantial impact on the overall poverty rate—the very large drop in their poverty rate reduced the rate for all persons by 1.5 points. Over the 1967–1982 period their poverty reduction was almost wholly attributable to increases in real Social Security and SSI transfers. Since these benefits are not expected to further increase in real terms in the next decade, we do not expect very large further declines in poverty for this group.

Poverty rates for nonaged men are affected more by changes in mean market incomes than in mean transfers, suggesting that economic growth could reduce poverty for this group without further increasing transfers. This optimistic assessment must, however, be tempered by the realization that poverty rates for nonaged males would already be low were it not for the current cyclical conditions. A return to full employment would have a substantial impact on the poverty rates of nonaged men. However, it would not have a very substantial impact on the aggregate poverty rate because this group represents an increasingly small portion of the total poverty population and the low rates become increasingly hard to reduce.

If economic growth is unlikely to make substantial inroads into aggregate poverty by reducing the poverty rates of the elderly or nonaged men, growth can only be an effective strategy if nonaged female-headed households gain substantially from increases in market income. We remain pessimistic that economic growth per se will have a large impact on their poverty rates. Our pessimism is based on the small poverty reduction experienced by this demographic group during the high growth period of the late 1960s and early 1970s.

APPENDIX

Time-Series Regressions of the Trend in Poverty

We regressed the natural log of the official poverty rate against the natural log of various measures of economic growth, cyclical conditions, and transfers.[1] Like previous authors, we interpret the coefficient on the growth variable as the partial impact of growth in raising the market incomes of the poor. Since transfers are also an independent variable, the coefficient on the secular variable measures the extent to which the working poor benefit from growth through higher market incomes.

Without an explicit theoretical foundation for these regressions, there is little to guide us (or the previous authors) in the choice of variables or functional form. Therefore, we used several alternative measures of the independent variables, time periods, and corrections for autocorrelation. We evaluate these equations on the basis of their ability to provide stable estimates of the impact of growth and transfers on poverty and to provide projections of poverty. Each is considered in turn.

Stability of Coefficients. Tables A.1 and A.2 show a sample of the many regressions we ran. Three alternative measures are used to capture the impact of secular growth. Two different time periods are used—1966 to 1982 in table A.1 and 1949 to 1982 in table A.2.[2] Following previous studies, we also show the impact of estimating with first differences rather than levels (i.e., changes in the log of poverty rather than the level of the log of poverty).[3]

We also estimate regressions adjusting for the receipt of in-kind transfers and regressions for major demographic subgroups of the population to account for the demographic shifts discussed earlier.

---

1. Aaron, "Foundations of 'War on Poverty' Reexamined," argued that the double log specification was appropriate if the income distribution was approximately log normal. Gallaway, in his "Reply" to Aaron, agreed that this was superior to the semilog specification he had used in his 1965 article on both "goodness of fit" and "ability to predict" criteria.

2. The Census Bureau annually publishes official poverty data gathered as part of the annual March *Current Population Survey*. These data provide consistent time series from 1959 to the present. However, the 1969 *Economic Report of the President* published a chart from which one can derive estimates for the 1949–1959 period. Since poverty rates based on microdata were not available in these earlier years, the quality of these data is less precise. We analyze them in Table A.2 because Murray, "Two Wars Against Poverty," used them. In our detailed empirical work, we are restricted to the 1967–1982 period because the March 1968 *Current Population Survey* is the earliest one for which a public use data tape is available.

3. Some authors (e.g., Thornton et al., Murray) use the absolute change in poverty as the dependent variable. This implies constant poverty reduction rates. Yet Anderson, Aaron and Hirsch ("Foundations of 'War on Poverty' Reexamined") have all made the case for diminishing marginal poverty reduction with growth when the poverty line is fixed.

TABLE A.1

Log Poverty Rate Regressions Using Alternative Measures of Secular Growth, 1966–1982

| | Percentage of All Persons with Incomes Below Poverty Line | | | |
	(1)	(2)	(3)	(4)
Secular Variable:				
Year	− .57			
	(25.0)			
Year^2	.004			
	(26.3)			
Log Real Median Family		− 1.7		
Income		(6.0)		
Log Real GNP per			− .09	− .14
Household			(.1)	(.2)
Log of Unemployment	.30	.04	.31	.30
	(21.5)	(.6)	(1.9)	(1.9)
Log Real Cash Transfers	− .25	.06	− .51	− .54
per Household	(5.5)	(.5)	(1.6)	(1.7)
Adjusted R^2	.99	.99	.97	.73
Level or First Difference	level	level	level	difference
Rho (if level equation)	− .84	.68	.91	NA
Standard Error of Rho	(.19)	(.18)	(.08)	NA
Predictions Based on Estimation through 1979				
1980	13.0	12.8	12.5	12.5
1981	13.7	13.4	12.4	12.4
1982	15.5	14.5	13.3	13.2
Predictions Based on Estimation through 1982				
1983	16.9	15.0	14.6	14.7
1984	16.9	14.2	14.6	14.8
1985	18.8	13.7	14.4	14.8

Note: t-statistics appear in parentheses.
NA = not available.

Real GNP is the traditional measure of secular growth (see Thornton et al.[4] and Hirsch.[5] However, it includes the effects of population growth as well as economic growth. Thus, we deflated real GNP by the number of

---

4. Thornton, et al., "Poverty and Economic Growth."
5. Barry Hirsch, "Poverty and Economic Growth: Has Trickle Down Petered Out?" *Economic Inquiry*, vol. 18, pp. 151–158.

TABLE A.2

LOG PERSON POVERTY RATE REGRESSIONS USING ALTERNATIVE MEASURES OF
SECULAR GROWTH, 1949–1982

	Percentage of All Persons with Incomes Below Poverty Line			
	(1)	*(2)*	*(3)*	*(4)*
Secular Variable:				
Year	−.16			
	(3.1)			
Year^2	.001			
	(2.9)			
Log Real Median Family		−1.8		
Income		(6.5)		
Log Real GNP per			−1.27	−.52
Household			(2.3)	(1.9)
Log of Unemployment	.17	−.03	.04	.12
	(4.2)	(.6)	(.5)	(1.9)
Log Real Cash Transfers	−.17	.14	−.18	−.15
per Household	(1.0)	(1.0)	(.9)	(.8)
Adjusted R^2	.97	.99	.96	.99
Level or First Difference	level	level	level	difference
Rho (if level equation)	.90	.61	.91	NA
Standard Error of Rho	(.07)	(.15)	(.06)	NA
Predictions Based on Estimation through 1979				
1980	11.8	12.7	12.4	12.0
1981	11.7	13.3	12.1	11.7
1982	12.0	14.2	13.0	12.1
Predictions Based on Estimation through 1982				
1983	15.1	15.0	14.8	14.8
1984	15.2	14.2	14.4	14.4
1985	15.3	13.6	14.2	14.1

NOTE: t-statistics appear in parentheses.
NA = not available.

households (see note 5). Real median family income is one alternative to real GNP per household. It has the advantage of being more consistent with the poverty data, since both come from the *Current Population Survey*. However, median family income does not average in the income of unrelated individuals, a growing proportion of the population. It also includes cash transfers, the effect of which we are trying to isolate. A drawback of both these measures is that they are collinear with the unemployment rate, the cyclical variable most commonly used. To minimize this problem, a quadratic time trend is our third measure of secular growth.

The first equation in table A.1 uses the quadratic in time.[6] The estimation period is 1966 to 1982. A maximum likelihood estimator is used to correct for autocorrelation. The results are consistent with those of Thornton et al.— increased transfers or reduced unemployment both significantly reduce poverty. For example, a 10 percent increase in real cash transfers per household reduces the poverty rate by 2.5 percent. The secular variable shows the "petering out" effect of economic growth. Taken together, the coefficients on time show that, if cash transfers and unemployment rates had been constant, poverty would have declined before 1975, but increased after 1975.

Columns 2, 3, and 4 show the sensitivity of the coefficients to the choice of secular measures. In column 2 the log of real median family income is the secular variable. Neither unemployment nor transfers has a significant impact, and the magnitudes of the coefficients are much reduced. Murray's conclusion that only growth matters is borne out. The equation in column 3 is identical to that in column 2 except for the choice of secular variable. When growth is measured in terms of real GNP per household, growth has no impact; only transfers and unemployment matter. This seemingly unimportant change reverses the conclusion.

The instability of coefficients may be due to multicollinearity. To lessen this problem some studies have estimated equations stated in terms of first differences rather than levels (e.g., Thornton et al. and Murray). This procedure is appropriate only if the autocorrelation coefficient is equal to one. Examining the value of this coefficient (rho) shows that using first differences would have been inappropriate for columns 1 and 2 but may be appropriate for column 3. Changing the column 3 estimation to first differences, shown in column 4, does not alter by much the size or significance of the coefficients. The secular variable is still insignificant and the other two variables are weakly significant.

Table A.2 presents the same four specifications as table A.1, but extends the estimation period back to 1949. The results differ substantially. Unemployment and transfers now have an insignificant impact in most of the regressions. However, when the estimation period is 1949 to 1965 (results not shown), transfers have a larger negative coefficient than in the 1966 to 1982 period, further showing the instability of the coefficients.

---

6. A constant term was included in each regression, but is not reported. Poverty rates, the number of households, and median family income are periodically revised by the Census Bureau. To ensure a consistent time series, we proportionately scaled earlier years up (or down) if the revised figure was greater (or less) than the unrevised figure for the same year.

While we show only the results of using the unemployment rate and the log of real cash transfers per household as cyclical and transfer variables, we experimented using several other variants for the independent variables (e.g., employment rate and cash public assistance per household or per capita) and the poverty incidence for households instead of for persons as the dependent variable. Our conclusion, that seemingly unimportant redefinitions have large impacts on the signs, magnitudes, and significance of the coefficients, is reinforced by these regressions.[7]

In the text, we discussed the role of demographic change and showed the different poverty trends by demographic groups. Table A.3 presents the regression from the third column of table A.1 for eight groups. We expected that such a disaggregation might yield more meaningful results, but the major finding again is the instability of the coefficients. For example, the real GNP variable has a negative sign and is significant only for the elderly and for

TABLE A.3

LOG POVERTY RATE REGRESSIONS BY DEMOGRAPHIC GROUPS, 1966–1982

			Percentage of All Persons with Incomes Below Poverty Line Who Live in Households Where Head Is:					
	Aged (1)	Non-aged (2)	White Male (3)	White Female (4)	Black Male (5)	Black Female (6)	Hispanic Male (7)	Hispanic Female (8)
Log Real GNP	−2.2	−.86	−.76	.15	.97	−.04	2.26	−1.43
per Household	(1.7)	(1.2)	(0.6)	(0.2)	(0.4)	(0.4)	(3.5)	(1.5)
Log of Unem-	−.22	.22	.42	.33	.53	.09	1.22	−.07
ployment	(1.3)	(2.0)	(1.8)	(2.4)	(1.3)	(0.5)	(10.5)	(0.4)
Log of Real								
Cash Transfers	−.44[a]	−.03[b]	−.77	−.87	−1.58	−.33	−2.18	.25
per Household	(1.7)	(0.2)	(1.7)	(3.3)	(2.0)	(0.9)	(9.1)	(0.7)
Adjusted R²	.97	.96	.93	.99	.95	.99	.99	.99
Rho (Standard	.59	.92	.91	−.35	.75	.39	−.67	−.44
Error of Rho)	(.20)	(.07)	(.08)	(.25)	(.19)	(.31)	(.23)	(.33)

NOTES: t-statistics appear in parentheses.
Poverty rates for Hispanics are only available from 1972 to 1982.
a.   Cash transfers primarily received by the aged.
b.   Cash transfers primarily received by the nonaged.

---

7. For example, consider the case where we decomposed the real cash transfer variable into public assistance and social insurance transfers per household and used the specification of regression (3) in table A.1. GNP then has a perverse positive and significant sign, and both transfer variables are also significant. These regressions are available on request.

Hispanic women, groups we expected to be among the least likely to benefit from economic growth, holding transfers constant.

We also noted that the poverty measure that includes in-kind transfers is quite different from the census measure. If a sufficiently long time series on persons with cash income plus in-kind transfers below the poverty line were available, we could have experimented with regressions like those in table A.1, using the log of the adjusted poverty rate as the dependent variable and real cash plus in-kind transfers per household as an independent variable. However, as column 6 of table 1 shows, we only have seven observations on in-kind poverty.[8]

With this limited amount of data, we estimated the following equation which allows increased in-kind transfers per household (INKIND) to reduce the gap between the log of in-kind poverty (IKPOV) and the log of official poverty (OFFPOV):

$$\log \text{IKPOV} - \log \text{OFFPOV} = -1.55 - .18 \log \text{INKIND}$$
$$(2.3)$$

$$\text{Adj } R^2 = .46$$

As expected, inclusion of in-kind transfers further increases the importance of increased transfers as a source of poverty reduction.

In sum, we conclude that previous estimates from time-series regressions of the relative importance of growth and transfers in reducing poverty should be viewed with a great deal of skepticism. Running such regressions with highly collinear series is a futile exercise if one is interested in understanding the relationship between economic growth, increased transfers, and poverty reduction.

Projecting Poverty. While the collinearity makes it very difficult to obtain reliable estimates for individual coefficients, the regressions, taken as a whole,

---

8. Morton Paglin, *Poverty and Transfer In-Kind* (Stanford, Calif: Hoover Institution Press, 1980) derived a longer time series. Timothy Smeeding, "Book Review of *Poverty and Transfers In-Kind*," *Journal of Economic Literature*, vol. 20, 1982, pp. 634–636, suggests that Paglin's study overstates the decline in poverty over time. He questions the technical merit and accuracy of Paglin's series on the following grounds. First, because Paglin did not use microeconomic data, he cannot account for differences in in-kind transfers by, for example, family size or age of head, and he must rely on exogenous estimates of the percentage of transfers actually received by the poor. Second, his estimates of multiple benefit recipiency were not from a nationwide study. We were surprised to find that the Paglin series shows a continuous decline in poverty from 1959–1975. For example, during the 1974–1975 recession, official poverty increased from 11.2 to 12.3, whereas the Paglin series declined from 3.8 to 3.6 percent.

Our doubts about the accuracy of the Paglin series were reinforced after we estimated equations like those in table A.1 using his poverty series as the dependent variable. For example, the sign on real GNP per household implies that increases in GNP significantly increase poverty.

do provide relatively stable projections of poverty. The high R^2s in all of the specifications indicate that projections will be reliable as long as the patterns of collinearity are similar over the projection and estimation periods. If this is the case, it will not matter very much which specification is chosen.

Also, projecting within the survey period allows us to identify unusual changes in poverty that are inconsistent with the estimated effects of the combined changes in transfers, cyclical conditions, and growth. For example, one might ask whether the large observed rise in poverty between 1979 and 1982 reflected anything more than the combined effects of the rise in unemployment, decline in GNP, and decrease in transfers in those years.

To answer this question, we reestimated all the regressions in tables A.1 and A.2 for the period through 1979. The resulting coefficients were used to generate projections, adjusted for autocorrelation, for 1980 through 1982. These are shown in the first three rows of the bottom panel of tables A.1 and A.2. Looking across the columns reveals that these projections are not very sensitive to the specification.

In virtually all cases the equations badly underpredict the increase in poverty that actually occurred in 1980 and 1981. This is particularly true for the regressions for 1949–1979. Only the equation in column 1 of table A.1 comes close to matching the actual 1980, 1981, and 1982 rates of 13, 14, and 15 percent, respectively. Other factors were clearly driving poverty up. While we cannot identify why these years are outliers, they do point to the need to look for additional factors.

The second potential use of these time-series regressions is to make conditional forecasts of poverty.[9] These projections are conditional not only on the projected values of the independent variables, but also on the stability of the underlying structural relationships. As we have seen, the latter assumption may not have been warranted in recent years.

The bottom rows of tables A.1 and A.2 show projections of poverty for the years 1983 through 1985. They are based on the Office of Management and Budget's official July 1983 economic forecast of GNP, prices, and unemployment found in its "Mid-Session Review," and projections of transfers

---

9. Barry Chiswick and Michael McCarthy, "A Note on Predicting the Poverty Rate," *Journal of Human Resources*, vol. 12 (1977), pp. 396–400, point out that the official poverty measure for a given year is not available from the Census Bureau until the middle of the following year. Thus, even if the projections are subject to the problems mentioned, they are timely.

found in the fiscal year 1984 budget.[10] Equations are estimated through 1982 and the projections are adjusted for autocorrelation. Comparing projections across the columns shows that they are not very sensitive to the functional form chosen if one projects only two years forward.

---

10. Median family income and the number of households are not included in any official forecasts and thus must be estimated for use in our 1983–1985 projections. The log of the number of households was projected using a quadratic in time. The log of real median family income was projected using the projected log of the number of households and the official projections of real GNP.

COMMENTS

June A. O'Neill

The paper by Gottschalk and Danziger attempts to assess the relative importance of economic growth and government transfers in explaining the incidence of poverty. They use several methodologies: standard time-series analysis, a more complex decomposition analysis, and a simulation. Their results indicate that both increases in earned incomes and increases in transfer incomes reduce poverty, and that the extent to which each reduces poverty varies according to the initial dependence of the poor on transfers.

I will first discuss some details of the authors' analyses, and I will then address some issues that are only passingly addressed by Gottschalk and Danziger.

Defining Economic Growth

Since economic growth is central to the discussion, how it is measured is an important consideration. Gottschalk and Danziger use different measures at different times: GNP per household, median family income, and the ratio of household income to needs (where needs are measured by the poverty level). The problem with each of these measures is that they capture more than economic growth, which should be an exogenous factor. GNP per household reflects voluntary decisions about household living arrangements which are themselves influenced by rising incomes.[1] Median family income is influenced by both voluntary and involuntary decisions about work as well as

---

1. A growing literature has noted the effect of income on living arrangements. See Robert T. Michael, Victor R. Fuchs, and Sharon R. Scott, "Changes in the Propensity to Live Alone: 1950–1976," *Demography*, vol. 17, no. 1 (February 1980), pp. 39–56; Douglas A. Wolf, "Kin Availability and the Living Arrangements of Older Women," *Social Science Research*, in press and "Changes in Household Size and Composition due to Financial Incentives," *Journal of Human Resources*, vol. 19, no. 1 (Winter 1984), pp. 87–103.

by transfers. Household income relative to needs is affected by these same factors as well as by variation in family size. If economic growth is to be interpreted as productivity, which I believe it should be, then a preferable measure of economic growth would be output per hour of work, or real hourly earnings adjusted for compositional changes.

Time-Series Regressions

The habit of many economic variables to increase over time and, therefore, to be correlated with each other is always a problem in time-series analysis. Gottschalk and Danziger are forthright in showing how their results shift and even reverse when the variables are measured in different ways. Multicollinearity aside, I do think that time-series analysis can be better used to identify the factors affecting the poverty rate. The following explanatory variables ought to be considered. The real hourly wage rate and the dispersion in the wage rate could be used to determine the effect of economic growth on earning opportunities. The unemployment rate would then capture cyclical variation in the opportunity for hours of work. Here I think it would be better to use a pure cyclical variable—such as the unemployment rate of married men or of all men aged 30 to 44—rather than the unemployment rate of the total labor force as the authors do. The total unemployment rate is less useful because it captures the trend effects of increasing turnover in the labor force as teenagers and women comprised a growing share of the labor force.

The propensity of the public to transfer income to the poor is likely to be a function of income.[2] This may be worth testing in a time-series analysis where transfer payments are the dependent variable.

The Decomposition Analysis

By decomposing the change in poverty rates into market income and transfer income (both expressed relative to needs) and by providing separate information on the contribution of the change in the mean values as well as the dispersion, the authors provide some new and useful information. But many crucial questions remain. Do market incomes grow more or less slowly and affect poverty differently in the various periods because of productivity, because of particular demand factors affecting low-skilled workers, or because of voluntary choices about hours of work? Moreover, to what extent are hours

---

2. There is some evidence of this. See Larry L. Orr, "Income Transfers as a Public Good: An Application for AFDC," *American Economic Review*, June 1976.

of work influenced by transfers or economic growth? Since income and poverty are measured relative to needs, demographic factors—the birth rate and family formation and dissolution—are important, and these demographic factors are themselves likely influenced by transfers and by economic growth. The analysis, therefore, helps to identify the immediate route into poverty, but it doesn't go far enough below the surface.

Future Growth and Poverty

Gottschalk and Danziger focus on the years 1967–1981, which is a period of slowdown in the rate of productivity change combined with two sharp cyclical dips. Although cash transfers grew relative to income up to the mid-1970s, they leveled off thereafter. Thus, it is not hard to understand the failure of poverty to decline during much of the period. The long-term prospect for reducing poverty below current levels depends on several factors that are hard to predict. The leading factor, of course, is economic growth, without which market earnings do not rise and transfers cannot be readily increased. Assuming, then, that growth rates improve, what is the likelihood of reducing poverty? Gottschalk and Danziger suggest that, among the poor, only households headed by nonaged males are likely to benefit from growth; since these households comprise a rather small segment of the poor population, the authors conclude that economic growth alone will not do much to reduce poverty. Whether this view is correct or not depends to a large extent on how economic growth affects poor households headed by nonaged women—a group that now makes up about 40 percent of all poor households. (Gottschalk and Danziger unfortunately include little analysis for this group because of difficulties in accommodating their model to the income distribution of this population.) The poverty rate of families headed by women has declined over time—from 43 percent in 1959 to 30 percent in 1979, rising during the recession to 35 percent in 1981. Poverty within this group, however, depends sharply on work status. In 1981 the poverty rate of women heading families was 55 percent if the woman did not work at all during the year (somewhat higher even than the rate in 1959!) and 7 percent if she worked full time year-round. A substantial portion of those who do not work are supported by welfare; thus the persistence of high poverty rates for this group is in part related to the decline in real cash benefits. But the percentage of women who do not work heading families has declined.

One can speculate about a number of possibilities. Recent changes have undoubtedly reduced the attractiveness of welfare. Economic growth would raise prospective earnings unless it was accompanied by a shift in demand away from low-skilled workers. On these grounds I would predict that sustained economic growth would encourage more females heading families to work. More speculative are the possible effects of economic growth on family formation and fertility. Rising incomes of prospective husbands could conceivably encourage more marriage and remarriage, thereby reducing the number of female-headed families. In sum, it would be imprudent to assume that economic growth cannot affect poverty because it cannot affect female-headed families.

THE SOCIAL POLICY OF THE REAGAN ADMINISTRATION

Nathan Glazer

We are a nation of assessors—even when the time for assessment is not yet ripe, and the facts on which we must base an assessment are not yet available. Yet the enormous impact of what I would call the first avowedly *ideological* administration in this century—to go no further back—makes an early assessment inevitable. The Reagan administration is something new on the American scene. Indeed, two major programs to assess the new administration's domestic social policy were launched as Reagan came into office. These are the Urban Institute's Changing Domestic Priorities project and Princeton University's Urban and Regional Research Center analysis. We also have the Brookings Institution's ongoing analyses of federal budgets in its annual *Setting National Priorities* (SNP) volumes.[1]

The published works of these enterprises deal almost entirely with governmental *intentions*, which have been only partially realized, and have been distorted by economic crisis, political realities, fiscal pressures, interest group resistance, and the like. We have detailed analyses now of the proposed

---

1. John L. Palmer and Isabel V. Sawhill, eds., *The Reagan Experiment* (Washington, D.C.: Urban Institute, 1982); referred to hereafter as *TRE*.

John William Ellwood, ed., *Reductions in U.S. Domestic Spending* (New Brunswick, N.J.: Transaction Books, 1982); referred to hereafter as *RUSDS*.

Joseph A. Pechman, ed., *Setting National Priorities: The 1983 Budget*, and *Setting National Priorities: The 1984 Budget* (Washington, D.C.: Brookings Institution, 1982 and 1983); referred to hereafter as *SNP 1983* and *SNP 1984*.

Another study of the Reagan administration came to hand after I completed this paper: Fred I. Greenstein, ed., *The Reagan Presidency: An Early Assessment* (Baltimore: Johns Hopkins University Press, 1983). My conclusions are very similar to those in the chapters by Richard P. Nathan, "The Reagan Presidency in Domestic Affairs," and Hugh Heclo and Rudolph G. Penner, "Fiscal and Political Strategy in the Reagan Administration," in that volume.

budgets—and the very different enacted budget—for fiscal year 1982, but only scanty analysis yet of the budget and budget process for fiscal year 1983. Actual expenditures may be substantially different from projected expenditures, and FY 1983 is not over as of this writing. By the time the administration presented its budget proposals for FY 1984 to Congress in early 1983, the analysts' initial fascination with the impact of domestic social program cuts and changes had been transformed into almost exclusive concentration on the crisis portended by huge deficits. The contrast between SNP 1983 and SNP 1984 is striking. While the former concentrates on the probable impact of the cuts in social programs in the 1982 budget, the latter deals almost entirely with the budget deficit and concentrates on those domestic programs (Social Security and Medicare) and tax policies that contribute heavily to the deficit. Thus, the analysis of the actual impact of the new administration's modest cuts in FY 1981 and major cuts in FY 1982 is still in a preliminary stage, though the new volume from the Princeton program is of great help.[2]

The problems of domestic social policy, initially overshadowed by the fear of inflation, are now, after a brief moment of prominence, being overwhelmed by the problem of budget deficits—and its threat of renewed inflation and the early strangling of economic revival. But we propose to ignore the problems of inflation and budget deficits in order to concentrate on the neglected issue of social policy per se. What has happened to the social policy that was initiated in the administration of John F. Kennedy and achieved brilliant successes in the first years of the administration of Lyndon Johnson? It was scarcely checked in the administrations of Richard Nixon and Gerald Ford as Congress enacted new programs and beefed up old ones. That social policy was sustained through the administration of Jimmy Carter and was expected to receive a decisive reversal in the administration of Ronald Reagan. Did it happen?

Initial Intentions

The Reagan administration came to office with a program having no resemblance to what had been considered for decades the necessities of Amer-

---

2. See Richard P. Nathan, Fred C. Doolittle, and associates, *The Consequences of Cuts: The Effects of the Reagan Domestic Program on State and Local Governments* (Princeton: Princeton University, Urban and Regional Research Center, 1983); and Richard P. Nathan *et al.*, "Initial Effects of the Fiscal Year 1982 Reductions in Federal Domestic Spending," in Ellwood, *RUSDS*; and Richard P. Nathan, "Retrenchment Comes to Washington," *Society*, vol. 20, no. 2, (January/February 1983), pp. 45–48.

ican domestic policy. It promised only that it would do nothing to affect Social Security benefits. Beyond that, it committed itself to reverse the course in social policy that had been set for almost twenty years. Admittedly the constancy of the course was less the result of presidential leadership than of the insistence of Congress, often dragging along a reluctant president. But in any case, large gaps in the American welfare state had been filled and the newer mandate of generalized risk-protection through new regulatory agencies afoot in the late 1960s was completed.

The Reagan administration campaigned not only against big government, big taxes, and big expenditures, but, more or less specifically, against the innovations in social policy that had characterized the preceding two decades. The only beneficiary group not in jeopardy was the aged. Everyone else was put on notice: the poor, blacks, Hispanic Americans, the handicapped, college students, and even the beneficiaries of strong environmental and consumer protection. None of these groups could be in doubt as to where the new administration would stand if elected. And sure enough the administration has tried to fulfill its promises.

Its proposed actions did not simply reflect annoyance with governmental intervention and high taxes but rested on fairly coherent ideological themes. The ideology attacked governmental inefficiency and the ineffectiveness of government programs, but its underlying force was a vision of how societies grow economically and what makes them strong. Individual action, unhampered by government, spurs an economy. Special consideration for the poor undermines the incentives that should encourage them to work. Government should get out of the way so that people can take care of themselves and, in so doing, can contribute to the economic strength of a society.

The Reagan administration seized upon supply-side economics as a more sophisticated rationale for what was basically a simple view of human nature and of society: Tax cuts would restore individual and corporate initiative; the resulting flood of increased economic activity would reduce inflation, take care of the poor, eliminate racial discrimination, reduce the deficit, and provide the funds for a huge national defense buildup.

An ideology can also be defined by what it does not believe. The Reagan ideology did not have confidence in the capacity of a central human wisdom, expressed in government, to plan for and manage the economy and to arrange the problems of the poor and the unfortunates of a complex industrial society. Admittedly, no ideology can escape the reality that the government is now held responsible and has been, at least since the Great Depression, for the general state of the economy. But the Reagan ideology, opposing Keynesian fine tuning and social engineering, promised to strike out on a new course. The government would recognize its limitations in dealing with the economic and social problems of a complex society and would place greater reliance on the initiatives of private philanthropy, local government, and the states. A commitment to the Federalism of the original Constitution buttressed various other grounds for reducing the role of the federal government in social policy. It was symbolic that the Reagan administration, in its ideological fervor, planned to eliminate both the education and energy departments.

So much was intended, so much was expected, so much was feared. What then ensued? Are we in the midst of a counterrevolution in social policy—one taking us backward, rather than forward? If so, how far back, and with what degree of permanence?

The Scale of Change

The ideology was so clear; the reality is so complex. It is much easier to analyze the administration's intentions than its effects. To assess its significance is even more difficult. It may be premature to assess the Reagan administration's social policy reforms. But in view of the increasing difficulties further changes will meet—as the élan of the electoral victory fades, as Congress becomes increasingly independent, as the various groups affected by the social policy revolution regroup and fight back—it may not be too soon after all. Perhaps most of what will happen has already happened. The big change was that signaled by the FY 1982 budget and the legerdemain of the Omnibus Budget Reconciliation Act (OBRA) of 1981. No subsequent change will be as great. (Even the last revolutionary burst in social policy, that of Johnson's Great Society, saw all its major legislation passed in a surprising two years.) The FY 1983 budget did not much advance the ideology and program of the Reagan administration; that of 1984, however it turns out, will do less.[3]

First, let me state that less has happened in the realm of social policy than the amount of anger, resistance, agonizing, and newspaper reportage suggests. There *have* been reductions in some key programs, particularly if measured against the size they might otherwise have attained in a severe recession. Undoubtedly distress has risen substantially, but this is probably

---

3. A review of the findings of the Princeton University study, which covers fiscal year 1982, suggests that study encompasses most of the change we are likely to see: "Congress has since been unwilling to give Mr. Reagan new cuts he has asked for, and the change from 1981 to 1982 is expected to remain as the domestic high-water mark of his current term." Quoted from John Herbers, "Study Tells How 14 States Countered U.S. Aid Cuts," *New York Times*, 8 May 1983.

more the result of the recession from which we are now exiting than of substantial social policy changes. It is difficult to document scale of change, especially when one does not know what baseline to measure it against. But various authorities who have examined the substantial cuts and social policy changes summed up in the 1981 OBRA agree the overall change was not very large.

SNP 1983 asserts that the FY 1982 budget (the only year in which the Reagan administration was able to get Congress to accept most of what it wanted) reduced total outlays by only $27.1 billion—hardly enormous in a budget of $725 billion.[4] Ellwood gives a somewhat larger estimate: He reports that the Congressional Budget Office estimated cuts of $35.2 billion in outlays, and even more in budget authority. Richard Nathan, in the same volume, thinks this is too high: "Estimates of the total reductions in the 212 federal budget accounts affected by the Reconciliation Act range from a high of . . . 33 billion in outlays to a low of . . . 15 billion. . . ." But Nathan concludes that "estimates in the lower range should be used in assessing the outlay cuts of 1982" because public officials have a strong tendency to overstate the size of the cuts—conservatives to demonstrate they are really carrying out their program, liberals to build up public support against further cuts.[5]

Palmer and Mills stand closer to *SNP 1983*: They estimate reduced outlays for nondefense programs of $31.6 billion, 6.4 percent of their baseline expenditures for 1982 (rising to $54.8 billion or 8.2 percent of the baseline expenditure for 1986).[6]

Where Change Occurred

In one sense, all these estimates understate the cuts, insofar as they take as a base all nondefense expenditures. Most nondefense expenditures were almost impossible to reduce, primarily for political reasons. Social Security, for example, was sacrosanct. Proposals that were obviously necessary to reduce the growth of Social Security expenditures—which had greatly exceeded growth in wages and were tied to an unrealistic cost-of-living measure—met total resistance from Congress, Democrats and Republicans alike. The huge Medicare expenditures were also very difficult to reduce. Here the problem was not so much massive political resistance as it was the difficulty

---

4. Pechman, ed., *SNP 1983*, p. 25.
5. Ellwood, ed., *RUSDS*, pp. 24 and 320.
6. John Palmer and Gregory B. Mills, "Budget Policy," in Palmer and Sawhill, eds., *TRE*, p. 78.

of reducing expenses without threatening the quality of health care. Pensions for civil servants and the military were as sacrosanct as Social Security pensions. So the reductions, perhaps a modest 4 percent of the total budget, could rise to a striking percentage of the parts of the budget that were considered negotiable. These relatively small cuts amounted to very substantial percentages of some programs and, as it turned out, those programs most focused on the poor. While Aid to Families with Dependent Children (AFDC), Food Stamps, and Medicaid might appear to be entitlements of the same order as Social Security or Medicare, the latter are based on taxes and contributions that are specifically designated for them. The public considers Social Security and Medicaid as insurance one buys (and therefore is entitled to), whereas the entitlements focused on the poor are not seen as such. Thus a common sense of justice, as well as simple political reality—the fact that far more people benefit from Social Security than from welfare, far more receive Medicare than Medicaid, and those who get the insurance-type entitlements participate more actively in politics and carry more political weight than the poor—combined to focus the cuts on benefits to the poor.

All told, the cuts were not massive, particularly since cuts in some programs showed up as unexpected increases in others. Moreover, many of the program cuts had been proposed by previous (including Democratic) administrations. Indeed, the growth of entitlement programs and of grants to states and localities had already received some check under the Carter administration.[7] Under the élan of the Reagan victory, a stunned Congress enacted changes that previous administrations wished for but could not bring about. The restructurings and reductions were only possible because they had already been previously considered by the Office of Management and Budget or in the agencies. Many of these cuts, then, could be attributed in part to ongoing efforts to streamline government and make it more efficient, an effort that goes on without great success under *all* administrations. Palmer and Sawhill offer an interesting evaluation of the kinds of cuts that were made (and those proposed but not made):

> Some of the program changes proposed by the Reagan administration have long-standing antecedents and were widely considered meritorious. Several had been advocated by earlier administrations, usually for reasons that went beyond simple budgetary considerations. Examples are reductions in the guaranteed student loan subsidy and support for physician education, reduced reliance on new construction in housing assistance programs, and the scaling back of public service employment.

---

7. See Table 2 in Greenstein, ed., *Reagan Presidency*, p. 59; and Table 2 in Benjamin A. Okner and D. Lee Bawden, "Recent Changes in Federal Income Redistribution Policy," *National Tax Journal*, vol. 36, no. 3 (September 1983), p. 349.

Other proposals, though representing a more marked departure from past presidential policies, were fully developed prior to the Reagan administration and had considerable bipartisan support. Examples are the reduction of direct federal housing finance operations and greater user fees for transportation services.

Several measures reduced or eliminated programs that many policy makers and analysts had criticized as being of dubious effectiveness, although such cutbacks had not been proposed by previous administrations. Examples include the Professional Standards Review Organizations (PSROs) and certificates-of-need programs in health, trade adjustment assistance, and several small regional economic programs.

On the other hand, Palmer and Sawhill assert that programs with a record of success or strong promise of success were also scheduled for severe cuts—for example, immunization grants; the Job Corps; the special supplementary feeding program for low-income pregnant women, infants, and children (WIC); compensatory education for disadvantaged children; and the new child welfare services program. And "other programs were prepared for broad cuts where trimming and restructuring were needed. Examples are the large Social Security benefit cuts for early and new retirees and the cap on federal Medicaid grants to states (both rejected by Congress) . . . and across-the-board reductions in CETA training programs. . . ."

Some of the program changes were called "gambles that could jeopardize stated purposes:" namely, reductions in income-related benefit payments, which will be analyzed further below.

Finally, they emphasize that poverty and social problems, because of their unequal distribution geographically, *do* require a federal involvement.[8]

To many, this will seem an overly benign evaluation of the program cuts. Yet many of the Reagan proposals were those of previous administrations. Moreover, both an increase in defense spending and a decrease in the personal income tax rate were already in the cards. The increase in the defense budget was already underway during the Carter administration. To quote Palmer and Sawhill again: "The ratio of federal taxes to GNP had crept up [in the years before 1981]. Another in the series of periodic tax cuts was clearly in order for the early 1980s, but it would have to be accompanied by greater spending restraint if it were not to result in a continued upward drift in the federal tax burden or high risk of large deficits. It was also evident that the burden of any such spending restraint would have to fall primarily on nondefense spending, since Congress (and the Carter administration) had recently initiated a program of real defense growth planned to be sustained well into the 1980s."[9]

---

8. Palmer and Sawhill, eds., *TRE*, pp. 17–19.
9. Ibid., p. 67.

Of course this says nothing about the scale of the tax cuts or about the rate of military buildup. Much criticism of the ominous budget deficits has concentrated on these two features. The Brookings analysts show a moderate rate of increase in real spending for defense, an increase between 1979 and 1985 (a period covering part of the Carter administration) of about 0.3 percent of GNP a year, with a bigger bump (0.5 percent) for 1982. These figures are from *SNP 1983*, based on the FY 1983 budget. *SNP 1984* shows a slightly higher rate of increase in defense spending as a percentage of GNP, but a slightly slower rate of increase as a percentage of total budget outlays. Between the projections in *SNP 1983* and *SNP 1984*, the rate of growth of the economy slowed, and expectations that the budget would go down as a percentage of GNP were revised.[10] Moreover, the tax cuts passed by Congress in 1981 went beyond administration proposals.

The Eclipse of Social Engineering

One of the most striking elements of Reagan's social policy was his rejection of *social engineering*, the idea that incentives and disincentives and sharply focused programs can be used to affect human behavior and improve the human condition. This had been a dominant ideology of the 1960s and 1970s; but it was decisively rejected by the Reagan administration.

A number of the Reagan administration's significant program reductions demonstrate this rejection of social engineering. Perhaps the most striking is the Reagan administration's rejection of what Leslie Lenkowsky calls the incentive approach to welfare. Economists and sociologists had theorized that by modifying incentives leading to family breakups and to reduction of work effort, enlightened social policy could bring forth socially desirable behavior without resort to direct prohibitions and requirements. This approach assumed that a high implicit tax on earnings of welfare recipients (imposed by reducing welfare benefits in accordance with earnings) reduced their incentive to work. It further assumed that a program aimed at income maintenance for mothers and their children rather than complete families reduced incentives for fathers to stay with their families and help support them. Therefore it lauded any change in the system towards more uniform support of working *and* non-working poor families, those with *and* without the father present. These were the underlying bases of the welfare reforms proposed by the Nixon and Carter administrations, and they were rarely challenged. What was challenged was

---

10. Pechman, ed., *SNP 1983*, p. 31; *SNP 1984*, p. 204.

whether sufficiently strong incentives could ever be enacted; few doubted that positive effects would follow such a reform.[11]

While AFDC is by no means the largest social program, and indeed compared with Social Security and Medicare it is minor (even the Food Stamp and Medicaid programs are larger), it has always been considered a key program in social policy. It is *the* major program providing aid to the destitute, it benefits a substantial proportion of the black population (more than a fifth), it is the major means of support of large segments of the population of many large cities, it includes a particularly high proportion of children, and it raises in the sharpest form the fears that many Americans will not be integrated into work and family life and will pass on their dependency to their children. This program, costing $8 billion in federal money, and similar amounts from state and local sources, has received more attention and analysis than any other program of its size.

The Reagan administration scrapped all of this analysis. Welfare dependency would be reduced by reverting to an almost primeval concept in social policy: It would become basic charity, providing limited benefits and administered sufficiently harshly that people who could work would be happy to get off welfare and would try to stay off welfare even if working did not provide more income than welfare.

Welfare: From Incentives to Norms

The Reagan administration practiced what it preached in its strongly criticized changes in the treatment of earnings of welfare recipients that were incorporated into OBRA of 1981. For a long time, the first $30 of earnings and one-third of the remaining amount was deductible in determining eligibility for AFDC. OBRA allowed these amounts to be disregarded only during the first four months of employment. It also placed a cap on the work expenses that could be deducted in calculating income and need—for child care, $160 per child per month; for work expenses, $75 per month. It also limited the total income any family could receive and still qualify for welfare.[12] Without question, these changes reduce the incentive to work while on welfare, which is why they were so fiercely attacked. Many argued that working welfare recipients would quit their jobs to stay on welfare.

---

11. For a fuller account of this attempt at reform, its underlying rationale, and ultimate rejection, see Nathan Glazer, "Reforming the American Welfare Family, 1969-1981," *The Tocqueville Review*, forthcoming.

12. These and other changes in AFDC are from Ellwood, ed., *RUSDS*, pp. 300–302.

I should like to make three observations at this point. First, substantial incentives to work had already been incorporated into welfare, making it very difficult to design an incentive-based, negative-income-tax welfare reform. Someone on welfare *and* also working, even for a low wage, could almost always make more than someone who was working for the minimum wage and not on welfare. If need (as assessed by number of children) was great, income from work and welfare benefits could be far higher than income from minimum-wage work alone. This raised the cost of any negative-income-tax program to a point where it was fiscally unacceptable. Furthermore, one objective of negative-income-tax welfare reform was to reduce the stigma associated with welfare. But the proposed reforms made many people fearful that the dependent poor would not be incorporated into the working world, but that rather the working poor would incorporate themselves into the welfare world. Under the Reagan reforms, welfare recipients can still work, but more of the work income is taken into account in determining benefits.

Second, some who favored a high minimum welfare benefit argued that since the poor wanted to work, their behavior in seeking work would not be affected by increasing the minimum support level. The Reagan administration turned this argument on its head: Insofar as the poor wanted to work, they would not reduce their work effort even if their welfare payments were more sharply affected by work earnings. In any event, preliminary research did not substantiate a rush by welfare recipients to leave their jobs so as not to lose their benefits. Thus, the Nathan study of the response of states and localities to budget cuts finds "the return rate for families removed from the welfare rolls due to the Reagan changes so far has been low—about 10 percent on average. This estimate is based on information from those states and local jurisdictions that had conducted studies covering the first six months to one year of experience under the new policies."[13] And a widely noted study by the Research Triangle Institute, which compared the behavior of welfare recipients leaving the welfare rolls before and after the Reagan changes, did not uncover a rush to return to welfare after the changes.[14]

Third, all the incentives that had been built into the welfare system to encourage work were not very effective anyway. This may have been owing to the incapacity of most adults on welfare (women with limited education) to work, the limited number of jobs, or the simple fact that for mothers

    13. Nathan in Greenstein, ed., *Reagan Presidency*, p. 62.
    14. I am indebted to Wendell E. Primus, staff member of the U.S. Congress, House Ways and Means Committee, for a summary and analysis of the Research Triangle study. For press coverage of the study, see Robert Pear, "Most of Those Taken off Welfare Are Said Not to Leave Their Jobs," *New York Times*, 29 April 1983; and Burt Schorr, "Study of Welfare Indicates Success of New U.S. Rules," *Wall Street Journal*, 2 May 1983.

without great prospects of earning much from work, welfare was preferable to work. But in those states with the most generous incentives to work, such as New York, few adults on welfare worked; in those states most niggardly in this respect, more people worked. Perhaps people worked because they *felt* they should and saw work income as a desirable substitute for welfare, rather than a reward for trying harder.

One other change in the treatment of earned income under OBRA should be mentioned. Low-income families had been eligible for some years for an Earned Income Tax Credit (EITC) or rebate if they worked. Now this tax credit must be taken into account in determining welfare eligibility, whether families apply for it or not. The tax credit reduces the welfare payment, but only by the amount of the credit. This should lead all who are eligible to apply for the tax credit. As a side benefit, it will encourage low-income welfare families to file income tax returns. It may also educate them to the fact that the federal government will do something *more* for those who work, which is a subtly different message from "we will not reduce your welfare payment if you work." One assumes that work is the norm, the second that welfare is the norm.[15]

Various other changes introduced into the welfare system indicate in which direction the administration was moving and how it was implementing its ideology. For example, part of a stepparent's income must now be considered as income available for support of stepchildren who receive AFDC benefits. Under previous law, as interpreted by the Supreme Court, a woman could live with a man who was not the father of her children, without that man taking responsibility for the support of her children. This may have encouraged women to take up with other men and encouraged men to live with women whose children they would not be held responsible for supporting. If limiting family breakup was one objective of welfare policy, here was one possible approach. But the Reagan administration was not trying to provide an incentive for family stability. Rather, it wished to promote stability by imposing a norm: that a man living with a woman and her children had an obligation to support the woman with whom he lived as husband, and the children with whom he lived as father.

Many social workers might argue that imposing a traditional norm is no way of getting traditional behavior: Making men liable for support might keep them from moving in, creating *more* female-headed families, not fewer. No matter. Reagan had consciously abandoned the incentive-based approach in

---

15. This interesting proposal was reportedly "on the shelf" before Reagan ever took office. Undoubtedly other proposals discussed in this article had also been around for some time. The point is that the Reagan administration dusted them off and *adopted* them.

favor of moralism or traditionalism: Men *should* contribute to the support of mothers and children with whom they live, whether or not they have an economic incentive to do so.

One final change deserves notice. Women with no previous children were made ineligible for welfare benefits until their sixth month of pregnancy. One of the presumed scandals of welfare is that girls are treated as women, with their own welfare grants, as soon as they become pregnant. Teenagers can thus achieve financial independence by becoming pregnant. The Reagan modification increases—admittedly by only a few months—the period during which a parent can exercise financial control over a child.

The various changes probably generated only modest savings to the federal government. But they indicate a direction—away from the social engineering of welfare recipients through a subtle pattern of economic incentives, and toward the simple insistence that the only purpose of welfare was to take care of the destitute. If welfare recipients worked, it would be because they should, not because the government offered them a reward for working that was not available to other low-income workers. The traditional incentives, to work and support one's family, were now assumed rather than paid for.

The Withdrawal from Education and Urban Policy

Other examples of Reagan's abandonment of social engineering can be cited. Twenty-nine educational programs were consolidated into a single block grant. While many of these programs were pet projects of various congressmen, others, such as the important grants under the Emergency School-Aid Act (ESAA), represented the social engineering approach. They targeted money to deal with a complex social problem in specified ways, with an underlying assumption that the federal government knew better how to deal with it than local officials. ESAA grants, for example, were supposed to help local school districts deal with the problems of desegregation—another of the difficult social problems the federal government proposed to solve with well-targeted money. By bundling twenty-nine federal programs having various origins and purposes into one program for states, the Reagan administration showed again that it rejected the belief it knew how to solve problems better than the local governments.[16]

---

16. Pechman, ed., *RUSDS*, pp. 196–198.

A third area in which the Reagan administration moved toward the abandonment of social engineering has been in housing and community development. The Reagan administration does not even speak of an urban policy—much less public housing projects, poverty programs, and model cities. It does not claim to know how to help the trouble-ridden older cities (and its dependence on free-market mechanisms suggests it wouldn't try even if it knew how). Reagan's major initiative in this area is likely to be a housing voucher plan under which the poor would find their own housing. Rather than subsidizing vast new housing developments for the poor, housing vouchers would be used to help pay for existing housing.

Each of the areas we have discussed is enormously complicated. (The reader is directed to the relevant chapters in *The Reagan Experiment*, which is still the best guide to the Reagan administration's intentions and budgetary and legislative changes in social policy.) But their overall thrust is clear. Under Reagan, the federal government has given up the effort to "do better." And it has given up the effort to complete the pattern of government services in a developed welfare state that was so marked a feature of the 1960s and 1970s. If there are gaps in the American welfare state, the administration seems to be saying, so be it. The government already does more than it should, more than any administration can dismantle; this administration will only be responsible for providing a social safety net to deal with the most serious cases of distress. This government accepts no responsibility for income redistribution. Quite the contrary, its tax cuts and other measures show a commitment to individualism and individual economic freedom, not to any concern for the poor and economic equality. When pressed, administration spokesmen claim that general economic prosperity will help the poor more than any program addressed directly to them and their needs. No one claims that it will produce more equality.

Ironically, the biggest hole in the American system of social policy— the absence of a system of medical insurance for the unemployed who are neither old nor poor—may get partially plugged because the high unemployment rate resulting from Reagan's policies showed how gaping the hole is. By lowering the income limits under which poor people can qualify for welfare—and Medicaid—the gap has been further spotlighted. Indeed, the desire to avoid losing Medicaid benefits may be a greater work disincentive than the desire for money benefits from welfare itself. Certainly, the loss of health benefits associated with jobs can be disastrous. Something may finally be done to fill part of this gaping hole in our health insurance system, although the Reagan administration would do so reluctantly.[17]

The Significance of Federalism

Another ideological theme that is strongly evident in the Reagan administration's social policy involves returning programs to the states and restricting federal controls. The Nixon administration also sounded this theme and proposed many block grants, some of which were enacted. The Reagan administration has been more successful, though hardly as successful as it wishes.

Many welfare advocates think this has the further effect of hurting the black and the poor. They prefer federal controls on social programs, which they believe they can better influence than state controls. Yet close federal control over welfare in the past has not prevented huge disparities between states in benefits, coverage, and regulations. This is true for education, housing, and other social programs as well.

Even after a period of enormous growth of the federal power, ours is still a federal (decentralized) system, with more of our taxes raised by state and local authorities than in any other developed industrial nation. Unquestionably, Reagan's new federalism will focus more attention on the states, requiring interest groups to build new connections with state legislators. But in a large and heterogeneous country, with varied ethnic and racial groups, striking regional differences, and different codes of morality dominant in different areas, a substantial degree of power should remain with the states and cities.

The major contemporary argument against the power of states built into the Constitution is that certain social problems must be dealt with at the national level. For example, if one section of the country is burdened with poverty and with limited resources, it cannot effectively deal with poverty on its own without transfers from wealthier parts of the country. This economic argument for "nationalizing" the problem of poverty, or welfare, or elementary education is in principle a good one. Historically, however, the federal government has intervened on sectional issues primarily to free large minorities from institutionalized prejudice and discrimination. Thus, the fed-

---

17. Robert Pear, "Stockman Opposes New Health Funds for the Unemployed," *New York Times*, 28 April 1983; "Health Benefits for the Jobless: The Middle Class Cashes In," Editorial, *Regulation* (May/June 1983), pp. 7–8.

eral government intervened massively in the South through the Civil Rights Act and Voting Rights Act to gain for blacks equality in political power and in access to jobs, education, and public facilities. Without this intervention, the revolution in the position of blacks in the South in the past twenty years would not have occurred. Thus, an emphasis on states' rights not only appears to hurt the poor, but also blacks and other minorities.

I would not negate the economic and political arguments for a federal role in social programs from which the Reagan administration is withdrawing or would like to withdraw. But two factors undermine their force. First, measures of sectional poverty and wealth become increasingly ambiguous as regions draw closer to each other in wealth and income. Second, the civil rights revolution succeeded in creating a measure of minority political power that ensures minority participation in state and local decisions. Further, many regional differences are the result of regional choices. Welfare benefits are high in New York; they are low in Texas. As a result, industries seeking low-wage labor will be attracted to Texas rather than New York. But this is the result of choices by those states. Is it up to the federal government to equalize the effect of these choices by creating social programs that provide more assistance to New York than Texas?

Far more, of course, could be written for and against a federal role in alleviating poverty and providing social services. But I believe the two points made above—the growing economic equality among the states and the increasing political power of minorities—argue forcefully for a lesser federal role in equalization of income, wealth, and political power than prevailed in the 1960s and 1970s.

These developments are also relevant to the role of the Reagan administration in enforcement of the civil rights laws. Civil rights advocates insist that support of busing of school children, for example, is a key measure of commitment to equality. By this measure, the Reagan administration fails. Similarly, the Reagan administration is unsympathetic to goals and quotas as techniques for enforcing equality in economic opportunity. Undoubtedly these have had some effect in getting jobs, and better jobs, for blacks; yet the institutionalization of measures that allocate jobs and education on the basis of race and national origin raises grave issues of law and principle. The administration wavers between defending itself on principle and insisting it is doing "as much" to promote civil rights as the Carter administration. Of course, it is not doing as much if measured by lawsuits to force school busing and quotas for minority hiring. But it is not politically expedient to argue that there are bona fide reasons for not advocating such measures. And it would be politically disastrous to argue that the economic and educational level of the black population *now* has very little to do with the level of enforcement of laws against discriminatory practices.

But beyond all arguments as to when and whether the federal government should try to solve social problems, is the Reagan administration's master vision as to how societies overcome poverty. Societies and people do it on their own, and help from government is likely to do more harm that good. The fact that the blacks seem as badly off as fifteen years ago and that American education is in chaos after twenty years of major federal intervention gives a certain plausibility to the view. With its master vision, the Reagan administration will be skeptical of any argument that the federal government should act on this or that problem. Yes, poor people and poor states deserve more, it will answer, but if the government tries to provide that more it will do them no good.

This skepticism of government—as well as the desire to save money—leads the Reagan administration to encourage private philanthropy and charity as a means of dealing with the problems of the poor and with the other problems of society in areas where the federal contribution is being cut back. Encouraging more private philanthropy appears difficult since it already exists on a greater scale in the United States than anywhere else. And reducing the rate of taxation is a disincentive to give to charities since it decreases the value of the tax exemption. But charitable contributions to hospitals, universities, and social agencies existed long before income taxes provided an economic incentive to contribute. Need also induces contributions, and the cutback of federal funds has increased the needs of many institutions. The effect of the Reagan administration's policies on private giving—reducing the economic incentive, while increasing the exhortation to give—will be one of the most interesting parts of a full evaluation of the Reagan administration.[18]

The Impact on the Poor

Most of the criticism of Reagan's social policy changes have emphasized a single theme—that the cuts have fallen disproportionately on the poor. For example, Nathan concludes, "The cuts that we made in federal domestic spending in fiscal year 1982 affected poor people—especially the working poor—more than they affected the treasuries of state and local governments."[19] Palmer and Sawhill write: "The net effect of these tax and social

---

18. For an initial survey of the issues, see Lester M. Salomon and Alan J. Abramson, "The Nonprofit Sector," in Palmer and Sawhill, eds., *TRE.*

19. Pechman, ed. *RUSDS*, p. 318.

program cuts through 1984 will be to provide no significant overall change in the purchasing power of those with incomes below $15,000, modest increases for the broad middle class, and substantial gains for higher-income families. Within the bottom group those receiving benefit payments of one sort or another are likely to find themselves worse off. . . .''[20]

Even stronger quotations could be cited from *Setting National Priorities* and from thousands of newspaper columns. Other papers in this volume also reach the same conclusion.

One way of understanding why the Reagan administration's social policy has had such adverse effects on the poor is to look at who runs it. The traditional advocates of the poor simply have no role in this administration. One this basis, one can conclude that the administration's policies result from blindness to the problems of the poor, at best, or positive malice, at worse.

I have suggested an alternative view: Ideology animates the current administration, but it is an ideology that operates under constraint. Part of this ideology dictates steps that are no different, in effect, than legislating selfishness. Reagan believes the economic problems of America (including America's poor) result from an absence of sufficient savings for investment. He further believes that government cannot plan or manage productive investment as well as the private sector can. Without selfishness, he can argue for cuts that help high-income people to save and invest rather than for low-income people to consume. I would not fault the administration for its ideology, but for its lack of political courage in trying to implement measures necessary to support it. If taxes are to be cut and defense spending to be raised, huge deficits are inevitable unless nondefense expenditure is brought under control. Yet the administration has as yet achieved almost nothing in bringing under control the most rapidly growing domestic programs—Social Security, Medicare, and government and military pensions. I do not underestimate the difficulty of making any headway on these issues. Yet I believe the administration should have tried harder, rather than let the axe fall disproportionately on those programs that benefited the poor rather than the broad middle class.

Perhaps political expediency necessitates giving up on these big-ticket items, concentrating instead on those programs that are less well defended and more easily cut. In any case, this is what the administration has done. Reviewing the income security area, James R. Storey points out, "The expected outlay savings in 1984 arising from 1981 actions . . . are about 4 percent of projected income security spending under previous policies. . . .

---

20. Palmer and Sawhill, eds., *TRE* p. 21.

Nearly 60 percent occurred in low-income assistance programs, though these account for only 18 percent of income security outlays.'' Program savings as a percentage of baseline amount is 1.6 percent for OASDI and 0.8 percent for federal employee retirement and disability, as against 16.3 percent for AFDC, 18.6 percent for Food Stamps, and 34.5 percent for low-income energy assistance.[21] One can make a case for this pattern, of course; but the main defense is inevitably political. Against political realities, what can be done? I would argue that the administration should have devoted more effort to educating the public as to why Social Security and the other retirement programs simply had to be revamped. Instead, many middle-income people smugly raised the issue of the selfishness of the rich, while they selfishly resisted well-argued reductions in the rate of increase in Social Security and government and military retirement pensions or in aid to middle-class college students. Without question, their resistance was rather more effective than that of the advocates of the poor.

In a rich society with a wide array of social programs, it is hard to make a case primarily on grounds of suffering—though there has certainly been some increase.[22] The grounds I prefer to argue are (1) equity—equal sharing of pain and (2) effectiveness—cutting big programs will be far more effective in bringing the budget under control than cutting small ones. Recall that an estimated 1.6 percent reduction in OASDI produced 25.2 percent of the savings in Storey's analysis. If, then, as we all agree, the enormous deficits are a problem, the wide middle- and upper-middle-income segments of the population must be willing to accept lower benefits.

Conclusion

The Reagan administration came to power with a coherent ideology guiding its actions in social policy. It believed people were self-sufficient and

---

21. Ibid, pp. 373–375.
22. Despite ominous predictions of riots in the summer of 1982 because of program cuts, it was a relatively quiet summer. See Nathan Glazer, "The Reagan Administration and Social Policy—Is a Counterrevolution Under Way?" The Tocqueville Review, vol. IV, no. 1 (Spring-Summer 1982), pp. 118–126. I was not aware of similar predictions for summer 1983. An interesting study conducted early in the summer of 1983 in Stamford, Connecticut, showed remarkably little perception of program cuts or of actual loss of services. Nor did the poor report significantly more loss of services than the rich. Oddly enough, the respondents named Social Security and services for the elderly as areas where they thought there had been or would be a real loss of services." See G. Donald Ferree, Jr., W. Wayne Shannon, and Everett Carl Ladd, "Stamford, Connecticut Weathers Reagonomics," Public Opinion (February/March 1983).

did not need sophisticated federal government programs to deal with their problems of poverty, inadequate training for jobs, urban decline, poor education, and the like. Insofar as governmental intervention was necessary or desirable, it believed this should take place on the state and local level. Many of the needs of the poor, as well as the health, education, welfare, and cultural needs and desires of society, should be met at that level too, as well as through private philanthropy.

The Reagan administration did not, however, make a head-on assault on the idea, established in the United States as far back as the 1930s, that government had the responsibility to maintain a safety net of basic social programs to provide for the income needs of the destitute. It also stressed its complete commitment to Social Security to provide for the aged and disabled, unemployment insurance for the unemployed, and health insurance (Medicare) for the aged and destitute. Thus, the Reagan administration completely accepted the New Deal welfare state programs, as supplemented during the Johnson administration in the 1960s. Reagan was neither the Goldwater of 1964, nor the Reagan of earlier campaigns; and his victory was that of a conservatism that accepted the major characteristics of the welfare state.

The originality of the administration—and the main dispute with its opponents—lay in its conviction that the key to national wealth and income growth and relief from poverty could not be designed by government and implemented by programs keyed to specific problems. Thus, the administration attacked almost all such programs, whether through efforts to eliminate them, reduce them, or package them in general block grants. If people could manage by themselves, what need for the hundreds of federal programs directed at specific targets—whether immunization for the poor, work training for dropouts, or the decay of inner-city housing? Yet if the Reagan administration does not believe in a federal role guiding society, how does one explain its conviction that tax cuts would lead to saving, encourage investment, and the like? But this, from the Reagan administration's point of view, is what people do naturally: They see their opportunities and seize them. The only role of government is to stay out of their way—hence, the tax cuts.

But once again, I speak of *intentions*. The tax cut was envisioned as an across-the-board cut which, in a progressive tax system, would automatically benefit most the well-off and the rich. After many special interests had their say, the tax-cut wound up being both less fair and larger than anticipated. The enacted tax reduction bill was riddled with exemptions and incentives to reward the earning of income in one way rather than another. Combined with a recession and substantially increased military buildup, the result was deficits of a magnitude never before seen in peacetime, and with potentially frightening effects on the economy.

Ideological commitments were, at this point, reinforced by necessity, putting further pressure on that part of the nondefense budget that had the least political support. Inevitably, these were programs focused on the poor, even though the major causes of growth in the budget were those programs that primarily benefited the middle classes. But, in time, pressure to reduce the growth of these benefits must come.

Our nation cannot escape from the major social programs that were developed under Franklin D. Roosevelt and expanded in the years since— Social Security, unemployment insurance, some form of health insurance. Nor did the Reagan administration wish to move in on these programs. But it did philosophically oppose the programs that intervened in people's lives and were characterized by detailed planning, specific incentives, and sharply targeted expenditures on specific problems. It cut these programs, and further cuts are probably in store. Undoubtedly, a widespread disillusionment with such programs—not justified in all cases—assisted in the dismantling of a good part of the newer social policy thrusts of the 1960s and 1970s.

Even the opponents of the Reagan administration no longer support such programs in their campaign rhetoric. The day of the "laundry list"—the array of new programs for all possible problems and constituencies—seems gone, at least for a while. The programs grew, in number and scale, but the problems remained. A time of respite was due, and it has come with the Reagan administration. Perhaps our nation's confidence in its ability to understand its social problems and attack them with specially designed scalpels will return. But three years into the Reagan era, nothing suggests that that day will come soon.

COMMENTS

Henry J. Aaron

Nathan Glazer's thoughtful and thought-provoking paper might have been titled "The Reagan Revolution: Less Than Meets the Eye." Glazer points out that, measured against the totality of public spending, the Reagan administration has caused a modest dent in the trend of public spending rather than a sharp break. The political ruckus surrounding the budgets enacted in 1981 and 1982 has been magnified by the disturbance caused by high unemployment. As Glazer observes, it was further amplified by the ideological cast of the president and, even more, of his cabinet, staff, and congressional supporters.

Most of the 1981 budget program was not new, Glazer correctly notes. On the contrary, nearly all of the specific proposals were already gathering dust on OMB shelves in January 1981, after having been seriously considered or unsuccessfully advocated by previous administrations. Not even the prodigious talents of David Stockman could so swiftly have constructed such a sweeping and professionally articulated array of budget amendments had not much of the staff work already been done.

To be sure, the new administration selected from the shelf those items that fitted its ideology. It also added some new items. The common element in nearly all of the budget proposals was the simultaneous reduction of federal domestic spending and federal regulation. The theme of a sharply diminished federal role also appears in nonbudgetary initiatives that Glazer does not examine, notably in the many-faceted rollback of social regulation—in health, safety, and civil rights.

In short, Glazer reports, the Reagan administration strove mightily to redesign the skyline of federal domestic legislation created in the preceding half century, but succeeded only in knocking down a few structures and in renovating a few others. Then the forces of historic preservation banded together to block his federal bulldozer. To be sure, the leveled buildings disproportionately had sheltered the poor, blacks, and others whose needs previous administrations and Congresses had felt justified federal actions.

241

But, Glazer stresses, the Reagan administration upgraded a host of other concerns to which less weight had been attached—reduction of taxes, increases in defense spending, minimization of federal interference in business and social life—all in the name of promoting private incentives and moving decisions to states or localities or, even better, to individuals themselves. If, in the process, such federal activities as financial and legal aid and social services to the economically or socially disadvantaged had to be curtailed, so be it. These services had not in many cases worked as planned; and even if a high price had to be paid in the short run, it would be amply repaid— for all—in the not-so-long run.

The problem with Glazer's paper, as I see it, is that he has tried so hard—and successfully—to step back from the immediate fray that he has lost sight of the battle and its meaning. Furthermore, his perspective causes him to get some facts wrong.

First, the purpose of this conference (and that of his paper) is to appraise the Reagan administration, not the American political system and its functioning. The fact that the Reagan administration appears unlikely to gain approval for many more of its domestic proposals and in 1983 appears dead in the water cannot be ascribed to the modesty of its objectives. The explanation, rather, is that the majority of both parties in Congress were prepared to accept a measure of budgetary and regulatory retrenchment, but were unwilling to endorse the full Reagan agenda.

It makes no sense to characterize revolutionary goals as modest because they were thwarted. The magnitude of Reagan's budgetary agenda can be read better by analyzing the change in projected outlays between 1981 and 1988 than from a comparison of 1981 and 1983. His program calls for a 47 percent reduction in the share of GNP devoted to nondefense spending other than entitlements and interest and a 30 percent reduction in entitlements other than the so-called social contract programs. Glazer claims that the aged were the only beneficiary group not in jeopardy as a result of Reagan's campaign positions. Yet even Social Security cash benefits for the aged, survivors, and disabled would have been slashed nearly 25 percent by President Reagan's May 1981 proposals. New retirees would have suffered cuts in benefits of up to 40 percent.

To confront these intentions and to write, as Glazer does, "Less has happened, much less, in the realm of social policy than the amount of anger, resistance, agonizing, and newspaper reportage suggests" in appraising the social policy of the Reagan administration simply doesn't make much sense.

Second, Glazer's fiscal history is, to put it gently, imprecise. He recognizes that budget deficits have become public policy enemy number one, but he fails to point out that President Reagan inherited a healthy budgetary situation, a projected structural (full employment) deficit of negligible proportions for 1984. To be sure, a tax cut was overdue because of bracket creep. But, even with a $50 billion tax cut, with 5 percent annual growth in real defense outlays, and with no change in nondefense policy, a balanced structural budget was in prospect by 1986.

A fiscally responsible president, persuaded that taxes needed to be cut still more or that defense spending needed to be increased still faster, would have presented a program of specific reductions in other areas sufficient to achieve those targets or would have delayed some of the tax cuts. Instead, President Reagan proposed a list of nondefense cuts sufficient to cover about one-third of the extra tax cuts and defense spending that his program would produce by 1986 and hid the remaining deficit behind an economic forecast no one except the supply-siders believed. Some cynics suggest that the president and his advisers recognized that their policies were fiscally irresponsible and wished to use the prospect of unending deficits to keep pressure on domestic spending. Others attribute this forecast to incompetence. Perhaps someone from the administration can set us straight.

Glazer's discussion of welfare arouses conflicting emotions. He states that the administration backed away from estimates of work incentives that, he strongly implies, had never been confirmed with sufficient reliability to support the artfully calibrated programs built on them. I am inclined to agree with this judgment and have long felt that gradual changes to improve the equity of welfare, linked to sensible work requirements, was a more promising strategy for reform than the comprehensive approaches put forward by Presidents Nixon and Carter. The Reagan administration began with a different set of values about government aid and about the best remedies for poverty. It curtailed eligibility for a variety of programs, thereby reducing federal spending and, incidentally, *increasing* work incentives by reducing benefit levels and narrowing the number of people touched by high benefit-reduction rates.

Some of Glazer's discussion of economics are either wrong or incomplete. Glazer suggests that the cuts in nondefense spending are small relative to the large impending federal deficit. But the enormous deficits were manufactured in Washington in 1981 and 1982 under the highly effective leadership of President Reagan. He did not inherit a structural deficit. His program created it. The discussion of incentive effects of welfare payments on labor supply confuses income and substitution effects. Also, he uses the presumed need for faster capital accumulation to justify tax cuts for the well-to-do, when any tax cut will reduce domestic saving unless those who receive the tax cut reduce their consumption in consequence. No responsible economist has ever made such a claim, except for Keynesian demand effects; and that assuredly was not the basis of the administration's defense of tax cuts for the wealthy.

In summary, Glazer's paper is useful in reminding us that the Reagan administration has so far accomplished only a modest part of its full agenda and that the achievement of the remainder will hinge on future political contests. It makes clear that the ideological stance of this administration has been unmatched in half a century. It reminds liberals and conservatives alike that conflicting desirable goals always vie for priority and that the Reagan program can be regarded simply as having upgraded certain of these goals relative to others.

But Glazer has not addressed the social *policy* of the Reagan administration. He confuses, rather than clarifies, the budgetary history of the past two and a half years. He omits or understates such relevant actions as the administration's assault on Social Security and the projected devastation of other nondefense programs. He tells us a fair amount about the political struggle but very little about the underlying strategy of the administration whose policy he set out to examine.

ABOUT THE AUTHORS

Henry J. Aaron is a senior fellow at the Brookings Institution and professor of economics at the University of Maryland. He is former assistant secretary for planning and evaluation at the U.S. Department of Health, Education, and Welfare. His current research is on the control of medical costs and tax policy. He is a coauthor of *The Painful Prescription: Rationing Hospital Care*.

Martin Anderson is a senior fellow at the Hoover Institution. He served in the Reagan administration as assistant to the president for policy development (1981–1982), having responsibility for coordinating the development of the domestic policies of the administration. Dr. Anderson is a member of the president's Economic Policy Advisory Board and the president's Foreign Intelligence Advisory Board. He is the author of *The Federal Bulldozer: A Critical Analysis of Urban Renewal, 1949–62*; *Conscription: A Select and Annotated Bibliography*; *Welfare: The Political Economy of Welfare Reform in the United States*; *Registration and the Draft*; and *The Military Draft: Selected Readings on Conscription*.

Michael C. Barth is a principal of ICF, Incorporated, a Washington, D.C. consulting firm. Dr. Barth was previously deputy assistant secretary for income security policy, Department of Health and Human Services. He is the author of several articles on various aspects of labor economics and the economics of welfare. Recently he has been working in the area of environmental economics and will edit and contribute to a 1984 volume on the effects of global-warming induced sea level rise on coastal areas.

D. Lee Bawden is director of the Human Resources Policy Center at The Urban Institute and editor of this volume. Dr. Bawden has conducted research on welfare policy, poverty, and employment and training policy for nearly twenty years, the last ten years at The Institute. Prior to that he was professor of economics and agricultural economics at the University of Wisconsin, Madison, and a fellow of the Institute for Research on Poverty. Dr. Bawden was one of the authors of "The Well-being of Families and Individuals" in *The Reagan Experiment* and the "Social Policy" chapter in the forthcoming book, *The Reagan Record.*

Blanche Bernstein, a former commissioner of New York City's Human Resources Administration and a deputy commissioner for income maintenance for the New York State Department of Social Services, is currently director of the Social Policy Research Institute, New School for Social Research. She is the author of *The Politics of Welfare: The New York City Experience* (Abt Books) and numerous studies of social welfare programs.

Barry R. Chiswick is a research professor in the Department of Economics and Survey Research Laboratory at the University of Illinois at Chicago. Professor Chiswick has researched the causes and consequences of labor market behavior, including welfare dependency. Most recently he has focused on the labor market adjustment and impact of immigrants, and the determinants of racial and ethnic group differences in economic success. His research has been published in numerous articles and books. He is a coauthor of *The Dilemma of American Immigration: Beyond the Golden Door* (Transactions Books 1983).

Sheldon Danziger is professor of social work and director of the Institute for Research on Poverty at the University of Wisconsin, Madison. He is the author of numerous articles on the trend in poverty and income inequality, and on the redistributive and efficiency effects of government income transfer programs. He is currently studying the impact of the Omnibus Budget Reconciliation Act of 1981 on the work effort and well-being of welfare recipients.

Stuart E. Eizenstat was President Carter's chief domestic advisor and executive director of the domestic policy staff at the White House from 1977–1981. He is a Phi Beta Kappa graduate of the University of North Carolina and obtained his LL.B. degree from Harvard Law School. He has written a variety of articles on legal and public policy issues. A partner in the Washington office of Powell, Goldstein, Frazer and Murphy, an Atlanta-based firm, he is also an adjunct lecturer at Harvard University's John F. Kennedy School of Government.

Nathan Glazer is professor of education and sociology at Harvard University and coeditor of *The Public Interest*. He was, with William Gorham, coeditor of *The Urban Predicament* (The Urban Institute, 1976), and his most recent book is *Ethnic Dilemmas, 1964–1982* (Harvard University Press, 1983).

William Gorham has been president of The Urban Institute since its formation in 1968. He served as the first assistant secretary of Health, Education and Welfare for Planning and Evaluation and as deputy assistant secretary of defense. He began his career in the economics division of The Rand Corporation.

Peter Gottschalk is associate professor of economics at Bowdoin College and project associate at the Institute for Research on Poverty at the University of Wisconsin, Madison. His published work has focused on the relationship between labor markets and income inequality and instability. His current research looks at the relationship between demographic changes and changes in the distribution of earnings of males.

Edward M. Gramlich is a professor of economics and public policy at the University of Michigan and chairman of the Economics Department. Dr. Gramlich specializes in applied public finance and macroeconomics and is the author of several books and journal articles on these topics.

G. William Hoagland is the deputy staff director of the Committee on the Budget, United States Senate. He served as the administrator, Food and Nutrition Service, U.S. Department of Agriculture in 1981, and prior to that appointment, he was employed by the Congressional Budget Office. He is the author of numerous papers on food and agriculture policies and public income transfer programs.

Deborah S. Laren is a research associate at the Institute of Public Policy Studies at the University of Michigan. She has written several journal articles on applied public finance topics, and is a frequent user of the data base analyzed in the paper.

Jack A. Meyer is currently a resident fellow in economics and director of the Center for Health Policy Research at the American Enterprise Institute in Washington, D.C. He is the editor of two recently published volumes: *Market Reforms in Health Care: Current Issues, New Directions, Strategic Decisions*; and *Meeting Human Needs: Toward a New Public Philosophy*.

Prior to joining AEI in 1979, Dr. Meyer served as an assistant director of the U.S. Council on Wage and Price Stability in 1977 and 1978. His work with the federal government included positions in the U.S. Department of Labor and the U.S. Department of Housing and Urban Development.

June Avis O'Neill is principal research associate in the Human Resources Center of The Urban Institute. Dr. O'Neill's current research interests include the determinants of women's earnings and occupations, the determinants of child support, higher education finance, and issues in taxation. Prior to joining the Institute, Dr. O'Neill served as a member of the senior staff of the president's Council of Economic Advisers and chief of the Human Resources Cost Estimates Unit of the Congressional Budget Office.

Isabel V. Sawhill is codirector of The Urban Institute's Changing Domestic Priorities project, of which this volume is part. Dr. Sawhill's areas of research include human resource and economic policy. She has directed two of The Urban Institute's research programs and has also served as director of the National Commission for Employment Policy and as chairman of the Department of Economics at Goucher College. Her publications include *The Reagan Experiment, Youth Employment and Public Policy*, and *Time of Transition: The Growth of Families Headed by Women*.

Timothy M. Smeeding is director of the Division of Social Science Research within the Center for Public Affairs and Administration at the University of Utah and associate professor of economics. He has written widely on the issues of poverty and income transfer programs, particularly noncash transfer programs. He is the author of the 1982 U.S. Census Bureau technical report, "Alternative Methods for Valuing Selected In-kind Transfers and Measuring Their Impact on Poverty."

PARTICIPANTS

Henry J. Aaron
The Brookings Institution

Tom Ault
*Department of Health and
Human Services*

Mary Jo Bane
Harvard University

Michael C. Barth
ICF, Inc.

D. Lee Bawden
The Urban Institute

Blanche Bernstein
New School for Social Research

Barry R. Chiswick
University of Illinois

Sheldon Danziger
University of Wisconsin

Frederick Doolittle
Princeton University

Gregory Duncan
University of Michigan

Stuart E. Eizenstat
*Powell, Goldstein, Frazer and
Murphy*

Shepard Forman
The Ford Foundation

Irwin Garfinkel
University of Wisconsin

Nathan Glazer
Harvard University

Nancy Gordon
Congressional Budget Office

William Gorham
The Urban Institute

Peter Gottschalk
Bowdoin College

Edward M. Gramlich
University of Michigan

G. William Hoagland
Senate Budget Committee

Kevin Hopkins
The White House

Frank Levy
The Urban Institute

Glenn Loury
Harvard University

Jack A. Meyer
American Enterprise Institute

Richard Michel
The Urban Institute

Milton Morris
Joint Center for Political Studies

Richard Nathan
Princeton University

Demetra Nightingale
The Urban Institute

June A. O'Neill
The Urban Institute

John L. Palmer
The Urban Institute

Anthony Pellechio
*Department of Health and
Human Services*

Wendell Primus
Committee on Ways and Means

Robert D. Reischauer
The Urban Institute

Isabel V. Sawhill
The Urban Institute

Timothy M. Smeeding
University of Utah

Eugene Smolensky
University of Wisconsin

Raymond J. Struyk
The Urban Institute

34.75

DATE DUE

HIGHSMITH 45-220